SEEKING SOLACE

The Life and Legacy of
Horatio G. Spafford

Horatio G. Spafford

SEEKING SOLACE

The Life and Legacy of Horatio G. Spafford

Author of the Hymn
"It Is Well with My Soul"

Thomas E. Corts

Sherman Oak Books
Samford University Press
Birmingham, Alabama

Thomas E. Corts (1941-2009) was the seventeenth president of Samford University, Birmingham, Alabama (1983-2006); Interim Chancellor, Alabama College System (2006-2007); Executive Director, International Association of Baptist Colleges and Universities (June 2007-September 2007); Coordinator, The President's Initiative to Expand Education and Coordinator of Basic Education, Office of the Director of Foreign Assistance, U. S. State Department (October 2007-December 2008).

Sherman Oak Books
Samford University Press
Samford University
800 Lakeshore Drive
Birmingham, Alabama 35229, U.S.A.
www.samford.edu
©2013, 2014 by Samford University Press
First edition 2013. Paperback edition 2014.

Printed and bound in the United States of America

ISBN-13 978-1-931985-20-8
ISBN-10 1-931985-20-0

Editorial Supervisor: Sandra L. O'Brien
Cover Design by: Monica W. Washington

Cover jacket photographs: Portrait of Horatio G. Spafford ca. 1860-1880; portrait of Anna Spafford ca. prior to 1873, both from Spafford family photograph album; *The Sinking of the Steamship* Ville du Havre, Currier & Ives, 1873; draft manuscript of hymn "It Is Well with My Soul," ca. 1873, American Colony in Jerusalem Collection, Manuscript Division, Library of Congress. Bulkley stained-glass window, The Church of the Good Shepherd, Augusta, Georgia. *Frontispiece:* Portrait of Horatio G. Spafford ca. 1860-1880. *See* Illustrations and Photo Credits for complete details.

Editor's Note

At the time of Dr. Corts's death, he had not yet prepared footnotes and a bibliography. I ask the reader's forgiveness if reference errors are found. My efforts were genuine and strong-willed, but it is possible a few things were missed. Dr. Corts was a skilled and gifted wordsmith, and therefore, only very minor textual edits were necessary. For those of you who are familiar with his writing, you will "hear" his voice throughout the book.

Sandra L. O'Brien, Editor

CONTENTS

FOREWORD

Dr. Thomas E. Corts and I first met in autumn 2004 near the end of his tenure as president of Samford University. Although only thirty minutes of his busy schedule had been allotted to interviewing me for the Billy Graham Chair of Evangelism in Beeson Divinity School, he generously hosted me for well over an hour. Our conversation had begun on the topic of Christian higher education and the place of the Divinity School in the wider university community, but it soon evolved into another area dear to both of our hearts—Christian biography. Only a year earlier Dr. Corts had edited a book on P. P. Bliss, the gospel songwriter and friend of evangelist D. L. Moody. Because I had written a biography of Moody just a few years earlier, Dr. Corts and I began to talk about several men and women whose lives were interwoven with Moody and Bliss, among them Ira Sankey, D. W. Whittle and Horatio G. Spafford. We agreed that these lesser known but important participants in the revivals of the late nineteenth century had led fascinating lives, and that if their stories were better known it would enrich our understanding of their era and the evangelical movement in which they invested their lives. Before our meeting ended, Dr. Corts and I agreed that we should consider coediting a series of minor-figure biographies and that both of us should contribute one or two volumes to the effort. I urged him to expand his seminal work on Bliss into a full biography. He agreed to give it careful consideration.

Alas, he did not live long enough to edit the series or write the Bliss biography. But we can all be grateful that immediately upon his retirement from the university, Dr. Corts immediately undertook this biography of Horatio G. Spafford. Consequently, he has bequeathed to us a portrait of Spafford that is important for several reasons. First, it is the only serious and objective biography of the man who is best remembered for the lyrics for "It Is Well with My Soul," written in the wake of the tragic death of his four daughters at sea in 1873. Second, this carefully researched and well-written book separates the truth from the myths surrounding the writing of the hymn. Third, the Spafford story enriches our understanding of the interconnectedness of business and financial leaders with the Protestant religious elite during the late nineteenth century when evangelical Christianity experienced unusually rapid growth. Fourth, this engaging biography reveals the devastating consequences that can occur when sincere Christians abandon the Bible as their guidebook and rely instead upon the leadership of one or two "prophets" who claim to hear directly from God. Finally, this fascinating biography shows that a man who brought great glory to God can be utterly corrupted by money in the twinkling of an eye.

Tom Corts wanted people to learn from the lives of the folks he called "Half-Forgotten Saints." He ably brought H. G. Spafford out of semiobscurity into the light that will enrich and caution all who read it.

Lyle W. Dorsett
Billy Graham Professor of Evangelism
Beeson School of Divinity

PREFACE

Having grown up in Ashtabula, Ohio, I knew about the Ashtabula Bridge Disaster of December 29, 1876, and about the death of well-known gospel musician Philip Paul Bliss and his wife, Lucy. That familiarity prompted me to inquire of Reverend Virgil Reeve about the possibility of a one hundred twenty-fifth anniversary remembrance of that event in August 2002. Preparing for the observance, I found more than I had ever known, including that much local lore had it all wrong. With the help of Jean Metcalf and Barbara Hamilton, I learned of a cache of old materials related to the Disaster that had gone unnoticed for about one hundred years. Subsequently, to dispel the myths and to strengthen the community's awareness of its heritage, we put together a book, *Bliss and Tragedy: The Ashtabula Railway-Bridge Accident of 1876 and the Loss of P. P. Bliss.*

Bliss wrote the music to the popular hymn, "It Is Well with My Soul," and Horatio Gates Spafford penned the words. Haunting my research and writing about Bliss was my inability to stop wondering about Horatio Gates Spafford. Bliss was such a devout, spiritually minded, selfless man, I pondered whether it could be possible that Spafford was, too. I set out to understand him better and began to believe he was. Eventually having to come to grips with Spafford's frailty, I was still able to recognize a devoted heart conflicted with the realities of finances, responsibilities, and possibilities unrealized.

I owe much to Dr. Barbara Bair, historian in the Manuscript Division of the Library of Congress, who has given me access to many documents, shared ideas, thoughts and judgments, and encouraged me from the very start. That a public servant could be so genuinely interested in the Spafford family and in a project such as this, should be satisfying to American taxpayers.

Many thanks are due my creative friend, Dr. A. Kenneth Curtis, of the Christian History Institute. With his warm heart and keen appreciation of church history, he encouraged me to refine and test some of my findings about Spafford in the Institute's *Glimpses* series.

Helpful British courtesy was extended by staff of The British Library, both at St. Pancras, and at the Newspaper Branch of the Library at Colindale, North London. Personnel at Moody Bible Institute were very cooperative. Barry Smith, historian of Lincoln Park Presbyterian Church, congregational inheritor of the surviving records of the Spaffords' Fullerton Avenue Presbyterian Church, provided materials and gave me helpful markers along the way. Barbara Dobschuetz, Chicago historian, also shared background on the city and on the Moody Church. Staff at the Lily Library of Indiana University and at Asbury Theological Seminary kindly allowed me access to pertinent papers of Hannah Whitall Smith. My friend Elizabeth Wells and staff at the Harwell G. Davis Library at Samford University have always responded expeditiously to every request or question, and have helped me find my way, even down blind alleys. I owe much to Darlene Kuhn, Becca Williamson, and Sandra O'Brien, who, until my retirement in 2006, made the President's Office at Samford University an efficient place, even when the President was inefficient—traveling or tracking the likes of Henry Drummond, Bliss and Spafford. Sandra O'Brien, particularly, offered the critical insights and advice of an experienced editor and researcher. My wife, Marla, our children and grandchildren, have come to expect my periodic withdrawal and isolation, fretting over Mr. Spafford. I owe them more than words can ever repay. Of course, the judgments and opinions reflected herein are my own.

It occurs to me that I probably owe my greatest debt to an unseen cloud of witnesses that includes my mother and father, brothers and sister, Daily Vacation Bible School leaders, Sunday School teachers, and literally hundreds of churches and music leaders. Somehow, from earliest childhood, the Christian message conveyed in hundreds of songs and melodies lodged in my heart, and, even today, flows through my consciousness in a never-ending stream of blessedness.

Thomas E. Corts
February 1, 2009

ADDENDUM TO PREFACE

For six years before his sudden death due to a massive heart attack on February 4, 2009, Tom devoted most spare moments to researching and writing on the life of Horatio G. Spafford. Just a few days earlier on January 28, Tom wrote in his journal, "I am trying to decide if I can have a couple of points researched further, but I am anxious to see if I can get that project concluded. I do think it is a much better manuscript now than earlier, and I hope it will do justice to the man and be a help and encouragement. He made some bad mistakes, but he has a continuing ministry even 120 years after his death. Not many people can claim that."

Wanting to finish the task, but unable to find a complete list of references, or a bibliography, I asked Sandra O'Brien, his assistant/editor while he served as president of Samford University, to complete the project, making it ready for publication. This she has done, patiently and painstakingly, returning to the manuscript again and again as her duties in the President's Office allowed. Without her inestimable help, this manuscript would remain unfinished.

I am deeply indebted to Dr. Andrew Westmoreland, current president of Samford University, for his support in seeing this through to book form. Gratitude is due also to Dr. Allen P. Ross, Beeson Professor of Divinity at Samford's Beeson Divinity School, with whom I and others traveled to Israel in June 2011. While in Jerusalem, he assisted me in locating and visiting the American Colony Hotel and Spafford's burial place. Olga Smoldyreva, our tour guide, accompanied me to both sites, helping with photographs and securing admittance to the Jerusalem Protestant Cemetery that was closed to the public.

Making my way up the slope of Mt. Zion near the Jaffa Gate and standing at the foot of Spafford's grave, I was able to put to rest a work dear to Tom and thus to me, giving life-meaning to the last lines of a bereavement poem, "Complete these dear unfinished tasks of mine, and I, perchance may therein comfort you."

Marla Haas Corts
June 4, 2012

PART ONE
LIFE IS A JOURNEY

1
ALL ABOARD

Befitting its status as the largest passenger ship in the world, the *Ville du Havre*, to the accompaniment of a slight breeze, rocked ever so gently as lesser vessels swayed in unison at the lower end of New York City's West Street. More sailing ships than steamships could still be counted that November 15, 1873, at the nexus of the Hudson and East Rivers. Through a tunnel of ship's masts, sails, and funnels, a stream of horse-drawn coaches and cabs seemed almost miniature as they made their way to offload passengers and luggage shipside along "the North River." Stocky steamer funnels, in a mile-long row, were slowly replacing the spindly masts of square-riggers, which in their dockside idleness that day waved canvas solicitations, "Immediate Departure," "Now Loading," and similar inducements. That particular area was to become "Steamship Row," but in that day steamers still had sails for auxiliary power and would for another twenty years, making sails dominant over funnels. Clearly, the quest for speed, heating up since the first regular steamships had carried mail across the Atlantic beginning in 1840, meant that man-controlled steam was outpacing the less-manageable variations of the wind.

At the wooden pier of the *Compagnie Générale Trans-atlantique*—for Americans, the sign read simply, "French Lines"—the *Ville du Havre* was proudly being readied from a wooden pier shed. The list was being checked: coal stocked, food and wine portered, potable water tanks filled. She was ready for her fourth voyage since having been lengthened thirty feet and converted from paddle wheel to propeller (or "screw," as they called it then). Originally built at a cost of 175,000 British pounds in 1865, she had been named *Napoleon III*; after the conversion costing an additional 100,000 British pounds, and after the fall of Napoleon the Emperor, she became the namesake of her home port of Le Havre. Despite the less imperial name, she reigned as the finest and most luxurious steamer on the Atlantic, and except for a cable-layer, she was boasted to be the *largest* ship afloat. Lloyds of London insured just her hull for 120,000 British pounds, proof that her size and luxury represented a significant investment. "Unsinkable" was the word used to describe her safety and sturdiness of construction. Eleven bulkheads were outfitted with watertight doors operable from the upper deck, and her lifeboats' capacity was reported at 290.

Advertisements touted the *Ville du Havre* as "a floating palace" with innovative steam heating and rapeseed oil-burning lamps throughout. Its public areas glistened with polished wood and marble, gilded-trim mirrors, and carvings, all highlighted by fine, upholstered furniture and plush carpets. It had a library of books and prints, a smoking room for men, and a boudoir for the ladies. The ship's saloon, the leisure sitting area, had the posh atmosphere of an elegant club.

Those Americans and British wealthy enough to have a choice preferred the French liners of the 1870s. The French liners were tended by veteran naval officers with twice the staff for table-waiting, housekeeping, and ordinary service, compared to their English counterparts. According to one London newspaper, the French ships "lack nothing in equipment that can conduce to their safety, or, indeed, their comfort. They are thus favourite steamers with Americans visiting Europe, and especially for invalids who at the beginning of winter are in search of the moderate climates of the south of Europe." The Paris correspondent of London's *Daily Telegraph* concurred that many Americans-in-Paris preferred ships of the *Compagnie Générale Transatlantique* to the English, believing the accommodations were better, "wine is given with a liberal hand," smoking was permissible, and communications were more friendly between passengers and officers.

As departure time neared that November afternoon, the hard work was below deck, where firemen stoked coal and monitored pressure gauges. On deck, stewards and chambermaids were helping passengers find their staterooms and settle in. Experienced stevedores pulled the levers on a steam crane, hoisting massive rope-net collections of passengers' luggage onto the deck where crew members could match them with their owners' rooms. The mostly French crew of one hundred seventy-two afforded an enviable ratio to the one hundred thirty-five passengers.

Boarding was a drawn-out affair. Several hours after second-class and third-class passengers were on board, the elite of first-class ramped up the gangways. Their beautiful trunks and cases, their stylish dress, their manner of conveyance to the pier—all were recreational scrutiny from the portholes of already-boarded, lower-class patrons. The staggered procession of passengers was orchestrated toward a three o'clock departure, carefully set to take advantage of the tides. Expected aboard were eighty-nine persons paying a first-class fare of $125 in gold; nineteen in second-class at $75 each; and twenty-seven paying $48 for third-class tickets. The cost of a ticket included transport, New York to Le Havre, France, lodging, three meals per day, including wine with each meal, and almost all available services.

Along with passengers, the *Ville du Havre* was bearing 3,200 tons of cargo, none of it uncommon for that day: 1,615 bales of

cotton; 550 cases of bacon; 30,877 bushels of wheat; 250 tons
of lard; 52 cases of canned goods; 30 barrels of potash; 1,800
bundles of hides; 5 cases of peppermint; 2 barrels of oysters; 2
casks of chinaware; 8 casks of copper; 51 casks of jeweler's rouge;
16 bags of shin bones; and a case of ribbons.

"Time and tide wait for no man," so a little before three
o'clock, the trumpet having sounded for guests to depart the ship,
the two gangways pulled back to the pier. A siren blew, erupting
a flutter of handkerchiefs and plaintive good-byes in antiphonal
shouts and hand signals from both ship and shore. The big engine
churned, smoke belched from the funnel masts, and a modest tug
eased the big vessel out into the river, so it could glide between
Hoboken and Jersey City, the profile of New York City slowly
shrinking in the distance.

Then, as now, travel excites a certain eagerness, a willingness to
confront the new and unfamiliar. It requires a feeling of risktaking;
in travel, one defies routine, taunts a sense of vulnerability, and
tests the laws of science. For example, though sailing ships had
crossed oceans for centuries, the first English steamer had crossed
the Atlantic in 1838; yet in that same year, Dr. Dionysius Lardner
"was demonstrating at the Royal Institution at Liverpool that,
'As to the project of making a voyage directly from New York to
Liverpool, it was perfectly chimerical, and they might as well talk
of making a voyage from New York to the moon . . .' ."

Sea travel in that era was not without danger, witness the
four ocean liners that had already been lost in the western ocean
the first ten months of that year, 1873. Passengers would have
been familiar with recent, well-publicized ship disasters and lost
lives involving the *President*, the *City of Glasgow*, the *Pacific*,
and the *Atlantic*. Sea transport was not fail-safe, especially as it
transitioned from sail to steam, and the industry at multilevels
adjusted to a new paradigm.

One accident, much on the public's mind, had occurred in March that year. Newest of the crack liners, the *Atlantic* had run aground on the rocky coast of Nova Scotia in a blizzard on its way from Liverpool to New York. Seas were so high, no lifeboat could be launched. One of the officers, in a herculean effort, heroically swam the frigid waters, bearing a line to the nearest rocks so that 450 of the 931 persons on board could be saved.

But no such thoughts troubled passengers as the *Ville du Havre's* sixteen hundred horsepower began to plow the open ocean that November day. Almost all aboard explored the hallways, staircases, long corridors on either side, and the decks—the floor plan of their temporary home. They wondered about unfamiliar buttons, levers, and compartments as they patrolled up and down three staircases, admiring the luxury at every turn, and hoping to remember how to get between their personal quarters and the deck, the saloon, the smoking room, and other haunts. They greeted fellow travelers, introduced themselves, dodged the children, and shared discoveries with anyone who would listen.

An official manifest of passengers had been posted on a bulletin board at the purser's office, but personalities are always more revelatory than mere names. Passengers were eager to become acquainted with fellow citizens of their newly formed floating village. Their first coming together would be at dinner in the saloon at 7:00 p.m., their initial opportunity to assess fellow travelers, to follow up on first impressions formed as they watched one another trundle aboard, to check the veracity of gossip, to see and be seen, and to hear and be heard.

Among those passengers best-known were Judge Rufus W. Peckham and his wife. The judge, with his well-earned dignity and courtly courtesy, had held several judgeships and had served a term in the U.S. House of Representatives. At the time of the voyage, he was a Justice of the New York Court of Appeals. He cut a striking figure, well-dressed in a high collar that accentuated a mustache, as white as it was well-curled, complemented by a thick crop of white hair crowning his impressive countenance. Truth to tell, the judge was near exhaustion from work; medical advisors and his associates had urged an extended foreign holiday to provide "relief from labor, and to recruit his energies by temporary absence."

A popular French performer was aboard. Using the stage name "Monsieur Collodion," an obvious play on words (since collodion was a solution of nitrocellulose in alcohol and ether originated by the French for developing photographs), he was styled as an entertainer and "caricaturist." During the mid-and-late 1800s, without practical means of reproducing photographs, black-and-white drawings involving political sarcasm and mocking well-known personalities became popular in both Europe and America. In America, their rise is well-documented in the career of Thomas Nast (1840–1902), whose cartoons for *Harper's Monthly* often drew comment from President Abraham Lincoln. The thirty-five-year-old Collodion, almost six feet tall, with an air of French insouciance, had so successfully mocked French President Thiers that Collodion had actually fled for his life. In England first, and then in New York and other U.S. cities, he had drawn considerable interest. Newspaper advertisements of his appearance with the Lydia Thompson burlesque troupe at the Olympic Theatre in New York, heralded "M. Collodion, The only acknowledged instantaneous caricaturist, engaged at enormous expense." It was said, "His facility in sketching with almost electrical rapidity the outlines of any well-known face" was remarkable, accomplishing a portrait with black chalk on canvas in about one minute. His representations of U.S. President Grant would have been known to his fellow passengers. He was returning to Paris with his wife following several months' stay in

Britain, as well as having made his American debut, September 1, followed by other appearances in the U.S., allowing time for the hostile feelings of the French government to abate. He had briefly considered opening a studio in New York but felt compelled to return to Paris due to recent political unrest.

Madam and Monsieur Theodore Jouanique, married only two years, were millionaire fashion designers with operations in Paris and New York. They had been in New York visiting her father, Mr. Roux, a well-known furniture dealer on Broadway. It is easy to imagine them as targets of whispered conversation— the accomplished, middle-aged businessman with the twenty-three-year-old wife.

Traveling to Paris to be married was Miss Caroline Turcas, a Creole girl about seventeen. The *New York Times* described her as "exceedingly beautiful." Her parents were French, but had been living in Cuba, where they owned large coffee plantations. Within the previous two years, both parents had died, and then a brother, who had gone to Cuba to settle the parents' extensive affairs, got sick and died.

The stylish Mrs. Abraham Bininger, forty-five, wife of a well-known New York wine importer, was traveling with her daughter, Fanny. She was planning to spend the winter in France after Fanny's enrollment in school.

Helen Wagstaff, a lovely nineteen-year-old, from an established Long Island doctor's family, was the companion of her close friend Sarah Adams Bulkley, endearingly called "Lalla" or "Lallie" by her mother, Mary Adams Bulkley. Equally at home in Paris and New York, the Bulkley family had extensive forestry holdings in New York and Georgia to support their papermaking businesses.

Lallie, a comely twenty-year-old, caught the attention of every passenger. Selfless in her attention to others, she proved to have a buoyant optimism, a contagious joie de vivre, and a gift for entertaining the children. On one occasion, fellow passenger, Reverend Nathanael Weiss described her: "This young American lady has golden hair, slightly disordered by the wind, and blue eyes, so gentle and compassionate, and features so delicate, and such a distinguished air, that she seems like a beautiful fairy of the olden time." Winsome and joyous—her presence so ideal as to be almost imaginary—Weiss affectionately called her "the Fairy." His fellow French minister Theo Lorriaux chose to call her more biblically, "The Good Samaritan" because "she succeeds in the most marvelous way in raising the spirits of those who are depressed." Almost instantly, she was known to all the passengers and crew.

Young Charles Burritt Waite, son of the owner of famous Brevoort House hotels in Manhattan and Chicago, with both New York and Paris addresses, was taking his seventh trip abroad. While normally athletic, he had only recently recovered from a serious illness and was traveling to relax and regain his health. Accompanying him was his twenty-one-year-old sister, Julia, noticeably motherly toward her recovering brother.

Affable B. F. Breeden, of the firm of Breeden & Southwick, agents for the Goodyear Rubber Boot and Shoe Association, had homes in New York and in Versailles. He and his daughter were to be reunited with Mrs. Breeden, and another daughter and son, who were already at Versailles.

Unconventional, slightly Bohemian in style and manners, Lizzie Putnam was bound for Paris, intent on living in the Latin Quarter and continuing her studies. She spoke of letters of introduction to some important French names in painting. Her sketch pen would be seen accurately portraying her fellow passengers in their far more traditional attire.

Celebrating his graduation from Princeton with the Class of '72, Hamilton Murray, with his sister, enjoyed social status

10

on both sides of the Atlantic. He had signed his Last Will and Testament only the night before the departure, designating Princeton University as primary beneficiary.

Mrs. John C. Kennet was traveling with her daughter, ten, and son, two, and the children's nanny. They had planned a European rendezvous to end a long separation from their U.S. Navy Lieutenant Commander husband and father.

The first secretary of the Belgian legation to Washington, bearded Alfred Barbanson, was returning to his homeland on leave. A tall, athletic Canadian, Francis Howard, was en route to Paris to marry his French fiancé. Andrew B. McCreary, among the San Francisco superrich, also Paris-bound, planned to reside the entire winter at his home in France. From the Massachusetts port of New Bedford, William R. Swift, partner in the firm of Swift and Allen supporting the whaling industry, was middle-aged with a slight limp. He had his wife and eight-year-old daughter at his side.

Captain and Mrs. Hammond were accompanied by their three children: Frank, Clarence, and Alice. Veteran traveler James Bishop, an entrepreneur with a Broadway, New York address, was carrying a lot of cash as well as gold. Seventeen-year-old McCloskey Butt spent most of his ship-time reading. Another passenger who kept to himself was Francisco Llado, a Spanish merchant specializing in cork and corkwood. He was headed for Catalonia and Andalusia, Spain, to see his family. Henry Beltknap was from a fine, Mount Vernon Street address in Boston.

Two families of special prominence planned to winter on the French Riviera, which was just then becoming a haven for the rich. Captain and Mrs. Hunter, from Newport, Rhode Island, had attracted the astonishment of fellow passengers when they arrived at the pier with an extra carriage overloaded with baggage to accommodate their three daughters, Annie, Mary

11

and Caroline, and their French maid. Their obvious abundance sent passengers in eager pursuit to learn their identities as they boarded. From Boston, Charles Mixter, about sixty, his wife, Mrs. Mixter's father, Nathaniel W. Curtis, seventy-six, and the Mixters' two daughters, Madeleine Curtis Mixter, seventeen, and Helen Kortright Mixter, nine, were hoping a change of scenery would revivify Mr. Curtis, mourning the recent passing of his wife. After living in France several years, the Mixters had returned to Boston earlier in 1873 when Mrs. Curtis had come down with what was to be her terminal illness. (That the Mixters were well-connected is evident from the fact that young Teddy Roosevelt, later President Theodore Roosevelt, as a freshman at Harvard in 1877, wrote a letter to his parents informing them that he had dutifully called on Miss Madeleine Mixter, "who unfortunately was out.")

The Mixter girls quickly became friends with Anna Spafford. She was traveling with her four daughters, Annie, eleven; Margaret "Maggie" Lee, nine; Elizabeth "Bessie," seven; Tanetta, two; and Mademoiselle Nicolet, her companion and the children's governess. In addition to her own children, Mrs. Spafford had been asked to oversee, William Barry "Willie" Culver, the extremely bright, twelve-year-old son of friends Mr. and Mrs. Belden F. Culver of Chicago. Mr. Culver, Willie's father, was a well-connected, prosperous real estate developer who had also been appointed by the governor as president of the Lincoln Park Commission. Willie would be attending school for a couple of years in Stuttgart, Germany, where he would live with his grandparents, Reverend and Mrs. William Barry, formerly of Chicago.

Anna Spafford's friend, Mrs. Daniel Goodwin Jr., whose husband was also a Chicago lawyer and successful real estate developer, was on her way to Europe with her three children,

Goertner, Julia, and Lulu. Goertner Goodwin, Willie Culver, and Annie Spafford were about the same age and instantly established the rapport that comes so naturally to their age group.

A contingent of five ministers, European delegates to the Evangelical Alliance Conference of 1873 in New York City, was returning to Europe. Pastors Nathanael Weiss, Emile Cook, and Theophile Lorriaux were bound for Paris, Reverend Antonio Carrasco for Madrid, and the scholarly, Reverend Doctor Cesar Pronier for Geneva. Through evangelical church affairs, they had met the Spaffords during their time in the States, and Pastor Lorriaux's sister had at one time served as governess to the Spafford children. The five clerics quickly became popular with passengers and favorites of the young. Weiss was especially delighted with American children, who, in his judgment, were growing up with proper pious training in contrast to children in his own country, hindered by what he called France's tendency toward agnosticism. While in America, Weiss had made a study of Protestant Sunday schools and was intrigued with the religious tone of American society. A special soft spot in his heart was reserved for children, whom he considered "charming creatures, whose careless gaiety could give pleasure to the saddest, and from whose naivete, in the midst of the astonishing objects they would meet on their voyage, he expected a rich harvest of amusement."

Weiss played games with the kids and gathered them about for a story or French fairy tale, told in his broken English. Playing the piano, he taught them songs, listened to their questions, and quoted rhymes. He showed them how to do gymnastic stunts, watched and cheered when they succeeded. On some occasions, groups of adults could be left alone in pleasant, unbothered conversation because the children were in Weiss's thrall. He became their counselor and referee as, for example, when mischievous Frank Hammond, twelve, teased nine-year-old

13

Maggie Spafford that "French children had black faces." It was Pastor Weiss who told her the truth.

Dr. Pronier was a professor at the theological seminary in Geneva. Sophisticated and reserved, he could not conceal his eagerness to be home with a sickly wife and their six children, the oldest of whom was thirteen.

The animated good humor of the Spaniard, Reverend Carrasco, eager to be home to see his three children, including one born during his stay in America, was cut short by severe seasickness. His self-containment and sophistication gave no clue to his prominence as "the most eminent of Spanish preachers," as he was called. Having once been jailed in his homeland, a fellow prisoner of Manuel Matamoros, he had been banished from Spain in 1863 for his religious convictions. He returned in 1868 after the revolution, having received in exile an excellent literary and theological education, as well as ordination at Geneva. He was chief of the Protestant Evangelical Mission in Spain and as recently as January 1873, had stirred a large crowd of Spanish evangelicals with a rousing address on the abolition of slavery. Still, the inconvenient confines of the *Ville du Havre,* seasickness, and a sharp disdain for the odors below deck prompted him to keep to himself, and to vow early in the voyage never again to travel the sea. Early on, he made plans to leave the ship even before it reached Le Havre, intent on saving a few hours en route to Madrid.

Ever conscious of his role as pastor, the devout Reverend Cook became the ship's spiritual leader. A graduate of the Wesleyan College at Richmond, he was the French Wesleyan pastor of Les Ternes and Rue Rosquépine Chapels in Paris. During the siege of Paris, he had been courageous, but his courage was almost fatal when the Communists mistook him for a German, and he was nearly killed. Aboard the *Ville du Havre,* it was he who proposed and then led an impromptu Sunday school that second day and the first Sunday at sea. Adults, overhearing him, and observing his manner with children in the after-lunch Sunday school, requested that Pastor Cook read the prayers of the English liturgy that evening, an event that ordained him in his role as unofficial chaplain of the voyage. He was a gentle, pastoral man, and his wife and seven children eagerly awaited his return home to France.

The Reverend Lorriaux had a friendly, if cautiously skeptical, curiosity. He could ask a timely question, was often ready with an answer, and was capable of easy exclamation. He kept up with the ship's happenings and seemed to know generally the gossip, tenor, and mood of the ship's citizenry.

Weiss, Lorriaux, and Cook, untroubled by seasickness, seemed to be everywhere talking with people. They were dubbed "The Three Musketeers," turning the voyage into a social event, their accents and cheerful goodwill making them especially appealing to Americans. In American railway carriages, Weiss observed, persons might ride from New York to San Francisco without a word between them; but in France, the general habit of conversation and the love of talking would gradually break down all barriers of etiquette.

Henry Sigourney was a young, well-read Boston businessman. Youthful LeGrand Cramer accompanied his middle-aged aunt from Troy, New York. Ruldolf Adolph Witthaus, already showing likeness to the professor he would become, spent most of his time on board reading.

Many others passengers are unknown to us, or known but slightly. A Roman Catholic priest was a passenger. "Monsieur M" was a colonel of the National Guard of Paris during the siege of that city. According to Weiss, he had been in America on business for several years and spoke of his regard for Americans' honesty in business relations, but in his opinion, Americans were "too daring and too much in love with their own ideas" to imagine that their commercial or financial arrangements might ever fail.

2
A CHOICE COUPLE

Reviewing the *Ville du Havre's* passenger list reminds us that every person has a fascinating story, if it can be collected and told. Some people openly share the triumphs and tragedies of their lives, day-to-day, everyday, in an almost play-by-play format of a modern media commentator, or almost as though they have been compiling and phrasing an autobiography in their subconscious over a long period of time. Some safeguard memories very privately, as though speaking them aloud might dislodge them from memory. Still others savor memories but are never able to put them into words, or choose not to do so. For some, life is over before they have the opportunity to string together the experiences of which it consists. Few have the good fortune to organize neatly the highpoints, descriptions, and incidents that summarize their lifetimes. For lives that end so tragically, such as the passengers on the *Ville du Havre,* we have only the aftermath.

Horatio Gates Spafford and Anna Lawson Spafford were no more children of destiny than any others separated from their families that fateful November day in 1873. Yet, with what we now know of the Spaffords, they inspire special interest, affording small insights through which we can better understand the human experience, ponder choices made at crucial intersections, and reflect on the consequence of tragedy and our response to it. The Spaffords' story begins in the East, crosses to Chicago and the Midwest, involves the mid-Atlantic and Europe, rebounds to Chicago, and ends in Jerusalem.

Horatio Gates Spafford, the author of "It Is Well with My Soul," was born October 20, 1828, in an obscure section of Troy, New York. His father, Horatio Gates Spafford Sr., ["Sr." is this author's designation] was born February 18, 1778, in Dorset, Vermont, about four months after the Colonial Army of General Horatio Gates had heroically forced surrender of British troops under General John Burgoyne at Saratoga. Gates's triumph was decisive for this young nation. The elder Spafford's father, Captain John Spafford, was a Revolutionary veteran, who had commanded a militia company of Green Mountain Boys under Ethan Allen. Obviously, Captain Spafford was attuned to military matters, and naming his son for the celebrated General Horatio Gates was an act of patriotism and respect.

The Spaffords were descended from John Spofford, who came to Rowley, now called Georgetown, Massachusetts, from Yorkshire England in 1638. The family motto was "Rather deathe than false of faythe." His family, with roots in Yorkshire, England, must have been of some note, for it was listed in the *Domesday Book,* the first formal listing of land holdings.

Horatio Spafford Sr. was a most uncommon man—an inventor, author, promoter of democracy, farmer, and an inveterate self-promoter. Seemingly well-educated, he carried on a vigorous correspondence that at points touched most of the prominent people of his day—Thomas Jefferson, John Adams, Noah Webster, James Madison, and Josiah Quincy, to name a few.

With a powerful curiosity, he early conducted numerous scientific experiments in light and heat or, as he called it, "the matter of caloric." His persistence resulted in winning a patent in 1805 for an improved fireplace, and began his lifelong complaint about the U.S. patent system. In 1814, he even had a conference in Washington with President James Madison, seeking improvements in patent laws and procedures.

The elder Spafford debuted as an author with publication of his *General Geography, and Rudiments of Useful Knowledge Digested on a New Plan, and Designed for the Use of Schools,* published in 1809, when he was thirty-one. Considerable attention and acclaim found him in 1813, with the publication of *A Gazetteer of the State of New-York; Carefully Written from Original and Authentic Materials, Arranged on a New Plan . . . With an Accurate Map of the State.* Its printing was the fruit of incredible persistence, made possible with assistance of a three-year, interest-bearing loan arranged by an act of the New York Legislature, a credit to the author's ingenuity and persuasiveness. Spafford was thrilled, after ardent solicitation, that the *Gazetteer* received the strong endorsement of former President Thomas Jefferson in a letter: "I have read it [the *Gazetteer*] with pleasure, and derived from it much information which I did not possess before. I wish we had as full a statement as to all of our States. We should know ourselves better, our circumstances and resources, and the advantageous ground we stand on as a whole. We are certainly much indebted to you for this fund of valuable information."

Surely a best seller for that time, six thousand copies of the *Gazetteer* sold well even at the then-substantial price of three dollars per copy. President James Madison ordered two copies. John Adams called it a monument of industrious research and indefatigable labor, and the volume earned similar plaudits from Josiah Quincy, as well as the presidents of Williams College, the University of Vermont, and many others.

For its time, the *Gazetteer* was an impressive compendium of facts, citing, for example, that New York City in 1811 had

1,303 grocery stores and 160 taverns where spiritous liquors were sold. Intermingled with statistical information, the author shared his editorial opinions, observing, for example, "there is hardly a street, alley, or lane, where a lad may not get drunk for a few cents, and be thanked for his custom, without any questions how he came by his money." It appears that among aspects of his "New Plan," a phrase used in the titles of both works, was inclusion of more wide-ranging commentary, advancing his own political and moral convictions, as well as a strong refusal to separate the nation sectionally—i.e., southern, middle, northern. Somehow, its author believed subdividing the country into regions would promote sectionalism, "likely to become merely political, and improper, because of evil tendency."

In 1814, Spafford obtained a patent for an unusual improvement to wheeled carriages, employing what was called a "crooked axle" in order to better distribute the load. With visions of fame and fortune, he could hardly contain his enthusiasm while trying to keep the idea confidential pending a patent. "Nothing of the present age will outlive it [the crooked axle] in fame," he predicted in a letter to Jefferson in 1814. In his estimate, he opined to U.S. President James Madison, his invention would "revolutionize the whole world of mechanics" and save a million dollars a year for the American people. Though obviously hyperbolic in promoting his carriage concept, Spafford, the inventor, also made reference to his farsighted improvement in carriage springs—remarkably, proposing something akin to the modern shock absorber. He realized that a "bladder, nearly filled with air, and enclosed in a strong case of leather, presents an action of elasticity, acting precisely on those principles which are best calculated to meet alike the wishes and wants of philosopher, and the mere economist."

But his greatest idea was expressed in "Cursory Observations on the Art of Making Iron and Steel, from Native Ores of the United States," an essay never printed, but read before the American Philosophical Society early in 1816. We cannot fully evaluate his proposed process, since patent records were destroyed by fire. However, it appears that Spafford had proposed the essential process that, with the sponsorship of Britain's Sir Henry Bessemer, was patented in the U.S. in 1856. If, in fact, he had held the idea years before Bessemer, and if it could have been patented and implemented, Spafford could have gained the fame and fortune he so relentlessly sought (Bessemer's royalties by 1870 totaled over one million British pounds). But slow progress and his need for money caused him to sell his patent rights prematurely for $5,000 and some stock. As his biographer has said of the elder H. G. Spafford, he had an "unrivalled capacity for turning every scheme into loss and ruin," and in so doing "left to other men the gathering of the laurels and the fruits of one of the really momentous discoveries of the nineteenth century."

All the while experimenting, dreaming, and proposing inventions, the senior Horatio Spafford found time for literary pursuits. In 1816–17, he successfully published *The American Magazine,* a wide-ranging miscellany of thoughts and ideas to spread its publisher's favorite themes: vibrant patriotism, faith in education, antipathy toward the patent system, and disapproval of lawyers. Overarching all was his expression of loyalty to the young country. "America is the favorite soil of freedom—and however tyrants, little or great, domestic or foreign, may sneer at this, the Star of America seems destined to rise till it become the Sun of the Firmament." The expanded title of the journal serves to demonstrate the capacious mind and intent of its editor: *A Monthly Miscellany, Devoted to Literature, Science, History, Biography, and the Arts; Including also State Papers and Public Documents, with Intelligence, Domestic and Foreign, and Library,*

Public News, and Passing Events; Being an Attempt to form a useful Repository for every Description of American Readers.

The parents of Horatio Sr. originally intended him to be a military man, but his admission into the Society of Friends about 1800, when he was twenty-two, negated that plan. It is unclear how he supported himself through life. He claimed to have long experience teaching school, though we have little information to confirm when and where, and teaching would hardly seem to support his standard of living. He had lands and farms, bought and sold in entrepreneurial fashion, and may have benefitted from a significant inheritance, since at one point he referred to his "fortune." Foreshadowing the real estate speculation that was to intrigue his youngest son in the Chicago of the 1870s, in 1817, Spafford purchased ten thousand acres of land in Venango County, Pennsylvania, ten miles east of Franklin, Pennsylvania, at a dollar per acre. He went there, cleared land, built a western cabin, was fascinated with a type of wild potato he discovered, and became postmaster of a frontier site he intended to become "Spafford's Settlement." But the slow pace of development and the lack of intellectual stimulus caused him to abandon the project and move back East after three years.

In another strange twist to his life story, in 1817 Spafford published a novel under the pseudonym Maria–Ann Burlingham. *The Mother-in-Law: or Memoirs of Madam de Morville* was a story of misfortune, seduction, and the triumph of virtue. While Spafford admitted his authorship of the book in a letter to Thomas Jefferson, and the story seems to have some tie to Spafford's family history, the "certain purposes" he used to justify publishing the volume, quite racy for its time, are unclear.

The elder Spafford was a member of numerous intellectual societies prominent in his day and was awarded an honorary Master of Arts degree by the University of Vermont in 1811.

Some time between 1815 and 1824, there is some indication that he may have been granted an honorary doctorate (LL.D.), but it cannot be confirmed.

H. G. Spafford Sr. was married to Hannah Bristol, by whom he had six children. He was granted a divorce from her on the grounds of her adultery. Perhaps it was that very public divorce trial, in which neighbors testified to seeing male visitors in his absence, that prompted the newspaper to write in his obituary years later, "In the death of Dr. Spafford, an interesting, but now deeply afflicted family have sustained an irreparable loss, and a large circle of friends will mourn his departure." His second wife was Elizabeth Clark Hewitt, of Canaan, New York, by whom he had five additional children, the youngest being Horatio Gates Spafford, the younger.

Since Horatio's father died before his fourth birthday in 1832, he may not have known of his father's inventiveness, his writing, his remarkable correspondence, or his eccentricities. His father seemed often to be on the brink of financial distress, and yet his son appears to have had many advantages common to persons of wealth and status.

As a youth, Horatio went to excellent schools and early showed a penchant for poetry and a fascination with the night sky that he regularly described as "always overcast." With a school friend, he stood one evening on the porch of his home as the friend spoke of the brilliant stars. Not seeing anything worthy of his friend's exclamation, with the simple candor of youth, Horatio asked if he had really seen anything of remarkable beauty up there. His friend, Charlie, stared at him a few moments and then made a diagnosis as accurate as it was amateurish: "Horatio, I believe you are nearsighted!" Then, handing over his own glasses to Horatio, Charlie watched as his friend viewed a night sky more beautiful than he had ever seen before. A few years later when he was twenty-one, he wrote a poem celebrating in its first stanza the transformation of his vision. A poem entitled "Night" was published in the April 1850 issue of *Wellman's Literary Miscellany,* which his daughter Bertha believed was her father's poem.

NIGHT

(published in Vester 1950)

Ye countless stars that tremble in the sky,
How bright and beautiful are you tonight!
I've known ye long, but never did my eye
So burn beneath the glory of your light
As it doth now; I kneel to ye—ye wear
The impress of the Deity that's there.

There is a spirit in the night that talks
To man, as man cannot. There seems to speak
A voice to him from out the depths. There walks
Amid its glowing halls a form that seeks
Communion with him—a pervading soul
That lives and breathes, and animates the whole.

How my whole being worships ye, ye skies!
How Godlike is illimitable space!
I see in every flashing ray that flies
Throbbing from forth your lights, the peaceful face
And aspect of divinity. Ye stand
As when first flung from the Creator's hand.

Ye are unchanged—the ceaseless lapse of years
Dims not your brightness—since the world began
And ye were summoned forth, the arch that rears
Proud and magnificent its giant span
Filling immensity—as now—has stood.
'Twill stand with time—eternity is God.

His experience of seeing the heavens as never before was later to become a useful, personal illustration in Spafford's evangelistic work with D. L. Moody.

As a young man, Spafford had been sociable and popular, though somewhat retiring prior to the correction of his vision. He loved outdoor sports and came to appreciate music and literature. In the tradition of his father, he reserved a special fascination for the great American West. Therefore after admission to the bar, he headed west to Chicago in 1856 where he began to practice law. He boarded at Clifton House with a contingent of bachelors, while his partner, Joseph Tucker, boarded at Mrs. Haight's on Michigan Avenue. Horatio must have immediately become active in local affairs. An 1856 newspaper made note of a Republican rally at Laporte, Indiana, where "[T]he principal speaker was H. G. Spafford of Chicago, who made a telling and able address. . . ."

Just three years later, H. G. Spafford, Esq., in addition to his law practice, was listed as professor of medical jurisprudence on the faculty of Lind University, later, Chicago Medical College, and still later the Medical College of Northwestern University. Among his involvements, he also taught a girls' Sunday school class—where his attention was arrested by a Norwegian girl—Anna Larssen.

Anna Tubena Larssen was born March 16, 1842, in Stavanger, Norway. Lars Larssen, her father, a farmer and cabinetmaker, emigrated to the U.S. when Anna was four years old. Settled in the growing Scandinavian community of Chicago, he eventually modified their name to "Lawson."

In the late 1840s, an epidemic of cholera fell upon Chicago, and few homes escaped its dreaded touch. As a child, Anna was the only member of her family to avoid the disease. Her mother, Tanetta, and baby brother, Hans, died in the epidemic. Her father survived, and he moved Anna's half brother, Edward, with him to Goodhue County in southeast Minnesota, hoping to outrun cholera's spread and hoping that a rural climate and farmwork would be healthful.

At first, Anna was left in Chicago in the care of a Mrs. Ely, a kind, stand-in mother. Anna responded positively to the warm, family atmosphere, her schoolwork and her music prospering. But, though only twelve or thirteen years old, when she got word of her father's relapse, she insisted on going to his aid, even though it meant living in an unfinished log house in a rustic, remote region of Minnesota. A powerful sense of duty called her to her father, even with the daily wiles of frontier existence: howling wolves, threats of massacre and scalpings, and isolation. She cooked, washed, milked the cow, tended chickens, and nursed her father, all heavy responsibility and arduous labor for an inexperienced girl.

When Lars Lawson died, the children were aided by neighboring settlers, though the nearest was seven miles away. Suddenly alone in the world, heavyhearted, bearing their loss in relative isolation on the unsettled frontier, Anna and Edward made the best coffin they could from the new lumber on hand, padding the interior with homegrown straw and covering with a linen sheet.

When a pastor, son of Norwegian settlers, came to visit his family in their remote vicinity, he held a memorial service for their father. Afterward, the preacher agreed to escort Anna through the country to the nearest railroad station, where she could return to Chicago.

According to plan, Edward drove his sister to the farm where the pastor's mother and stepfather resided, hauling the one trunk that held all her earthly belongings. When the horses had rested, Edward bade farewell to Anna, hastening back to attend his own farm chores that could not wait. One can imagine the sad parting of the two survivors of the Lawson family—Anna walking beside Edward in the wagon, dreading to let go, until Edward finally insisted that she turn back. As he rounded a turn in the road, he disappeared into the horizon, and Anna never saw her brother again, though Edward Lawson lived to old age, with children and grandchildren.

At the farmhouse where Anna was to lodge, temporarily awaiting the traveling pastor's escort to the rail station, a congregation of settlers had gathered for special services, taking advantage of the parson's rare presence. Disappointment fell hard on Anna when, as the service concluded, she heard the pastor say he had decided to stay one more week to baptize infants born in the interim since a cleric last visited the countryside. As guests departed, the pastor accompanied them on a baptizing circuit, leaving Anna to privately sorrow at the thought of an unplanned lapse of one week in the household of complete strangers. Since Edward was gone, and wolves and Indians discouraged even the thought of the long trek home, Anna was marooned.

With the rare presence of a minister and religious services, baptisms to celebrate, and a good reason to come together, something of a festival atmosphere prevailed. But Anna did not enter into festivities. At that age when self-consciousness is natural, feeling alone, abandoned, mourning the loss of her father, sad at saying good-bye to her brother, uncertain of her future and, by that time speaking English better than most settlers' Norwegian, she observed the services and the gaiety from a distance, more as spectator than participant.

Before leaving Chicago, Anna had an unfortunate experience with a man who claimed to be a Christian and a leader in the church, but who was mean-spirited. Whatever happened was always vague in Anna's recollection or in what she chose to disclose. She had witnessed some form of abuse or cruelty to the man's own defenseless dependents, and Anna herself had been subjected to some unseemly experience. The man's inconsistent or hypercritical conduct settled in her mind a distaste for Christianity, and from that time she did not attend church or Sunday school, nor did she pray.

Then, with all her earthly belongings in one simple trunk, facing an unknown future, she awkwardly found herself a guest in a stark, frontier household. Worse, the traveling minister's mother was blind, and the stepfather was a strange man who leered at pretty Anna in a sinister way that the sightless mother could not observe. The couple lived in the open main floor space with a fireplace for warmth and for cooking. A dark, dirty attic was the only available space where Anna found a pile of straw, and in her tired and weary-spirited state almost immediately dropped off to sleep.

During that first night, Anna was startled awake by something pawing at her face and incoherently mumbling, as if in Norwegian. Too frightened and too cold to move, she remained motionless until the unknown creature shuffled off to another corner; then, she listened carefully until she heard the creature snoring. For the first time in a while, she prayed earnestly, "O God, deliver me, and I will never be discontented again." When morning broke, she cautiously detected that the creature was a sleeping woman, later identified as the adult, mentally disabled stepsister of the pastor.

Anna dreaded another night in the attic, but she was also fearful of the stepfather of the house, who continued privately to make intimidating gestures toward her, veiled from the mother by her blindness. Cold, dingy, and scary as it was, the attic was the safest place. To her surprise, she discovered that the stepsister was not dangerous. She responded instantly with gratitude to Anna's kindness. The week was difficult, but it became just another event in her life when she confronted despair and deliberately rejected it.

Finally back in Chicago, Anna was welcomed by her half sister, Mrs. Rachel Frederickson, and she resumed her music and voice training. At Dearborn Seminary, initially through Rachel's kindness, she was at last exposed to a proper educational environment. She quickly established herself as a brilliant student. She made close friends with girls from prominent families. Among them were Mary Morgan, later to become Mrs. A. Halsey Miller, wife of a prominent Chicago jewelry store owner, and Bertha Madison, later, Johnson, who after marriage moved to Paris where she was to be exceedingly hospitable to Anna in her later time of great need. Anna was also a friend with Jessie Bross, daughter of the lieutenant governor of Illinois, who was one of the owners of the *Chicago Tribune*.

When Anna Lawson was fifteen years of age, she was mature beyond her years in character and experience. According to a friend at the time, Anna, "had the bluest eyes, and abundant fair hair, with beautifully molded mouth and chin, and very white and even teeth. Her ears were so pretty they were often compared to seashells. She had a merry, kind, and affectionate disposition that won the hearts of many people, but she could be mischievous, too, with a keen sense of humor. Her voice was lovely, and people predicted that when it was trained, a great future lay before her."

One friend Jenny Simpson urged Anna to attend Sunday school with her. In what must have been a most uncommon circumstance for that day, Jenny said their teacher, Mr. Spafford, did not talk down to them, gave them a chance to express opinions, and loved an argument. Though not recorded, it could be imagined that fifteen-year-old girls were also mightily impressed by the handsome lawyer, unmarried, and ten to fifteen years older than most of them.

Yielding to her friend's persistence, Anna agreed to attend the Sunday school class just once, but that one appearance was sufficient to seize the lawyer's notice. In one brief encounter, he eyed her as a special attraction. Physical beauty was one thing, but she had intelligently entered into class discussion, and he liked the way she looked him straight in the eye as she spoke. So attractive and mature in manner did she appear that Spafford did not at first guess her true age. He imagined what unique experiences she must have had to be able to make such comments and to display such confidence.

On a visit with Mrs. Frederickson, Spafford hoped to learn more about the mysterious girl appearing unannounced in his class. From that visit, a friendship blossomed between Anna and Horatio, and a year later, he asked Anna to marry him. Surprisingly, only at that point did he discover that she was a mere sixteen, too young to marry. It was then arranged among Anna, Mrs. Frederickson, and Horatio that Anna should attend the Ferry Institute for Young Ladies in suburban Lake Forest, about twenty-eight miles from Chicago. Ferry Institute was a highly selective "finishing school," stressing normal subjects, but also manners, customs, and propriety, as understood by society's privileged young women of that day.

How the parentless girl was able to finance such an education is not clear, though it seems likely that Horatio was her sponsor. In December 1860, Anna wrote Mrs. Ely, with whom she maintained a lifelong friendship: "I wish you were acquainted with Mr. Spafford. He is a true and noble man. I owe him a great deal, but still I would not marry him merely from gratitude."

Anna's daughter Bertha wrote of her own visit to Ferry Hall years later. She noted that her mother was still remembered and that on a windowpane was etched a heart, enclosing the initials, "HS–AL." Bertha believed they had been etched with the diamond of her mother's engagement ring.

When Anna attained marrying age (nineteen), she and Horatio, almost thirty-three, were wed at Second Presbyterian Church on the south side of Chicago, September 5, 1861. The Civil War was in progress, and the national mood was somber. Weddings tended to be simple, so the church was decorated only slightly with white flowers and ferns. The invitation list was confined to close friends; yet when the day arrived, the church was full.

After the ceremony, the couple drove straight to Lake

View township and their rented home, a vine-covered cottage surrounded by ten acres of lawn on the north side of Chicago, some distance from the city. It was an impressive beginning for newlyweds who would later purchase the house. Each day, her husband was chauffeured to his law office in the city by Peter, the houseman. If guests came to Lake View for dinner, they usually traveled by train and stayed the night, since the last train left too early in the evening for guests to linger over dinner and conversation.

Lake View was a distinctive place, as a contemporary writer glowingly described it.

> One of the most attractive places in the old township of Lake View in the seventies was a residence—ivy-hung and tree-embowered—that seemed in its surroundings the chosen abode of peace and happiness. The house, a picturesque irregularly shaped cottage, not far from the Lake Shore, displayed in each nook and corner a rare taste and refinement. Grace, simplicity, and beauty everywhere prevailed. . . .

With four daughters after ten years of marriage, the Spaffords were comfortably situated in a grand house and grounds, with a growing reputation among Chicago's leadership, a strong devotion to Fullerton Avenue Presbyterian Church, an ardent supporter of the YMCA and other good causes, and a friendship with D. L. Moody. To appearances, their enviable life style was made possible by a thriving law practice, where Horatio was senior partner in the law firm of Spafford, McDaid & Wilson. The Spaffords were blessed with the material things of life, and they conscientiously used their resources in religious and charitable work.

3
CONFLAGRATION

Horatio was across the state line in Indiana in real estate negotiations on October 8, 1871, when headlines informed the world of the Great Chicago Fire. Abandoning consideration of a land deal, he dashed home to find that Lake View escaped the carnage and devastation. He would later learn that his law office was not so fortunate.

From the vantage point of Lake View, Anna, the children, and others had seen the billowing flames reflected in Lake Michigan. The eerie flashes of fire against the sky, combined with periodic explosions, added an ominous sense to the tragic night. Even in an age without television or radio, it became obvious that a great tragedy was underway, and no one knew where it would end. Only gradually did it become clear that the Fire had spent itself, and Lake View would be safe.

In the Fire's sweep and aftermath, pandemonium erupted. Driven by the fire from the city to Lake View, people were looking for safety, solitude, and temporary shelter. First to enter the carriage lane at the Spaffords' was a complete stranger, a woman refugee laid across a wagon. Granting her shelter, the Spaffords were to find the woman highly eccentric, but ultimately she lived the rest of her days at Lake View as "Aunty Sims." Completely unknown to the Spaffords prior to that night, Aunty Sims was taken into the Spafford household with nothing but the clothes on her back. Over the next many months, the uninvited visitor promised never to leave Anna, and Anna never had the heart to send her away. Aunty Sims had a husband somewhere, who treated her shabbily and whom she was suing for divorce. As she mended and sewed for the Spafford household, she would also offer unsolicited (and often unappreciated) advice and admonitions, even as she could occasionally amuse and entertain the children with stories. She was alternately a delight and a trouble.

As Chicago burned, another unannounced arrival at Lake View was a load of people transported in a handsome but sooty carriage. In due course, they were recognized as Anna's former schoolmate and friend, Mary Miller, her husband, A. Halsey Miller, their two children, and Mary's mother, Mrs. Morgan. Mary's father had been separated from them during the escape from the fire. Halsey Miller owned the large, prestigious jewelry store opposite the Chicago courthouse, known as the "Tiffany of the West." Even such prominent folks had to battle two days and a night, through fire, traffic, and smoke, just to get to safety at Lake View. They stayed several nights until they could get word of their home and business situations.

Less than two years after the Fire, Anna Spafford was advised by the family friend and physician, Dr. Samuel P. Hedges, to enjoy a change of scenery. Though more fortunate than most area Chicagoans, Anna seemed struck by a vague notion of undefined weariness or fragility, nowhere specified. (Bertha Spafford, Anna's daughter, believed that Aunty Sims might have been a contributing factor, being a nerve-rattling, chattering, always-in-the-way individual, who needed to be considered in all plans and activities.)

Horatio, not wanting his family to be separated, decided

to take the entire family on a two-year sabbatical in Europe. He recalled a business trip he made three years earlier to the British Isles. He was fascinated by the difference in customs, and he longed to take Anna to see the enthralling museums and galleries, and to meet the great Baptist preacher, Charles Haddon Spurgeon. So, in late summer 1873, reservations were made to go first to France, then to Switzerland, over a period of about two years. He made plans for Maggie and Annie, the two oldest girls, to attend a Swiss boarding school. Mademoiselle Nicolet would accompany as governess for the two younger girls, Bessie and Tanetta, and they would lodge nearby. Horatio and Anna would be free to travel for several months in Europe as a second honeymoon. Horatio felt that such a casual journey would revivify Anna's spirits, renew her physical strength, and provide a welcome release from Horatio's pressures of business, while the children would benefit from exposure to different languages and culture. It was a grand plan, not uncommon among the well-to-do.

Oblivious to the "Panic of 1873" that had rocked financial markets only a month earlier, producing a storm of caution, hesitancy, and wait-and-see, first class passage awaited the entire Spafford party on the *Ville du Havre,* the most luxurious ship afloat, to depart New York, November 15, 1873. Not long before they left Chicago by train for their New York port of departure, Horatio Spafford informed his wife that he had received an offer for part of the land constituting his great real estate investment, the cornerstone of his financial future. They concluded that Anna, the children, and Mademoiselle Nicolet should depart for Europe as scheduled, and Horatio would come after the land deal was resolved.

With business weighing on his mind, Horatio Spafford dutifully escorted the coterie of eleven women and children via train from Chicago to New York. Strangely, as the group and their baggage went on board the *Ville du Havre,* Horatio felt a special urge to have his family's cabins changed, moving them closer to the bow of the ship. He said later that he argued with himself about whether to bother exchanging the cabins he had so carefully selected only a few weeks previous, but the urge was so strong, he went to the purser, and it was done.

Ironically, just before departure, as he was getting ready to bid farewell to his family and the band of Chicagoans, Horatio, as he later told it, was handed a telegram stating that the man planning to buy the Chicago real estate had suddenly died of heart failure. He later explained that he silently chose not to let the family start the voyage with the disturbing news that the real estate sale had fallen through. All along, Anna had been reluctant to go without Horatio, and he knew the bad news telegram would only intensify her feelings. Never at the time, or afterward, did Horatio disclose the name of the prospective buyer or elaborate with any details, the severity of circumstances diminishing such details.

4
THE SEA IS THE LORD'S

Aboard the *Ville du Havre,* that first Saturday night's dinner was a social icebreaker. The day had been sunny and mild. Though some were obviously still suffering the pains of separation from loved ones, the spontaneous glee of children's games, the excitement of a new adventure, meeting fresh faces, a hint of flirtation among the young, the bouquets of fresh flowers, the calm of the sea, the obvious confidence of the Captain—all combined to allow good humor to dominate the evening. A fine first dinner was easy to arrange with all the fresh ingredients available so soon after embarking, and it made a positive initial impression. Usual activity would include a walk or at least an appearance on deck after dinner, though only a few braved that evening's November chill and only for a few minutes. Most were still unpacking, sorting their baggage, and getting accustomed to their personal quarters; soon, hardly an after-dinner voice was audible throughout the public-gathering spaces.

No one commented much on the fact that about four hours out of New York, they had stalled in the water for about an hour and a half to arrange some machinery being transported in the hold. What did call for much reaction at breakfast the next morning, however, was a discovery made overnight when a band of six stowaways came in from undercover. Somehow, they had sneaked aboard at the pier and lain concealed under the tarpaulins of two deck boats. About 4:00 a.m., desperately cold and with the deck clear, they abandoned their hiding places and explored their way by stealth through the shadows, happening onto the alleyway next to the engine room with its welcome rushes of heated air. Warming themselves there, a night steward spotted them and arranged their capture. The stowaways were stashed in the crew quarters under guard until morning. At first light, they were hauled before the Captain, who dispassionately sentenced them to manual labor—peeling vegetables, washing dishes, and emptying slops—until the intended turnover to municipal police at Le Havre.

Word of the stowaways created a buzz among passengers—gossip multiplying their number from six to ten, and infusing the story with dashes of mystery and danger, even claiming the freeloaders had knives and guns. Actually, after suffering the abuse of the Captain's most extreme French, the six were absorbed into the workforce of the ship and virtually forgotten. Later, it appeared that the six were immigrants who had not met with success in America and were returning to Europe. There was even a suggestion that the stowaways may have been aided by some of the crew.

As the ship forged its way northeast at twelve or thirteen knots per hour on the sixteenth of November, passengers were charmed by the sea's tranquility as they savored their Sunday morning breakfast. Then the children entertained, as they chased one another on deck and followed the flying-diving exploits of sea gulls. Late morning, newly impressed by the American tradition of Sunday school that his colleague Reverend Weiss had so carefully studied, Reverend Cook made the suggestion that they have an impromptu Sunday school for the children on board.

Following lunch, the children with parents and adult observers went down to the saloon and seated themselves at red-covered tables. To begin, Reverend Cook led a short prayer. When he asked the children if they knew Sunday school songs, they called out many before settling on "I Want To Be an Angel." Their little voices blended into a cherubic choir:

> I want to be an angel,
> And with the angels stand;
> A crown upon my forehead,
> And a harp within my hand.

Then Reverend Cook read from the New Testament Matthew 18:21-35, the passage that raises the question, "How often should we forgive our neighbor?" In the style of Socratic dialogue, the pastor quizzed the children: "Jesus replies to Peter that he must pardon how many times?" "Seventy times seven," came an alert response. "That makes—" interrupted before his question was complete, he heard the correct answer, "four hundred and ninety times."

Seeing an opportunity to make the real point of the Scripture, the pastor posed: "And suppose one should offend four hundred and ninety-one times, must he not be pardoned?"

"Yes, sir," came an enthusiastic response, "for seventy times seven means always." The children's quick answers greatly impressed the French clerics.

Lesson well grasped, they sang another hymn, agreed upon a Scripture lesson for next Sunday, and heard Reverend Cook's benediction.

An afternoon at leisure was absorbed by activities available within their mobile neighborhood. More familiar with their fellow travelers, there were fewer introductions, and fewer queries about hometowns, families, and occupations. Groups were in quiet conversation, while some read. At one point there was a gathering about the piano for a sing-along, collectively remembering words of well-known songs. A flurry of observers suddenly clustered about the few sailors gathered on deck to "heave the log," the time-honored method of determining the ship's speed. Sailors dropped overboard a six-to-eight-inch diameter block of wood, unreeling an attached rope with properly spaced knots. Counting the number of knots slipping through the sailor's hands in a specified time was the crude speedometer, confirming they were then traveling about twelve or thirteen knots.

A lazy Sunday afternoon culminated in dinner, which again brought everyone together. Many then made their way down to the saloon to participate in Reverend Cook's reading of the liturgy. Europeans were fascinated by Americans' early retirement to private quarters, when, by their traditions, the night was just beginning. Except for only a couple of European pedestrians, the darkened deck on Sunday night was the quiet domain of the crew.

Monday morning, November 17, was a different story. Overnight, the tranquil sea was disturbed and began pitching erratically in ways not conducive to sleep. Few appeared at breakfast, arriving after being buffeted about, bouncing from wall to wall in narrow corridors, and striving to maintain balance. Two of the ministerial corps were among those who had succumbed to seasickness. Mrs. Spafford appeared with friends, intent on breakfast. They watched as shelves, hanging suspended by chains, visibly swayed in small circles like foucault pendula, somehow not letting go of water bottles, glasses, salt cellars, and lamps. A row of lounge chairs, pushed by a great wave, collapsed seriatim like a row of dominoes. On deck, the Captain, with his boots seemingly planted in the deck, had his sea legs and did not falter, while passengers held to anything they could grasp. As the waves mounted higher and water spilled over onto the deck, even a serious walker could appear inebriated. More than one risktaker went sprawling and nearly washed overboard in a failed attempt to impress onlookers by walking in a straight line. Those venturesome few who dared come on deck could see the ship actually rise up high enough that the propeller often would be above the water line, and for an instant, having no resistance, it would release a shrill, unaccustomed sound.

Leaving port, passengers are at the mercy of the sea, the ship, and the weather; that Monday morning, the weather took charge. Troubled waters tormented the *Ville du Havre* and seasickness, the travelers. Among the nauseated, most tried to be discreet, but no one objected to tin buckets so obviously at hand, and more than one person on deck simply rushed to the rail. Here and there groups of passengers seemed to prevail, though the salon looked more like a hospital than a lounge. Ladies were pale, weak-looking, and resigned to their fate. But remarkably, Lallie Bulkley, the "Fairy" or "Good Samaritan," was enthroned in a corner with a congregation of children worshipfully watching her every move, catching every detail as she artfully distracted them from the rock and roll of the sea, acting out in English the fairy tales of Perrault. Weiss had observed her earlier that morning, like an unofficial angel of mercy, taking care of some, amusing and encouraging others, seizing every occasion to pit her calming presence against the common enemy. It was as though even the sea chose to respect her. While the children were pale and not in the best humor, their minds found their way to splendid castles and make-believe countries, led by the "Fairy" as she spun her story. Reverend Weiss described it, "Such is the power of the imagination awakened by a loving heart, that the grown people insensibly draw up their armchairs to the enchanted circle, leaning over to hear every word of these stories so vividly portrayed, that, for the time, they regain the charm and freshness of their early years."

Doctor Ouadint, the ship's physician, though seasick himself, kindly roamed the corridors. He extended sympathy, responded to questions, and offered relief and comfort where possible. The afternoon was abbreviated, with darkness settling in about four o'clock and an early dinner. The clergy group observed that the hanging shelves swung more vigorously, making an arc of ninety degrees, as the ship pitched and yawed, forcing the waiters to resemble tightrope dancers. In momentary flashes of calm, diners' eyes diverted to see again the American "Fairy" with a band of her friends, as she sat at the piano and charmed her audience in preparation for dinner. Reverend Cook struggled to eat amidst the motion and commotion, until his plate was thrown from the table by a sudden roll. For all, dinner was shortened by such unpleasant circumstances. Afterward, many passengers came to the salon or to the vestibule, toting mattresses and coverlets, hoping to wedge themselves into some stability, if not comfort. Passengers at the front of the ship were likely to be irritated by intrusions of seawater seeping through the decking and the deadlights. Others could not relax enough to sleep. If they simultaneously kept a strong enough grip not to be tossed out of their berths, they became so tense that no rest was possible. The makeshift sleeping arrangements resembled a pajama party, with everyone looking for some niche or adaptable corner, some accommodation amidst the turmoil.

It was on Tuesday, the eighteenth, at the lightly attended breakfast that passengers heard the bad news that a blade on the propeller had broken during the storm's fury. A few passengers voiced their feeling that, perhaps, it was a bad omen. The latest news included the consequence that since the propeller would turn less regularly and more slowly, they could not make normal speed. Someone said that the loss would likely add three or four days to their journey. Down in the engine room, the crew kept close watch on the imbalanced thrust of the propeller. If further problems were to develop, counseled the Captain unbeknownst to the passengers, they would have to complete the journey by sail, adding two or three weeks to travel time.

Further eroding passengers' good cheer, during the after-breakfast hours on the eighteenth, when the sea was only slightly less rocking, a thick veil of fog and mist descended. The fog added the annoyance of the shrieking howl of the fog horn, deafening if you happened to be nearby. It sounded as a precaution every two or three minutes, with the hope that it would be heard up to three miles at sea to alert any approaching vessel. It was also, of course, an obvious reminder of the potential for collision under such conditions, only further unsettling passengers' frayed nerves. The fog's moisture seemed to dampen almost everything—including bedding and other fabric. The less fortunate found the moisture so condensed that leaks appeared. One passenger said exaggeratively that the fog was so dense that it actually crept under the bedclothes.

In the tight grip of fog, the unwelcome darkness fell even earlier in the afternoon. The attitude of most was one of resignation and endurance. After countless games of chess, long hours of reading, and efforts to accelerate the passage of time, one of the clergymen's conversations ended with an old proverb that could have been the passengers' motto for the day: When we cannot get what we like, it is necessary to like what we have.

All during the journey, but especially during the bad weather of Monday and Tuesday and the fog of Wednesday and Thursday, the foremost admiration of the children and adults was saved for Miss Lallie Bulkley, the "Fairy" or "Good Samaritan." Had there been a vote for "Most Valuable Passenger," she doubtless would have won by a landslide. As one of the small number unfazed by the sea's commotion, with an angelic countenance, a quiet patience, and an unaffected altruism that avoided undue self-concern, hers was ever a tranquilizing presence. Even when the waves were most raucous, she moved among young and old, amusing and encouraging, spreading a contagious cheerfulness. There was about her a distinguished air that seemed to intrigue all ages. "One than whom no nearer an angel ever lived," was the way Charles Waite said he thought of her. Weiss artfully described one occasion when, just after the news broke concerning the damaged propeller, Lallie appeared.

> She is there to some purpose as usual, smiling, active, and helpful; she occupies herself immediately with the ladies and children, making them more comfortable, arranging little things about their clothing, and in some mysterious way beautifying everything she touches. Wherever this opening rose passes there is left a breath of the fresh Springtime, which reanimates hope. The little ones call her by name, and follow her with their eyes, and when she takes her accustomed place in the midst of them, with her beautiful eyes brightened with loving sympathy, she encounters the light of many others, sparkling with pleasure and moistened with the truest welcome. As usual, she soothes all suffering which sleeps cradled upon the wings of her poetical imagination.

But, as nature has limitless surprises, Friday, the twenty-first, their seventh day at sea, was made the finest of their journey by the presence of the sun. Pastor Lorriaux opened his porthole to brilliant sunshine piercing the room like a spotlight and gilding the crests of the waves. Fog, that cruel intruder, had unregrettably slipped away in the night leaving no trace of its oppressive presence. The *Ville du Havre* was at last beyond Newfoundland, where the crew had told them fog would often attack.

On deck, the freshly polished rails glistened, and the deck had been swabbed as though a special ceremony were planned.

The vestibule, the saloon, and the salons had been cleaned, removing the clutter and righting the upheaval brought by rough seas and the makeshift sleeping arrangements. En route to breakfast, people had a spring in their steps, and many were humming, whistling, or singing melodies. The children were content just to be with each other, allowing their "Fairy," Lallie, the freedom to join her own peers for a change. Minister that he was, but French by nature, Weiss wrote that Lallie seated herself apart from others, and he watched as the sun seemed "to take delight in gilding her abundant hair, in illuminating her lovely, sympathetic countenance, and making her charming features even more beautiful."

Pastor Weiss talked with Mrs. Spafford, who allowed that she would not feel strange in France after enjoying the cordiality of the Frenchmen on board. They observed that even the waiters seemed to have more zeal and enthusiasm for their work, given the brightness of the day. Speaking of the day's beauty inspired each of the clergy to sermonize briefly.

"It has often seemed natural to me," said Pastor Cook, "when the sun appears, after being hidden for many days, to thank God from the bottom of my heart; but I have never felt this grateful joy so strongly as today." Dr. Pronier explained, "It is because in the middle of the ocean the sun is the one necessity for us more than upon land."

"Upon land," Pastor Lorriaux opined, "bad weather is nothing in comparison with storms and fogs at sea; there, one has always a home in which to take refuge, and can make himself happy there in spite of gloomy surroundings."

Pastor Weiss remarked, "The vividness of our impressions while at sea seem to me to result from the fact that we are there in a transitory state, uneasy and disagreeable in itself. Our enjoyments or anxieties there depend almost entirely on our surroundings."

Sunlight was therapeutic, erasing passenger's recall of the recent distractions. No more disordered hair and disheveled looks existed among men or women. Indeed, everyone seemed to present his most winsome self. Buoyed by sunshine, even the French joined in the hearty American-style breakfast. Weiss was surprised that, when half the crowd toasted the health of the other half, the Americans did so only with ice water, despite the French clergy's urging.

With a crew of 172, plus six stowaways, the *Ville du Havre's* 135 passengers were less than fifty percent of capacity, making the ship a comfortable neighborhood. On the way from France to America the previous September on a smaller ship, Weiss had been among 793 passengers and crew, more than twice the current number. As with all gatherings of human souls, people seemed to divide according to undefined lines of affinity: a group that prefers to be alone and left to themselves to read or study, less interested in others; the gregarious extroverts, mutually attracted and eager to know more of one another; still others include those who avoid solitude and in-depth conversation, but employ imagination, intelligence, and even cunning, to flit about and to know almost at all times what is going on. But having been sprayed by the same seawater, drenched in the same mist and fog, roiled by the rolling of the same ship, by the seventh day, it was as though they had been ritually joined in a fresh fraternity.

As nothing is so sweet as difficulty overcome, by afternoon, joyful sunlight had become accustomed, and people settled into a more blasé state. Passengers were now familiar with one another. Children played together. Everywhere she went Tanetta, the youngest Spafford, was singing "In the Sweet Bye-and-Bye." There were spelling bees, card games, chess matches, songs around a piano, and guesses about whether they might reach port by next Thursday, even with the damaged propeller. Passengers read, matched up in conversational clichés, tried to organize in their minds the disorganization of the previous four days, and napped.

An amazing, close-of-the-day sight that caught everyone's attention came at sunset when a ship was spotted on the distant horizon. With full sails spread, taking advantage of a favorable wind, the last rays of the day's sun lit up the sails. Passengers felt a strange kinship at the sight of fellow travelers, and as they hailed their co-adventurers, far too distant to notice, the sailing ship glided off the horizon, just as the last crescent of the flaming disc sun slipped into the sea.

Nightfall began a soft ending to an almost perfect day. Without ritual, the lamps were lit, the bell rang a welcome gong, and the dining room filled with almost perfect attendance. Weiss observed that, among the ladies, even the indifferent seemed to have paid extra attention to their dress and makeup, giving the surround the aura of a fine hotel dining room. Conversation was lively, invigorated by all the activity of a splendid day. Reverend Dr. Pronier asserted that the Louvre was one of the most beautiful museums in the world, only to be challenged immediately by the Spaniard, Reverend Carrasco, who was adamant that the Louvre could not compare to the museums of Madrid. It was an evidence of how relaxed the group had become that an opinion tug-of-war could dominate dinner conversation. Everyone seemed lively, except the Captain. Alone and silent, his vigilance wearied, the four days of foul weather had taken their toll.

As was customary, the children dined separately before bursting into the dining room to find their parents. Pastor Weiss, while men smoked and ladies went on deck, instinctively chose to amuse himself by amusing the children. They performed for him, to him, and on him: they climbed the columns, did gymnastic feats, and finally surrendered to bedtime, but only after Weiss promised more of the same tomorrow. In the manner of a close-knit family, the children bid goodnight. Then, with self-conscious propriety and an affectionate handshake for each parent and friend, the children retired to their rooms. The children en route to bed, the adults drifted informally into social games.

Pastor Weiss dutifully looked for Mrs. Spafford, who, he was certain, had already said prayers and tucked into bed her four girls. He proposed a starlight walk on deck. Making their way up the staircase, the pastor commented on the magnificence of the night sky: "The stars are unusually bright, the mantle of night seems studded with diamonds, sparkling from a thousand points, and, although the moon does not shine, the atmosphere is clear and transparent."

"Yes, the night is beautiful," replied Mrs. Spafford, "and I am contented."

"You were not contented before, then?" asked Weiss.

"Oh, no! I was so sick, and so sad at the separation from my husband and home, even for so short a time," she answered.

"But you have been very well for these two days," the pastor counseled. "There is every reason to hope that the weather will remain fine, and you will find these few weeks, before Mr. Spafford joins you, pass very quickly in France and Switzerland, where you will meet many agreeable persons, who will welcome you cordially."

"O, I know all that, and I have struggled against these feelings," she responded. "I know, too, that I am going only because my health makes it necessary, and that God watches over us always, but —."

"But these feelings will pass away," Pastor Weiss interrupted. "You must remember that this is the first time you have been separated from your husband for any length of time."

"It is true; but it seems to me almost impossible that a ship *can* cross this immense ocean without danger," mused the young mother. "When I think that a few planks are all that separate us and all these charming people from the depths of the sea—."

The pastor admitted, "I have often had the same thought, and it has caused me to admire the greatness of man in the strength and wisdom which God has given him, and the goodness of God, which He so graciously shows in the undeserved protection He accords us."

"This thought should fill us with confidence and hope," Mrs. Spafford observed. "I have certainly done wrong in allowing myself to be so depressed, for everything has gone on well. My children have borne it marvelously well, and everybody is so kind to them."

"You should add that your little girls are very gentle and charming," the pastor added with a dash of French chivalry.

"If you knew how little trouble they give me, and how happy I ought to be thinking of them," the mother confided.

"I am sure that in truth you are so," agreed the pastor. "It is not astonishing that you should suffer a little in the separation from your husband, but that will soon pass."

"I hope and believe it will. Good-night," bade Mrs. Spafford, as she turned, humming a Sunday-school tune that her children loved, and went down to find her beloved children already fast asleep.

On deck, many such conversational groupings had taken advantage of the starry night serenity to walk before bedtime. It was clear but cold with a consistent breeze. Charles Waite walked a few laps arm-in-arm with his beloved sister, Julia. With the storm and weather, she had hardly appeared on deck, restricting herself to her stateroom, the saloon, and dining areas. About 9:00 p.m., with fresh air enough, her brother escorted her to her stateroom, where they joined others in conversation until about 10:30 p.m. Though Charles said goodnight, not sleepy, himself, he put on a thick sweater and returned to the deck, where, a soft, multidirectional cacophony of conversations on diverse subjects floated in the night air, several amateur astronomers identifying the better-known constellations. The lull of the engine under the twinkly black sky was a pleasant comfort, savored in relative quiet until midnight, when Charles Waite retired.

Pastor Lorriaux had been hobnobbing with the ship's doctor, Monsieur Ouadint, a somewhat eccentric man who preferred the southern seas toward Greece and India over the Atlantic. Stories and experiences aplenty were at his recall. A veteran ship's doctor, he had spent most of his time in the Mediterranean. He both hated and feared the Atlantic. As a physician, his compassionate sensitivity endeared him to all during the episode of seasickness. Curiously, he had an obsession, surprising for such a veteran, regularly bending over the rail to observe the water line. The thought lurking in his mind was that the water line was rising, indicating that the ship was slowly sinking. Seeking to prove his point on the particular night of the twenty-first, with Pastor Lorriaux, he insisted on two separate checks of the water level. At Lorriaux's suggestion, he even brought the Captain to observe a third check. The doctor told Lorriaux that the Captain had laughingly dismissed his concern, saying that if the ship was lower in the water, the engineers would be the first to notice and would at once inform him.

His concern not fully assuaged, the doctor turned to expressing his eagerness to arrive at Le Havre, to see his family, and to check on a sickly child. Lorriaux tried to change the subject, telling about his own observations on America, and talking of religious matters. Eventually, they shook hands and parted as old friends, confident in being able to pick up tomorrow where they left off.

In the darkness, two male forms sheltered by the port lifeboat were discussing the stowaways. Henry Sigourney was pointing out to Francis Howard, the Canadian on his way to France, his fiancé, and his wedding, "This is the boat the stowaways hid themselves in."

"I wonder how many people a boat like that holds?" Howard asked.

Sigourney said he had read an article in *The Tribune* when the *Ville du Havre* first came to New York and it stated, "The six big ones will take altogether 210, and the two smaller ones will hold twenty each."

Quickly computing that 250 lifeboat seats for 313 people would be insufficient, Howard exclaimed, "There's not enough boats to take everybody, if the ship was sinking!" His exclamation drew a laugh from Sigourney, along with the proclamation, "God willing, we won't need them. I don't anticipate having to take to the boats. Gosh! It would be mighty cold out there a night like this." Agreeing, Howard suggested they go below and get a drink that would drive out the cold.

On the opposite side of the ship, LeGrand Cramer walked with his aunt and an acquaintance made on the voyage, Rudolf Witthaus. Their conversation turned to the ship's personnel, and Cramer criticized the casualness and lack of discipline among the crew. Witthaus said he had made the same observation; the crew did not seem to respect their officers; they were too free and easy; they were too excitable and quarrelsome. Witthaus summarized his feelings: "The food is excellent and the ship is a very fine ship. And, I have always found Captain Surmont to be a gentleman. Nevertheless, I don't feel happy about the crew. They seem to be each man for himself. One feels very unsafe with them. They seem so undependable." Cramer affirmed his regard for Captain Marius Surmont and concluded that you'd have to admit the crew was "picturesque" or colorful. After the men joked about whether the crew were pirates, Cramer's aunt, noting it was 11:45, suggested they retire. At the foot of the staircase, they bade each other goodnight and went to their rooms.

Pastor Cook had spent most of the evening playing chess. When the match finished, he came out for a stroll on deck with his colleague Dr. Pronier. They walked a good while before intersecting with Weiss, to whom they bade goodnight, as he continued in animated conversation with the American B. F. Breeden. Weiss and Breeden traded compliments of the other's home country, and concluded that of all the European nations, France was still most compatible with the U.S., proof that the spirit of Lafayette still flourished.

The deck was almost clear except for the two French clerics who seemed to have outlasted all others. Weiss spoke of teaching the ladies some of the chants in preparation for Sunday's devotional service. Then, the night ambience settling its full weight on his thinking, he mused aloud: "[N]othing impresses me with the idea of infinity, of the power of God and the weakness of man, as does the ocean."

"Yes, that is very true," Cook agreed, "and I cannot tell you how often, since we set sail, I have felt our absolute dependence upon God alone." As though their comments had been a benediction on the day, the two ministers separated, Cook to his room and Weiss to drain the night of whatever essence might be left. Having spent virtually his entire day in courteous fellowship with others, Weiss was not unhappy to be alone. A man of sincere personal faith, he leaned on the rail at the stern, his favorite part of the ship, and pondered the majesty of God's creation: the consistency of the waves, the smoke gently rising from the stacks, the white foam spray like glow-in-the-dark; the trail left by the ship as its mighty engine divided the waters; the deep and mysterious velvet of the night sky sprinkled with stars glowing like diamonds. All to himself, the deck bereft of passengers, Weiss momentarily considered spending the night there—but the cold made him think better of the idea. He ambled below to the salon and fumbled his way in the dark to the piano. To his mind there came an Neapolitan barcarolle or folk song, "Santa Lucia," which his fingers softly translated into a little night music.

Sul mare luccica	On the sea shines
l'astro d'argento.	the silver star.
Placida è l'onda,	The waves are placid,
prospero è il vento.	the wind is favorable.
Venite all'agile	Come into
barchetta mia,	my little boat,
Santa Lucia! Santa Lucia!	Santa Lucia! Santa Lucia!

Fearful of waking sleeping passengers nearby, he closed the keyboard. He slowly felt his way in the dark to his shared stateroom, where he found his deliberate quiet to be wasted effort, as Lorriaux was lying wide awake. Tired, though not having slept well, Lorriaux said that for the first time, the bed felt comfortable to him. Far from home, the two shared many things, including a longing for their families after eight weeks' absence. In a reverent, devotional quiet, the two Frenchmen of faith, hope, and charity, voiced their gratitude and delight in the calm after the storm, and eased into a deep sleep.

The syncopation of the engine was unrelenting, but any other sign of life on board was sparse. In the night quiet, while most slept, at least twenty-five pairs of eyes were on the sea. In the engine room, firemen fed coal to the hungry boiler, and watched the wiggle of the gauges as it metabolized into steam; engineers squirted oil and lubricant at crucial joints. In the Captain's quarters, Captain Surmont, watchfully awake through the nights and days of trouble and fog, had finally retired at eleven o'clock, directing that he be awakened if there were any change in weather. Lieutenant Auduvaard, officer in charge, capable and intelligent, paced the bridge. He was experienced and known to have only one weakness, if any: a slight willingness to take risk. Two lookouts kept vigil. On a calm Atlantic, fifteen hundred miles from New York, the passengers could rest easy. There was a favorable breeze. Topsails and headsails were set. They were progressing at about nine knots per hour. Most passengers would have agreed with Madeleine Mixter, who later recalled that the sea was calm, the heavens were covered with stars, and "all seemed to favor us."

With pre-bedtime rituals complete and dressed in snug pajamas, Lallie came to her mother and repeated, "The Lord is my Shepherd, The Lord is my Shepherd." She kissed her two or three times and went to sleep. In almost every cabin, some such tender rite of closure ended the finest day of the entire trip.

5
TRAGEDY IN THE NIGHT

Unknown to anyone on the *Ville du Havre,* that same resplendent sky was being studied by the crews of two other ships, destined to make history together in the early morning hours of Saturday, November 22, 1873. Each was applying the technical formulae that proved the respective locations of their vessels on the Atlantic thoroughfare.

Cradled in the arms of the sea, lullabyed by the hum of the engines, relaxed by the delight of an almost perfect day—even the night-owl passengers of the *Ville du Havre* were sleeping soundly. Just before 2:00 a.m., with all the terror of noise in the night, what sounded like two terrific claps of thunder exploded, bringing horizontal passengers upright. Rudolf Witthaus awoke to a violent shaking of his cabin and a tearing, grinding noise. Recognizing some emergency in process, he fumbled in the dark to don trousers and shoes, in the process, noticing that the engines had stopped. Studious and orderly by disposition, rather than dashing to safety, he hurriedly groped for his coat and cap before feeling his way in the darkness to the deck. To his surprise, already a flock of bewildered passengers had congregated in fright, an incredible array of pajamas, nightgowns, housecoats, bare feet, coats, and cloaks. In the astonishment of interrupted sleep, their minds could hardly comprehend what their eyes seemed to perceive: the railing and deck on the starboard side of the ship had disappeared.

Charles Waite cried out to Julia and the other ladies in their area not to be alarmed and to keep quiet, as he ran on deck to find out what had happened. He was told there had been a collision. Looking at the starboard side, he saw a hole from the kitchen aftward, a length of about forty feet, penetrating from ten to twenty feet into the abdomen of the ship, and reaching well below the water line. Waite dashed back to his cabin to urge the ladies, already dressing, to hurry though he reassured them that everything would be all right. He dressed quickly, and they all went together on deck.

Waite immediately saw the large starboard lifeboat lying partially on the deck, one of the davits that held it aloft having been broken in the crash. Quick-thinking, he placed Julia, Mrs. Bulkley, Lallie Bulkley, and Helen Wagstaff in readiness to board, just a few feet from the lifeboat. With two other men, he set to work hacking the cover off the lifeboat, and they were about to get it afloat when the ship suddenly plunged forward, submerging the lifeboat. In the nick of time, Waite sprang from the lifeboat to the deck, thinking it was only a wave, and embraced the three ladies, simultaneously sheltering them and herding them to a dry place.

Sparks were shooting like fireworks from the engine room below, giving visibility sufficient to see a large ship about three hundred yards away. Two lifeboats were already afloat in the water, filled with sailors but no passengers, in the charge of Brest (France) pilot Conillandre and First Officer Gaillard. Other French crew members were wrestling to get more of the *Ville du Havre's* lifeboats launched.

Among the clergy squadron, Lorriaux had leaped from his bed, asking, "Did you hear that?" Answering the question with his own exclamation, Weiss said, "I am sure there has been a terrible collision—listen? The screw turns again, twice—and now it stops!"

While they dressed quickly, they heard Captain Hunter descending the stairs, returning from the deck. "What has happened, Captain?" they asked excitedly.

"Oh, it is nothing—nothing. A little vessel has struck us that is all," the Captain responded.

Noting that whatever happened seemed to have been enough to have shut down the engine, Weiss and Lorriaux, completed dressing, determined to go on deck to make their own assessment. They found passages crowded with people calling to the waiters, "What has happened? What should we do?"

The waiters replied with perhaps as much as they knew, though it was too little, saying only, "It is nothing. Stay quietly in your beds." It was becoming apparent that there was no safety or disaster plan, and no central announcement of what was wrong or what anyone should do. No clear voice of authority was heard.

On deck, the crew was rushing about in all directions. Passengers were using everything imaginable to loosen the fastenings of the life preservers suspended along the guardrails. Weiss came to one man prying life preservers loose with an enormous beam, large enough to demolish the whole railing, and asked, "What are you doing? Is there a man overboard?"

"A man overboard?" he asked. "You do not know then that we are sinking?" Weiss sought to find a knife, the better to accomplish his task.

Women? Children? Passengers? Rather than duty-first, the crew all seemed bent on following natural instincts toward personal safety. With naive politeness, seeking information or direction, passengers, numbed by the rude awakening and chaos, were mostly bewildered. Their ship was not moving and was damaged; in the distance a sailing vessel appeared poised.

Clearly there appeared to be an emergency. No one seemed to know what happened, or to direct the necessary response.

As soon as minds recovered from the disruption of deep sleep, any passenger could see that two of the *Ville du Havre's* lifeboats had been crushed in the collision. Two others, numbers four and six, were fully loaded with people, but not yet launched. Struggling seamen sought to swing overboard the two largest lifeboats, normally in the charge of the Captain and Second Officer, but they appeared to be jammed or stuck, and the press of people wanting to climb in only frustrated the sailors' efforts.

Witthaus remembered seeing a sailor's sheath knife stuck in the socket of a flagstaff at the stern. He ran to get it and used it to cut the lashings holding strings of life belts. A supply of cork preservers seemed ample, and Witthaus got one for himself, then lost it in the confusion. He gave his knife to Henry Beltknap, who had wasted his own penknife chopping at the painted-stiff lashing to a life belt. Even Willie Culver was last seen grappling to loosen the ropes of a life belt with his pocketknife.

In the dark, with only starlight, Weiss and Lorriaux, in true ministerial selflessness, were still trying to find out what should be done. "Can you tell me," Weiss asked a sailor, "if there has been a collision, and whether the ship is much injured?"

"Do not be anxious, sir, if there has," he answered. "Even if the water did come in through an opening, it would not sink a ship such as this with so many decks. You need not be troubled."

Dr. Pronier, the Swiss minister appeared, seized the hand of Weiss, and said quietly, "We are lost." His face wrinkled in worried despair, he said he feared Reverend Carrasco "is probably dead, in the ruins of our stateroom. I did not see him, poor fellow."

The third of the Three Musketeers, Reverend Cook, had still not been seen.

Momentarily, Lorriaux reappeared having encountered Mrs. Spafford, cuddling Tanetta in her arms, and linked to her other three girls. Among the first passengers to reach the deck, she and the children were nearest a lifeboat being freed. But other people, scrambling selfishly, pushed in front of her and the children as she argued with her Christian conscience: whether she should fight in behalf of her children for space on the lifeboat, space to which the children were rightfully entitled; or, possessing the resources of a Christian, whether she should yield to others, who were bereft of mercy, as they in their frantic tried to save themselves.

The ship's doctor, seeing her difficulty in getting a boat for the children, sought to encourage Mrs. Spafford. "We will try to put all the women and children in the lifeboats, and be assured that I, with the Captain and officers, will be the last to leave the ship." The good doctor made his statement not realizing that already two boatloads of crew members floated safely alongside the crippled *Ville du Havre.*

Mrs. Spafford came immediately to Weiss, pleading, "You will stay with me, will you not?" As he answered her assuringly, Maggie Spafford, seeking the same guarantee, clinched Weiss and cried in fright, "Oh! You will not leave me. You will take me with you?"

"Yes, yes, my child," Weiss responded. "Do not be afraid. Stay here. I will take care of you. But you are shivering with cold in this little gown. I must look for something to cover you. You, Lorriaux, try in the meantime to keep these little ones together and find a small boat," Weiss commanded.

Weiss descended the stairs, rushed to his stateroom, grabbed his topcoat and whatever he could snatch of shawls and wraps for the children. Passing through the vestibule, he saw Reverend Cook, standing dazed, clad only in his nightshirt and talking aloud, greatly agitated.

"What are you doing here? Why are you not dressed?" Weiss asked.

"Why am I not dressed?" Cook replied. "You do not know, then, that my stateroom is broken in and that I am saved from the midst of the ruins—that while helping a lady look for her child under the rubble, I found the water rising fast. We must have been struck, then, on the starboard, across from the main mast. Do you know anything of the others?"

"Pronier seized my hand just now. He believes we are lost," Weiss said.

At that moment Doctor Ouadint came into the vestibule and, seeing Cook, called out, "Cover yourself, Mr. Cook, you will freeze!" Taking the coat from his own back, he implored, "Wait! Put on my overcoat!"

By that time, passageways into the vestibule were filled with Americans, dressed with bulky life preservers around their waists. They were like sheep, waiting quietly to be led or to be told what to do.

Mrs. Charles Mixter, concerned for her daughters and her aged father, had dashed into the passageway the instant of the crash. She was very excited, but the rest of her family was calm as they put on their clothes and went to the deck. Mr. Mixter went back down to assist his father-in-law, Mr. Curtis. The stately Mr. Curtis stood quietly in his gray cap and overcoat, his hands in his pockets, a confident smile, ready to face whatever would come. Despite the subsequent confusion, Mr. Mixter had the presence of mind to run to their stateroom, cut the life preservers from under the beds and quickly tie them around his wife and his daughters, Madeleine and Helen. Madeleine begged their grandfather, Mr. Curtis, to take her life preserver, but he declined, maintaining his statuesque stance. Mr. Mixter ran back down to see if he could rouse others but to no avail.

Nearby stood Mrs. Bininger with her daughter, Fanny, and two stewardesses. A lifeboat was next to them, but it had not budged. Someone said it had been smashed in.

The "Good Samaritan" was among the group, quietly supporting her mother and her friend Helen. When the crash first occurred, her mother immediately feared they might have to take to the lifeboats. She had advised them to dress warmly, gather a few of their most precious belongings into satchels, and dash on deck into the night's chill.

"How will our friends in New York bear the news of our death—those who love us so much," Mrs. Bulkley wondered.

A priest who had hardly been seen on ship suddenly appeared, passing among the groups, saying, "Are you Catholic? Repent, and I will give you absolution," as he made his way to try to get into one of the lifeboats.

Two or three Americans with life preservers strapped on decided to take no chances on a lifeboat and jumped overboard into the sea.

There was massive confusion. What to do? What to do? It was the question everyone asked, but no one answered. Children were screaming, and terror was mounting. A crowd had gathered near the starboard.

Suddenly, there was a mighty shudder, prompting Weiss instinctively to shout, "Let us go over to the other side with Madame Spafford and the children—quickly." At that very instant, the mainmast fell with a terrifying crash, flinging into the sea the two loaded lifeboats from which Mrs. Spafford and family had just been preempted. The horrifying screams coming from the wounded and dying on the crushed lifeboats and in the water brought an agonizing reality to the surreal context. Though Mrs. Spafford was slightly wounded, she realized that had she insisted on a place for herself and her children on those lifeboats—a place rightfully hers as first on-the-scene and as a mother with children—the family would have perished.

By that time, one group that had come together on deck, included Mrs. Bulkley, Miss Murray and her brother, Mrs. Platt, Judge and Mrs. Peckham, Mr. and Mrs. Montague and their fifteen-year-old daughter. As the mast fell, Mrs. Platt cried aloud, "Good God! We are shipwrecked!" Mrs. Bulkley, thinking there still must be some organized attempt at rescue, suggested, "Perhaps it has been cut away on purpose." Suddenly, Mrs. Platt burst out in fervent prayer. Their group was joined by Caroline Turcas, urgently pleading, "May I stay with you?"

Pastor Weiss and the Spafford cluster could see only a fraction of the frantic actions, as myriad groupings of family or friends or hastily formed groups debated what to do, how to face the end. Some in resignation and despair threw themselves on deck in earnest prayer. Judge Peckham, resolutely clasping his wife's hand, cried out, "Let us die bravely!" Lallie prayed in the midst of a small circle of kneeling women, all calm and resigned. They had dropped their satchels of valuables, so useless now. Embracing her mother, Lallie offered comfort. "Don't be frightened, Mamma and Helen, it will only be a moment's struggle and then we will be in heaven together."

LeGrand Cramer, with some other men, was still attempting to wrestle the big starboard lifeboat free of its strictures. Captain Hunter, who had originally told Weiss the crash was "nothing," seized a settee, thrust it into the hands of his two daughters, and told them, "Do not let go of it under any circumstances whatever." Ironically, Doctor Ouadint, ever fearful of the ship's water level, had at last been quite suddenly proven correct—the ship was by that time, indeed, lower in the water than ever, and soon to be even lower. To his everlasting credit, despite his own anxieties, the Doctor stayed in the lower levels throughout the crisis. He tended to the wounded with bed sheets and did his duty with whatever makeshift supplies might be at hand.

Once the mast had fallen, the dazed bewilderment intensified. Helen Wagstaff, who had spoken hardly a word, said with astonishment, "I cannot realize anything and don't believe we are in danger." At that very moment the ship pitched, flushing a rush of cold water over the side, splashing their knees. Lallie, still calm and collected, besought her mother, "Forgive me, Mamma, if I have ever done anything wrong."

James Bishop had taken time to fully dress. He calmly told Andrew McCreary that he had left everything in his cabin but his money. "I've got seven hundred pounds in English bank notes and French gold louis on me," he said. McCreary told him to get rid of the gold because it would weigh him down. But cavalier Bishop gave a laughing shrug, saying, "I've a notion I'll come out of this. Folks at home say I got a charmed life. Once was in a train wreck: train in a river. Another time in a gunpowder explosion. Came out of both. This is the third time."

By then, there was no doubt that the *Ville du Havre* was sinking. Charles Mixter, encircled by his family, lifted up his hands to heaven and said, "God has given us many blessings, and now we all go down together."

Maggie Spafford, holding Pastor Weiss's hand, looked up into his compassionate face and pleaded, "Pray!"

"God pardon us. God have mercy upon us," murmured the pastor.

Mrs. Kennet, standing with Mrs. Platt and Miss Murray, was observed holding her two-year-old son, who had been such a favorite with all the passengers. She passed him off to their nurse and went to clasp the hand of her daughter.

Another loud crash split the tense air as the bow ripped from the ship and sank in an instant, leaving remaining passengers on a floating hulk of metal, no longer even a ship. Maggie Spafford was terrified, quickly dropped Weiss's hand, and went to her mother, telling the pastor, "Oh, it is all right now." Lifting her dark eyes and lowering her soft voice, she addressed her mother, "Mama, God will take care of us."

Tanetta Spafford, her arms around her mother's neck, was quiet. Annie Spafford had earlier seen her mother straining to hold up Tanetta, and she was still selflessly providing reinforcement to her mother's arm. Bessie Spafford, silent and pale, held fast to her mother's knees. The five of them joined their governess Mademoiselle Nicolet, and pastors Lorriaux and Weiss to form a quiet, united huddle. Suddenly when the bow split, Charles Waite, trying his best to outsmart the circumstances, called out "Rush to the other side!" Annie offered her sweet counsel amidst the mayhem: "Don't be afraid. The sea is His and He made it" (Psalm 95.5).

6
MAYHEM

There was no time for strategizing. There was no way of escape. In an unannounced instant, the dark sea overwhelmed the floating hulk, swabbing the deck with massive waves, plunging everyone and everything into the frigid waters. The *Ville du Havre* had been rammed midship by the *Loch Earn,* a three-mast, medium clipper ship of the Loch Line of Glasgow. Both ships remained afloat for awhile, but in no more than fifteen minutes, the *Ville du Havre,* the $1.5 million creation of the ingenuity of man, the most luxurious ship afloat at that time, spiraled downward, breaking into scrap, irreverently hurling 226 people to their final resting place.

Of course, only *surviving*-passengers' sensations are known, and while similar in some respects, the experience was distinctive to each individual. Weiss's description was, "We feel ourselves whirled round and round as if in a vast funnel, and roll over in the depths of an abyss which seems immeasurable."

Mary Bulkley, in one of the few firsthand accounts of survival, wrote of her separation from her daughter, Lallie.

> Some tremendous force parted us as we went down together. I clutched desperately at her dress, but it slipped from my fingers, and I knew I was drowning alone; the sufferings of strangulation were on me, and I thought that I was falling to the very bottom of the sea;

with almost a start of horror I found myself rising to the surface . . . as I arose my hand struck a hard, cold substance; I grasped it, and found it had been an iron chain, suspended from a boat which was upside down in the water; a number of French sailors were clinging to the upraised keel. I spoke not a word, as these men shrieked for help, for I felt it was better they should not know a woman was clinging to the bottom of the boat. In a few moments the boat broke to pieces; for a second the shattered fragments held together like a raft, then scattered by the surging waters, all disappeared. I saw not a human being around me. As the boat broke to pieces a beam struck me in the chest. I remembered that persons could be supported in the water by resting lightly on a plank; so as the chain was drawn from me this beam supported me. I was surrounded by barrels and broken timber, etc., and my faculties were keen enough to distinguish the smell of liquor on the surface of the water; thus, I lay on the waters, not struggling for life, but passively waiting God's will. A woman once floated quite near me, and I heard her say "*Sauvez moi;*" so I knew she was French. I could no longer see the ship, and not a life-boat had I seen, or knew that one soul had been rescued. I felt that I was drifting far away into the ocean, and never dreamed of being saved; still physical instinct kept me on the plank. I was alone with my God, and prayed that He might take my soul. I was cold and benumbed, and knew I could not live many minutes; suddenly I felt something under me, and stretching my feet downwards, I felt them sustained by a triangular piece of timber; again, with this support under my feet, and the plank at my breast, I raised my head higher above the water, but soon a faintness seemed to come over me; I felt the waters going over my head, and raising my eyes for the last time as I supposed, towards Heaven, I saw a great white boat above me. Here I screamed for the first time: "Help a woman." The next instant strong arms were about me, and when I asked, "Who are you?' a voice replied, "An English sailor, come to save you."

Seventeen-year-old Madeleine Mixter, who later amazed everyone with her maturity, wrote her story.

> There was a sudden surging of the water, a rushing
> sound, and I found myself carried down, down,
> down. I thought I should never rise again . . . all my
> soul was merged in one ardent prayer . . . I rose to the
> surface, seized a board and lay there . . . alternately
> swimming and resting amidst a sea of forms crying
> for help. Not a vestige of our ship was to be seen. The
> English [the English ship, the *Loch Earn*] was in full
> sight. I was picked up by one of her boats in about half
> an hour and carried on board.

Safe on board a lifeboat, Madeleine found her sister,
Helen, also saved. She had clung to a cork ladder, where Fanny
Bininger was also holding tight, and both were soon picked up.
Helen was rescued crying aloud, "I do not wish to be drowned.
I will not be drowned." She repeated her declaration to one of
the French sailors as he reached out to hoist her aboard the
lifeboat, where, even shivering in the cold, she repeated, "I
didn't want to be drowned!"

The Mixter girls learned from Mrs. Swift that their father
had swum up to her and asked to take hold of her life preserver.
She answered, "Yes, but do not pull me under." LeGrand Cramer
had been sharing the same life preserver. A lifeboat fortunately
approached, and as Cramer was being pulled aboard, Mr. Mixter,
suddenly and unexplainably, gave a groan and sank at once.
Madeleine Mixter wrote, "I fear it was a cramp—oh! it is so hard
to think he was almost saved and then lost again!!"

But what of Anna Spafford and her children? As she was
sucked downward, she felt Tanetta torn from her arms by
a blow inflicted by some random piece of debris, a strike so
violent that her arm was severely bruised. She flailed at the
water trying to catch her baby, who clung to her gown just for
a moment before another smashing wayward timber tore the
gown away. Reaching out again, all she could clutch was a man's
leg in corduroy trousers. Instantly, Anna was rolled about in

a whirlpool and pressed to the edge of consciousness before coming to the surface near the ship, instinctively clutching a small plank. The next thing she recalled was the splash of an oar that awakened her to full consciousness, making her aware that she was unexplainably lying on the bottom of a lifeboat, severely bruised all over her body, sick with sea water, her long hair matted with salt, and her dressing gown shredded. From a surviving passenger's pocket watch, it was later determined that Anna had been in the sea for one solid hour.

At the moment of sinking, Charles Waite had his arms around a quartet of ladies: his sister (Julia), Mrs. Bulkley, Lallie Bulkley, and Helen Wagstaff. He was intending to hurry them with the coterie that included the Spaffords and others to the drier side of the deck. For an instant, they were together; then, as the ship washed away beneath him, Charles Waite was struck on the head by a piece of debris and was momentarily senseless. When he became fully aware, he was alone in the sea with no one around him. Swimming for a time, he found a piece of lumber he assumed to be part of the wooden frame that held the cover to the lifeboats. He got astride it almost like he had mounted a horse and allowed it to sustain him for some time. Then, he caught sight of two girls paddling furiously. He swam over to them and recognized Maggie and Annie Spafford. Waite, fully dressed except for his shoes, told the girls to do as he directed, and they would be all right. "Take hold of my coat," he admonished, "till I can find a piece of wreckage." Each girl took hold of one of the side pockets of his coat. He towed them until coming upon a board large enough to support all three. He then tried to maneuver the girls onto the board, keeping their heads above water, and supporting them with his arms. No one could know what the girls had already been through, but they appeared too weak to coordinate their movements with his. Waite frantically hoped for one of the rescue lifeboats to come to them but saw not a trace. The idle weight of the exhausted girls pushed down Waite's arms. With his own strength ebbing, he realized the girls were not responding to his pleading. Gradually, the tired eyes of the girls closed in exhaustion, and he could gain no response from them. His muscles strained beyond the point of numbness. Waite was helpless as first one, and then the other floated from his powerless arms. A lifeboat from the *Ville du Havre* finally came alongside, and sailors lifted him, physically spent, from the sea. Waite melted into a tearful collapse, the entire experience more than his composure and nerves could bear. He later realized that he was one of the first persons saved from the sea.

Pastor Lorriaux, unable to swim, was fortunate to encounter successively a scrap of wreckage to which he could cling, then a life preserver, and finally a raft—probably a piece of floor or roofing from the *Ville du Havre*. He was able to float his raft to the side of the *Loch Earn,* from where he could take in the entire mayhem, awaiting his rescue.

When Pastor Weiss found himself alive on the crest of the sea, and surprisedly looking up at a velvet, star-pierced sky, he began swimming, until nearly suffocating with exhaustion and almost dead, he allowed himself to float. Buoyed by the sea, he struck a short plank that increased his buoyancy and helped him reach a lifeboat. Consciousness left him just as rescuers, taking him aboard, realized he was covered in blood from wounds to his head and his right hand.

The last of the Three Musketeers, Pastor Cook, had been dazed by a blow when his cabin collapsed before the ship sank. He was bloodied, disoriented, and barely clothed in the moments right after the collision. As the *Ville du Havre* sank, Pastor Cook, like so many others, had the sensation that his body was going down into a dark, whirling funnel of water, with the sinking ship at the bottom of the funnel. Rolling over and over in a spinning centrifuge of bodies and wreckage, when the spinning slowed and he struggled to the surface, his wobbly consciousness left him unsure: was he dead or alive? A voice seemed audible, and as it came closer, he was sure it was an English voice, and that, indeed, he was alive. An English sailor, not at all encouraging, was saying, "He's pretty far gone, but he's alive. Here, put this 'round him."

After the same plunging experience others described, Rudolph Witthaus discovered himself on the ocean surface. In the dark, spying a topmost spar of the sail rigging, he swam to it and was later joined by two French sailors and Henry Beltknap. To prevent overweighting pulling his crude raft under water, Witthaus had to push away floating corpses that tended to entangle the rigging still attached to the spar. After about thirty minutes floating with the spar, the weary Witthaus kicked off his trousers to lighten his load. Hauled out of the water after about an hour, he had nothing but his shirt and underwear and was virtually comatose with cold.

LeGrand Cramer had been last seen trying to free the ship's big lifeboat when the deck was swept away beneath his feet. Having floated to the water's surface, he found a piece of debris, probably a grate, that provided buoyancy. His head barely above water, he scanned the surround for any signs of his aunt, but all he could see was a sea surface dotted with the heads of unrecognizable people, their hair wet and matted, their faces grim with fright, swimming, paddling, desperate for rescue. Cramer could see a boat picking up people about a hundred yards away, but he was too far away to attract their attention. Bobbing along, he came upon others desperately trying to survive. The instincts of each was to grab the grating. Twice, Cramer was pulled under by the acts of panicked, drowning people. In anxiety, he thought he had been in the water for hours before a lifeboat found him and brought him aboard. Afterward, he learned that he was picked up only thirty minutes after the collision. His watch had stopped at 2:30 a.m.

As touching as were stories of selfless heroism, there were also many accounts on the darker side. Lorriaux saw in a distance a log floating on the water with ten or fifteen people hanging on. An already overcrowded lifeboat passed near them but unable to take on any more passengers, the lifeboat hastened to the *Loch Earn*. The boat yielded its passengers and returned immediately within a half hour to the spot where it encountered the log ladened with survivors. By that time, the log and those clinging to it had succumbed.

One survivor seen wafting in the water viciously struck a girl in the face when she approached the plank that was sustaining him. Weiss saw a man, crazed with fright, arrive at a rescue boat at the same time as a woman. The man had a life preserver but still attempted to clamber into the boat ahead of the woman. The sailors begged him to wait a moment, but he seized the woman by the hair to drag her back into the sea and in a rage began biting those who disentangled his hand from her hair.

Ropes were suspended over the sides of the *Loch Earn* to support anyone who came near. One woman, buoyed by a life preserver, was seen with a child in her arms. By exceptional stamina, she had been able to reach the ship, but all the lifeboats were away picking up survivors. The lady was seen making a valiant lunge to reach one of the ship's overhanging ropes. She missed, and as though having used up the last ounce of strength, she and her child fell back into the sea never to be seen again.

Obviously, many were killed or drowned instantly. Others were seen floating in the icy waters amidst bodies and body parts, swimming or paddling, aided by pieces of floating wreckage, but as waves uncontrollably dashed about, the dense flotsam had the capacity to inflict serious injuries. In the frigid waters, no one could expect to endure for long. As it turned out, all the survivors had been rescued within an hour, and all were safely on board the *Loch Earn* by 4:30 a.m., two-and-a-half hours after the collision. But persisting, just in case, lifeboats from the *Loch Earn* continued to roam the site until 10:00 a.m.

As would become clearer in retrospect, it would be difficult to imagine a more wretched situation. In the dark, on a cold November night in the North Atlantic, with everyone roused from sleep, the *Ville du Havre* and the *Loch Earn* collided. In saving themselves first, the French crew of the *Ville du Havre* disobeyed orders, disobeyed laws of the sea, and even disregarded common chivalry and courtesy. Lifeboats and life preservers were not readily accessible on the *Ville du Havre,* immovably stuck in place by multiple coats of paint. The lack of a safety drill or even an authoritative voice to instruct at the instant of the accident was a glaring omission. Apparently, some of the *Ville du Havre* crew did not believe their ship would sink, as there were no flares lighted and no distress signal. A confusion of language delayed an all-out rescue effort by the crew of the *Loch Earn.*

Immediately after the accident, as the two ships were idly adrift, Captain Robertson of the *Loch Earn* saw a boat rowing in his direction with four crew members on board. With no idea of the catastrophic damage sustained by the *Ville du Havre,* he merely assumed the small boat had been dispatched in a calm, orderly fashion to enlist assistance since, as Captain Robertson said later, if there had been any danger of sinking, such a boat would have been crowded to capacity with passengers. Momentarily, the different languages befuddled communication. Captain Robertson called out to the four crewmen in the boat, "Is your ship badly hurt?" The men in the boat, all French, did not understand and so gave no reply.

When the Captain again called out, one of the seamen replied, *"Comprends pas"* (I don't understand).

As terrible as the tragedy was, amazing calm was the reaction of people on deck. Absent leadership, they cried, prayed, drew together, looked for direction and instruction, stood in amazement, worried about others, considered where to stand, what to do. Such feelings must have ricocheted within their heads as they faced the end.

It would be days before the toll of the tragedy could be fully known and told. But for each survivor the grim toll was already becoming clear. Mrs. Spafford, for example, held out hope, at first knowing only that Tanetta was ripped from her own arms and lost. She later learned from Charles Waite about Maggie and Annie, and she never heard a word about Bessie.

7
CAN THE SAVED BE RE-SAVED?

It was half past four in the morning when the last person from the *Ville du Havre* was lifted aboard the *Loch Earn*. With the excess adrenalin, the frenzied activity, and the darkness, the full impact of the wreck had not been assessed. All attention had been properly devoted to clothing and compassionate care of the survivors—the soft, human side of the mishap. Fortunately, the *Loch Earn* had not been fully loaded and was in ballast, and a quick analysis left the *Loch Earn's* Captain Robertson not unduly concerned. Although he realized that the four available small lifeboats, should they have to abandon ship, would never contain the more than a hundred persons on board or would put the boats so low in the water that they would be imperiled, he was confident that the ship was able to make land within two weeks. With the ship's carpenter, he had earlier descended in the darkness to the huge engine compartment to survey with lantern light the effects of the collision. It was clear that damage had been done, but the ship was made of iron, and at that point, it was not taking on water.

There was no celebration of survival aboard the *Loch Earn*. There may have been a few joyous reunions upon recognizing that someone was safe, but the prevailing cloud of gloom suppressed any suggestion of joy. Every *Ville du Havre* passenger was cold, drenched, hurting—feeling somewhere between deep gratitude for their own survival, guilt that they were still alive when others were not, and anger that their loved ones were so undeservedly snatched from them. Each was physically and emotionally spent, and probably theologically spent as well. They were walking wounded, with physical exhaustion dominant, and many with cuts, bruises, broken limbs, as well as undiagnosed aches and pains. As with survivors of any tragedy there was nagging denial or disbelief that it could happen so suddenly—through no cause they had initiated and amidst circumstances that they could not have prevented. Broken and wounded spirits were likely the most severe injuries.

A roll call yielded eighty-seven passengers and crew of the *Ville du Havre* present. Officers and crewmen totaled fifty-nine; twenty-eight were passengers, ten of whom were women. Helen Mixter was the only child to survive. That meant that 226 persons had been lost. No one was rescued after the first hour following the collision. Not a single passenger was saved directly off the deck of the *Ville du Havre*. Not one of the rescued passengers was taken from the ship in a lifeboat. In one way or another, each survivor had been victor in a cold, wet tussle with the sea and its fury.

A rope ladder had been thrown over the side of the *Loch Earn,* but most of the shipwrecked had been hoisted up the side of the ship by a rope slung under their arms. Shivering from shock and the cold, from grief and sheer fright, they were compassionately ushered into the main saloon and greeted with hot coffee. Mrs. Bulkley later wrote, "As I recognized faces of the passengers about me, I felt as if it were a resurrection of the dead." Every piece of spare clothing was generously donated by the *Loch Earn's* British crew. Too stunned for modesty, the passengers' various stages of undress went almost unnoticed, even as they scavenged for dry garments. Women changed salt-soaked nightgowns for men's heavy woolen shirts, flannel underwear, and serge and canvas trousers so that whatever they had been wearing when rescued could dry out. At first, passengers simply laid on the floor in complete exhaustion of spirit and body that utter futility imposes. Gradually, they made the best of circumstances. Mrs. Bulkley wrote: "Not a toothbrush among us; only such clothing as we had upon us when saved, which has been dried for us and the flannel underclothing of the sailors. Only two ladies have shoes, the rest are in woolen stockings which the English sailors gave us. . . ."

Only hours before, the same ladies could have chosen the best from their closets, resplendent imported fabrics shaped stylistically and expertly tailored to their exacting standards by the finest fashion seamstresses of the day. Suddenly, [l]adies and gentlemen who before had never known a single privation were standing there shivering and destitute, Charles Waite later wrote, as though making the best of castoffs at a charity giveaway.

Most survivors had physical injuries—cuts, gashes, severe bruises—from the destruction aboard ship or from the flotsam flailing the sea's surface in the mayhem after the collision. Like most passengers, Anna Spafford scanned the ragged forms there assembled, as though at any moment one of her dear children might come into focus, perhaps miraculously hand-in-hand with a rescuer. But soon, it became clear that the quiet, wet, dispirited band was all there would be—a meager token of surviving grace from a night of hell. The realization fell hard: no one else was saved, and no one else would ever be saved from the *Ville du Havre.*

That four Spafford daughters were lost was a realization their mother reached with an overwhelming finality. Her instinct was to rush out of the cabin and to look for them as though to be sure they were not looking for her. Almost hysterical, she thought of jumping into the sea to die with her girls if they were not to be found. With great difficulty, Reverend Lorriaux physically restrained her. As with heaviness of his own pastoral heart, he considered the horror of a mother's loss of her own flesh and blood, multiplied by four, a loss he had never considered when Horatio Spafford days earlier had asked him to watch over his wife and children.

In the stunning quiet of the survivor's circle, where each dealt with bereavement in his own way, Anna Spafford was the focus of the greatest sympathy. Charles Waite wrote, even several days after the accident, that she had been very low and that they had feared for her life. As she wept, she said, "God gave me my four little daughters; it is He who has taken them from me. He will make me understand and accept His will."

The four clerics were in difficulty. Cook was alive and had come aboard the *Loch Earn* almost naked; yet in the stark cold, he declined to accept even a blanket until every woman was covered. Lorriaux, primarily occupied with Mrs. Spafford, found Weiss lying in blood on the deck, exhausted, incapable of a single step, heaving each breath through allover pain, and with wounds to his head and hands and bruised ribs. As essential as breathing was, it was his most painful chore. Lorriaux had the presence of mind to realize that his friend had a temperature and was approaching a state of delirium. He insisted that Weiss get to a cabin, but the poor victim said he could not bear to be touched. Selfless, even in his pain, Weiss inquired about Dr. Pronier, who, according to Lorriaux, was last seen in the *Ville du Havre's* saloon with a severe gash on his head, and who was now nowhere to be found. He would never return to his wife and six children, awaiting him in Geneva. At the beginning of the trip, he had told friends of a premonition of disaster, and that if he returned safely, he would never venture on the ocean again. Reverend Carrasco, the courageous and eloquent Spanish pastor, who had shared Pronier's stateroom, had already promised never to sail again and had not been seen after the collision.

Through bitter tears, Fanny Bininger was inconsolable as she realized her mother was lost. One American, never named, was taken aboard, frightened and alone, the only survivor of the six stowaways. Captain Hunter's last-minute admonition to his daughters to hold on to the settee he placed in their hands and to not let go, had proven an adequate instrument of survival, for Annie and Mary when rescued fell into each other's arms. Alone, a poignant picture of grief, Mrs. Kennet was coping with the loss of her two children.

"If only"—was a conversational theme heard a lot. Weiss reflected on how he should have kept hold of Bessie Spafford's hand when in those last moments on deck, she let go of him to be at her mother's side. I might have saved her, he reasoned. Madeleine Mixter wondered how it was that her father unexplainably sank just as he was about to be rescued. Mrs. Bulkley was absorbed in a mystified stupor, reminding herself over and again, that she, unable to swim, survived when Lallie, an excellent swimmer, did not. Many were like Pastor Cook, overwhelmed with a sense of remorse that they were alive, when their friends died. Some openly criticized the French crew of the *Ville du Havre* as undisciplined, not respectful of authority, and engrossed in their own rescue, totally without conscience for the passengers.

Captain Surmont of the *Ville du Havre* spoke to no one. He made his way about the *Loch Earn* in the manner of a guest, almost dumbstruck by what had happened, fatefully banished in disgrace from his own ship by circumstances beyond his control. As Captain, he had watchfully stayed awake with only catnaps during the days and nights of storm and fog, and when finally able to sleep, his ship fell victim to an entirely avoidable, unthinkable collision at sea. Through his weariness, he regretted that he had ever gone to sleep. He must have considered that had he been on the bridge, the accident never would have happened. A graduate of the French Navy, tall and impressive-looking, clean-shaven except for a tuft of beard under his chin, he had at about age fifty a fine reputation for seamanship. At the pinnacle of his career, he was carefully selected to take command of the world's greatest passenger ship. Now, clad only in a workingman's ill-fitting shirt and trousers, without gold braid, epaulets, or command of the most luxurious steamship afloat, by Providence he had suffered the disgrace of having captained a sunken ship. By the law of the sea, he was now subject to the authority of a mere sailing ship captain.

No passenger found it in his heart to blame Captain Surmont. Weiss recalled that earlier in their journey, during the period of heavy fog, it had been a comfort to see this man so deeply penetrated by his own responsibility that he scarcely permitted himself to leave his post even for a few minutes. In the end, he had gone down with his ship, and only by a twist of fate had he resurfaced and been picked up. Others would wonder that the lack of discipline aboard ship was the Captain's responsibility, but at that time, the surviving passengers did not mention it. For his part, the Captain remained in a silent cloud of gloom, standing for hours staring at the sea as though questing to understand the mystery that had placed him in the center of such tragic circumstances. Few ever knew that Captain Surmont would live only a few more years, and bearing his sorrow, would be judged to have died of a broken heart.

Gradually, each of the odd-looking tribe of survivors was given brandy, wrapped in a blanket, gathered within the cabin of the ship, and enfolded in the warm bond of friendship and support common to those surviving a close confrontation with death. Twenty-four slept on improvised beds, covering almost the entire floor of the cabin. Several who had lost family members chose to remain on deck, hoping against hope that by some miracle their loved one might appear. To economize space, surviving crew members wedged themselves into the crew quarters of the *Loch Earn,* built with cargo as its first priority, rather than passengers.

Despite lack of creature comforts, the *Loch Earn* was the vessel of salvation for the survivors, so none could complain. At the same time, once on board and acclimated to the hardship that would be theirs until touching land again, the group became more aware and began to discuss openly the apparent frailty of the ship that saved them.

As the morning daylight of Saturday, November 22, 1873, had crept up the horizon, an eerie stillness dominated the *Loch Earn.* Those who could, rested or slept, the physical and emotional exhaustion self-evident. The three boats that had been circling the wreck site since shortly after 2:00 a.m. gave up their search. The crewmen, weary of rowing and dodging wreckage debris, were near exhaustion and had to be helped aboard. A reluctance to abandon the loved ones so suddenly swallowed by the ocean without a trace seemed to hold the *Loch Earn* in suspense. At points, even the sailors took off their hats and bowed their heads as though acknowledging that the sea had become a vast burial ground only hours before.

About 8:00 a.m., a glimmer of excitement began to shine among the melancholy group as a ship was sighted off the leeward bow, an estimated three miles away. The French sailors enthusiastically discussed the sighting, and the Captain, yielding to his best judgment, had the red ensign run up and the ship's Union Jack flown upside down—the international symbol of distress. While Captain Robertson was confident, the veteran Captain Surmont confessed to some anxiety about the durability of the *Loch Earn*. Rudolf Witthaus and Henry Beltknap had already made their own assessment, a very negative one, and shared their grave doubts with Captain Surmont first, and then with Captain Robertson.

The oncoming ship had slowed its pace, a sign it was coming to aid the cripple. It was clearly flying American Stars 'n Stripes, and about a half mile away, the crew made out the name *Trimountain*. Captain Robertson sent out a small boat from the *Loch Earn*. He instructed the first mate: tell the Captain of the American ship that we have eighty-seven survivors of a collision with a French steamer during the night, and could he take on board fifty of the passengers? He also wanted the mate to be sure to tell the Captain that it was Captain Robertson's opinion that his ship was safe, and they could reach England unaided.

After an excited conference, the boat returned. Emissaries brought the sympathy of the *Trimountain's* Captain William W. Urquhart, as well as offers of hospitality and assurance of his willingness to take the entire roster of survivors, including the crew and Captain Robertson if necessary. The *Trimountain,* a cargo vessel with full rigging of sails, had extra space between the decks, and they reported, though it had limited drinking water, would be glad to have any the *Loch Earn* might spare. Later, Captain Urquhart would explain the amazing miscalculation, that for the first time in his life, the charterer had left a vacant space of about seventy feet in the upper between-decks that could not be filled because the *Trimountain* was as deep in the water as underwriters would permit for that season of the year. It was as though the hand of Providence again had allowed for some unknown exigency.

While passengers doubted the *Loch Earn's* durability and wasted no time gathering their things to abandon it, Captain

Robertson did the captain-like thing, exuding confidence in his ship and calmly stating his plan to see his ship to port—even as plans were worked out for transferring the rescued passengers.

Conveying passengers from one ship to another on the high seas was not simple, even in calm weather. To all but wizened sailors, getting from the *Loch Earn* to the *Trimountain* was again to confront frightening hazards. The crew nonchalantly demonstrated how to step from the ship into the small boat at the exact moment when the crest of a wave vaulted the boat highest and closest to the *Loch Earn's* railing. As an extra precaution, lifelines were fastened around the waists of the transferees, in case a misstep dropped one of them into the sea. With all the survivors had just been through, it was torturous even to consider such a maneuver, and only self-preservation in the face of the debilitating condition of the *Loch Earn* could motivate the survivors. Then, when the boats reached the *Trimountain,* Captain Urquhart thoughtfully ordered that each woman passenger be placed in an armchair that was fastened to a rope and hung from the arm of the main yard. With a lanyard belted around the chair, the women and one child were hoisted aboard—slowly, one-by-one—like valuable cargo.

The male survivors were treated less delicately. Crew members from the *Ville du Havre* scampered up the lines thrown over the *Trimountain,* and the other men were hoisted on board via bowlines. Farewells were resolute, but softened as parting words of encouragement were appended. Thus, the hardy band of survivors experienced their fifth ocean-borne transport since departing New York: the *Ville du Havre*, the rescue boat, the *Loch Earn,* the transfer boat, the *Trimountain.*

The transfer had been successful in about three hours but not everyone transferred. As soon as news of the planned conveyance had unofficially made its way through the crew and surviving passengers, Lorriaux had gone immediately to the injured Weiss. Wracked with pain and semidelirious, Weiss seemed gradually to understand that an able ship was alongside, willing to take everyone on board and see them to England. But Weiss knew that his pain was so great he could not be moved.

Lorriaux, taking his dear friend's hand, told Weiss that he was of a mind to remain with him, but Mrs. Spafford was determined to transfer to the new ship. Lorriaux, still very concerned for her mental state and conscious of his parting commitment to her husband to look after her, was pondering aloud his dilemma. At that moment, Pastor Cook entered the stateroom. Coughing, looking frail and ill, Cook still readily volunteered that he would remain with Weiss. "So, as you wish," Weiss muttered, wan and motionless, eyes closed, too sick to take issue, or to compel Cook to go with the others.

Leaving Weiss to the dark quiet of his quarters on the uncertain *Loch Earn,* Lorriaux and Cook confided to one another their dismay and helplessness. Lorriaux spoke first: "He is gravely hurt. Some of his ribs are broken and he has lost all hope."

In what must have seemed a challenge to his theology—the possibility that Weiss might be saved from perishing *in* the sea, only to die a few days later *on* the sea—Cook agreed, saying, "Yes, I see that. I am afraid that before we reach land I may have to close his eyes. I don't think he will live."

Cook was watching over Lorriaux's hoisting to the *Trimountain* when Captain Robertson came beside him, confidently expounding on his ship's strength, and opining that in all probability their *Loch Earn* would even arrive a day or two before the *Trimountain.* So, just in case, Cook called out to Lorriaux the terms of an agreement: "He who arrives first will send word to the wife of the other." Captain Urquhart noticed among the first boatload of women a lone man, who, immediately on board, took the arm of a woman weeping hysterically. He learned later that it was Pastor Lorriaux, keeping close watch on Mrs. Spafford.

With its passenger manifest pared to three, the *Loch Earn* was left only with *Ville du Havre* fireman, Leopold Zaffiere, who appeared to have serious internal injuries so that he likely could not have endured the rigor of being moved, Pastor Weiss, continuously pleading for water and fading in-and-out of delirium, and Pastor Cook, who appeared to have been the freest of the three, but even he was held by bonds of friendship and pastoral compassion.

As Captain Urquhart prepared his crew to set sail for the onward journey, Mrs. Mary Bulkley voiced the thoughts of many survivors, pleading with the Captain to remain a little longer. I cannot believe my daughter was taken from me. God would not be so unjust. You cannot leave while there is still hope. She may be on a piece of wreckage, alive and praying for us to come to her. She may have floated out of sight. It would be wicked to leave without searching. The Captain, knowing there was no hope, consented to survey the area, sighting only a couple of casks. At dusk, his one last offer to those remaining aboard the *Loch Earn* was declined, allowing the *Trimountain's* sails to billow and head for his destination.

Experienced even at the age of thirty and serious about his religious faith, Captain Urquhart opened wellsprings of compassion to the survivors. Touched especially by the half-clad and ill-clad ladies, the Captain remembered some old dresses left behind by a passenger and found some extra clothing of his own. He made arrangements for two meals per day, one at midmorning and one in the afternoon. With the workers from the *Ville du Havre,* he had sufficient staff to operate the bakery all night, and cooks to make advance preparations.

Captain Urquhart was well-known for speed, having made some of the fastest crossings of the Atlantic. In the trade, many people called him Lucky Urquhart, because things seemed often to go his way. His cargo ship, suddenly loaded with an unanticipated "cargo" of anxious people who freshly escaped with their lives, enjoyed a value far beyond the 200,000 pounds of oil cake, 1,475 gallons of fish oil, 36 hogsheads of tobacco, 47,860 bushels of wheat, and 700 barrels of flour. Before their disembarkment, Captain Urquhart would become reasonably well-acquainted with almost every rescued soul.

So recently face-to-face with their mortality, each *Trimountain* passenger was unusually sensitive to spiritual considerations. On board, Pastor Lorriaux conducted services every evening at eight, according to the Captain's wishes, alternating one day in English and one day in French, the rescued officers and passengers attended regularly. Lorriaux reported: "No words can render the meek and submissive attitude of the ladies after the catastrophe. The poor mother whose four children had gone down, almost dead with cold and fatigue, told me, when we met on the *Loch Earn,* 'The Lord had given me those dear little ones; He takes them away. I will submit to His will.' "

As the *Trimountain* streaked over the horizon, making such excellent time that Captain Urquhart alarmed the sullen Captain Surmont and others, the *Loch Earn* was helplessly listing while proposals for repair were posited. With its residual population of thirty crew members, Captain Robertson, and the three passengers, the powerless *Loch Earn* seemed a vessel so small on a sea so large. Cook concentrated on his role as Weiss's nurse, in order to divert fearful thoughts about the *Loch Earn's* seaworthiness. The mind of each man must have replayed their long, philosophical discussions those evenings when they had strolled the *Ville du Havre's* deck, summarizing their experiences in America and sharing a longing for home. Their conversations had covered the Americans respect for Sunday as a day of worship; the American churches effective use of Sunday schools; the marvels of God's creation as seen from the sea. If the most valuable theology is that which is tested in the reality of hard times, theirs was becoming dearer by the moment.

Whether only a stiff upper lip or whether Captain Robertson actually believed in his ship's durability, things were at first upbeat aboard the *Loch Earn,* alone with the silence of the Atlantic. For passengers, there was plenty of elbowroom, and the surround was quieter. But their spaciousness contrasted sharply with the situation for those aboard the *Trimountain.*

Though never intended for passengers and certainly not passengers accustomed to luxury, the *Trimountain* had inadvertently been lightly loaded, and for those newly and narrowly saved from the clutches of death, it was enough to be alive and to feel increased chances of reaching terra firma. With great relief, the rescued had no immediate desire for the finer things of life. Twelve men crowded into one small cabin, and eleven women occupied the other.

While on the rescue ship Mrs. Bulkley wrote her mother:

> I have a pair of gentleman's slippers, and fortunately had my flannel wrapper on when I went over-board. All must use the Captain's comb; but one of the young girls, a wonderful child of seventeen, Miss Mixter [Madeleine] of Boston, combs our hair every morning—no hairpins, so we must wear it down our shoulders (brackets added).

But as with all the others, Madeleine Mixter was less concerned about appearances, thinking a lot about her new life without her parents or grandfather, her guardianship of her younger sister, and the adjustments necessitated by their harrowing experience. Though it would have to await mailing, she wrote her uncles:

> We all escaped with a few bruises. Helen is well and happy. She is too young to realize her loss. I feel she will be a sacred charge to me and I pray God to give me strength to direct her aright. Providence has been very merciful to us in saving our lives, and we should never forget how very near death was to us.

Mary Bulkley wondered: "It is mysterious to think why have I been saved, when with Lallie my life's work is done."

Thoughtful Charles Waite later told his parents about the sad ruminations he had after his own rescue.

> Finally, when the last boat came, I gave up all hope of ever seeing Julia [his sister] again (brackets added). It is so sad that she should have been lost for me, as she would not have come had it not been for my comfort; so, in a certain degree, it is my fault that she is lost. I suppose I ought not to feel thus, as God, in His all-wise providence, plans all things to His liking, and so has taken Julia to her home in Him.

Two weeks later, Anna Spafford was still bereaved, and Charles Waite was still reflective.

> My greatest sorrow, next to losing the best sister who ever lived, was my inability to restore those two little darlings [the Spafford children] to their sorrowing mother, who has nothing to console her (brackets added). Four dear little ones, aged three, five, nine and eleven years, are all gone to return no more.

Such heavy hearts slowed the march of time, but aboard the *Trimountain,* Wednesday, November 26, someone commented to Captain Urquhart that the next day was the last Thursday in November, the American holiday—Thanksgiving, but that they had nothing for which to be thankful. The Captain mentioned the approaching Thanksgiving holiday to the women who sat at his table for the afternoon meal. While some thought a religious observance would be a comfort, Anna Spafford was overcome and went to her cabin in tears. Nevertheless, Pastor Lorriaux agreed to hold a Thanksgiving service the next day.

The pastor, perhaps mindful of fragile emotions, strictly followed the holiday ritual. When he concluded, Captain Urquhart stepped forward to make sympathetic remarks, and to tell a story, his story, that encompassed seven remarkable "ironies"—though the Captain professed, "I believe that the chain of circumstances that led the *Trimountain* to the scene of the shipwreck was not chance, but part of a preordained scheme." The Captain ended with a quotation from George Eliot:

> Our life is determined for us—and it makes the mind
> very free when we give up wishing, and only think of
> bearing what is laid upon us, and doing what is given
> us to do.

He looked around to see some of the women in tears, whereupon he proposed they sing the well-known hymn, "Abide with Me," concluding the service.

8
YET ANOTHER RESCUE

Both an instrument of the disaster and the instrument of rescue for the survivors, the iron-stout *Loch Earn* was left alone on the Atlantic, seeking to work out her own salvation. Captain Robertson's confidence remained so great that the morning after their farewell to the *Trimountain,* when the *M. A. Marshall* came near enough that her captain could shout, "Do you require assistance?" Robertson had roared back, "No." Then, he explained what had happened, and urged the *Marshall's* captain to report on his three survivors "*if* you should arrive first, and I'm not saying ye will . . . ."

Soon, Robertson had the entire crew laboring with the ship's carpenter to secure the foremast and topmast, very difficult to do with the sides of the ship gone. They toiled at covering the huge holes, using the heaviest canvas normally used for sails to stretch across the expanse of the openings. Fifteen hours after the accident, the Captain had felt sure his ship could make land by dinner of November 22. Now, with more accurate evaluation and continuing surveillance of winds and waves impact on his troubled craft, Captain Robertson was cautious about the *Loch Earn's* future. It took the crew three days to erect a defensive barricade against the bow in order to keep it from smashing the bulkhead, to patch holes, and to attempt to stabilize the main masts. They were taking on water. To avoid exposing their most vulnerable sides to the current, they had to keep the ship in the trough of the sea, drifting. To attempt to make headway using the topsails caused the bulkheads to start to separate from the frame and made the ship vibrate.

Unable to make rapid progress, in moments of leisure, conversation always turned back to the tragedy in which they all had been unwilling participants. In the candor of their small, private setting, Captain Robertson confided that at the last moment, the *Ville du Havre* made a rapid movement to pass before the prow of the *Loch Earn*. The *Ville du Havre* was struck on her starboard as she was passing, since the *Loch Earn's* wind-driven course could not be diverted as quickly as could a steamer. Zaffiere declared that he saw the officer on watch on the *Ville du Havre* at the time of the collision in his shirtsleeves and, thus, wondered if his incomplete dress indicated that in a hurry, without fully assessing the situation, he gave a fatal order; or, was the proper order given, but badly executed?

"I am scarcely thirty years old, and I have been shipwrecked three times in my short life, but I have never witnessed a scene of such horror," the Captain confided to them. "If I had only known six or seven minutes sooner what was the state of the steamer," he said, "I could have given much more efficient help."

Cook wondered if the extent of the damage had been communicated by Captain Surmont's officers immediately at the time of the accident?

"Certainly," replied Captain Robertson, "but all that I could understand of what he said to me in French was that he did not think the *Ville du Havre* was badly injured. Six or seven minutes would have been enough for me to approach you, to send our boats to you, and perhaps to have saved all. It is fearful to think of all those ladies and children, whose cries came to us from the depths of the water and through the darkness."

Collectively, they remembered the beauty of the evening and were amazed that such a terrible incident could defile such a lovely night. Someone had seen a baby, alive and well and floating in a tub, but the tub overturned before they could get to it. The loss seemed especially agonizing and depressing when their stories of the children were repeated. With so few people left aboard the *Loch Earn,* everything and everyone were interesting. Five men of color were among the crew, fascinating the French clerics and French crew by their quaint manner and distinctive customs. Each maneuver assigned was accompanied by singing or a chant, sometimes a succession of mournful or monotonous cries, sometimes in unison and sometimes in almost-harmony—all seeming to the French to be sad and mournful. When furling the sails to steady the ship, for example, the sad sounds mingled with the rumblings of the storm, producing a melancholy mood among the riveted French.

Despite slow progress, with distance from the *Trimountain,* Captain Robertson had become more communicative, regularly checking on his two ministers and the injured seaman. He enjoyed the intellectual stimulation of conversation with professional men and confessed to Cook and Weiss that, while raised in a profoundly religious environment, he had simply allowed his religious life to lapse. It was at the Captain's request that Reverend Cook began short religious services daily. Cook was pleased that the crew attended and seemed to appreciate his efforts, even prompting the Captain to bring out the large Bible he maintained as a memorial to his parents.

Through severe stormy weather on the twenty-seventh and twenty-eighth, the clerics were particularly pleased with the Captain's assessment that the religious services were having a profound effect upon the crew, not normally considered among the devoutly religious, making them more steady, more willing to take courage and inspiration. Zaffiere, for whom Weiss had been translating Cook's daily Scripture lessons, requested a French New Testament. To everyone's amazement, an English cabin boy had one to give.

Surprisingly, Weiss was daily showing visible improvement in his physical condition. Assumed to be dying, he had unexplainably overcome an insatiable thirst. Despite terrible nightmares, he was able to rest and to sleep. By the twenty-fifth, Weiss was dramatically improved, and now, it was Cook feeling the symptoms of a bad cold and fever, restlessness and lack of sleep. In a scene of ironic foreboding, soon nurse and patient were to exchange roles.

By the twenty-seventh of November, having gained not a single mile by sailing but having drifted pretty far north, the *Loch Earn* and its skeletal crew had passed up four or five opportunities to abandon ship. But time was clarifying the extent of their damage, and crew members were checking the lifeboats, suggesting the possibility of building a raft and studying navigational charts. Cook and the ship had together grown feebler almost daily. The Captain did not talk about it, but the crew was worried about mere survival. They fretted openly to Weiss and Cook, and even used Cook's devotional time to express their concerns, to pray, and to ask Cook to pray for their safety.

On the twenty-eighth, about 6:00 p.m., a vessel with three masts appeared, and with telescope they thought they identified the American flag and the name of the ship, the *British Queen*. Earlier, they had declined to abandon ship, but this time, the ship's steward immediately started packing, the Captain lowered the lifeboat into very rough seas, and sent the chief officer to go aboard, report their distress, and ask the oncoming *British Queen* to stand by. At that point, while the crew acknowledged that the Captain could *compel* them to remain with him on board, they spontaneously refused to do so. Only one crew member, a Mexican soldier, volunteered to stay; so the decision was made *for* the Captain. Anyone could see the bulkhead was completely separating from the frame on both sides, and the ship was taking on water in torrents. (Much later, after he was safe on land, Captain Robertson reported they had eight feet of water in the aft hold and three inches of water in the well.)

Another boat was lowered. The three passengers with some of the crew went into the boat, along with the ship's instruments, books, and clothes. Cook, weak and sickly, but with his survival instinct still strong, managed to scale the rope ladder onto the *British Queen's* deck. With his right hand wrapped up and helpless, Weiss was raised by a rope. Seeing their wet clothes, the *British Queen's* Captain Marsters offered them his wardrobe and assured them of safety, although they were short on provisions. The pastors urged the Captain to go back and retrieve some of the *Loch Earn's* ample supply of food, but Captain Marsters insisted that they were astraddle only a lull in a big storm, and weather conditions demanded that they get on with their journey.

An hour later, all thirty-one *Loch Earn* officers and crew plus the three transients—Weiss, Cook, and Zaffiere—were comfortable on board the *British Queen.* While safe, they were not on a speed ship; as one of the crew told them, their petroleum hauler had already been twenty-five days on the journey. Still, feeling grateful and great relief, the crew celebrated with Cook and Weiss, saying "Thanks to your prayers, we are saved. God has heard our prayers." A *British Queen* officer then confided that because of the severity of the storm, they had twice changed their course during the night, and that absent the storm and those changes, the *British Queen* would never have been in position to rescue them. Cook was not surprised. With a sense of Divine

Providence, he told them, "It was necessary that you should come to our aid."

Unbeknownst to them at the time, the story of Reverend Cook's faith was later shared at the Moody–Sankey midday meeting at Free Church Assembly Hall in Edinburgh. When American Evangelist D. L. Moody finished his devotional, Dr. Thomson, one of the local pastors, read a letter he had received just that morning from an Edinburgh lady whose son had been on the *Loch Earn*. The letter relayed the son's testimony that the day before the rescue, everyone on board knew that shortly the ship would go down.

> The wind had changed, bringing them nearer the track of ships, but they had little hope of being saved. The Rev. Cook told the group, that death to him would be eternal life, and he urgently entreated them to put their trust in "Him who is mighty to save." At the same time, he told them he had no doubt that he would be rescued, that even then a vessel was speeding to save them, that God had answered their prayers, that next day as morning dawned, they would see her. That night was one of great anxiety. As morning dawned, every eye was strained to see the promised ship. There truly she was, and the *British Queen* hove down upon them. You may think with what thankful hearts they left the *Loch Earn*.

9
LANDFALL AT LAST

L eaving New York, the *Trimountain's* destination had been Bristol, England. After the rescue, Captain Urquhart, shortened the journey of his disconsolate passengers and decided to put in at Queenstown. Making good time with favorable winds, as he got closer, he changed his mind and decided on Cardiff, so as to hasten his passengers to land and to facilitate their getting trains onward to London and Paris. When the *Trimountain* dropped anchor at Cardiff Roads at about ten o'clock Sunday evening, November 30, 1873, and as soon as the Captain could get a tugboat for conveyance, two passengers were sent ashore. Charles Waite and James Bishop, with four fistfuls of carefully worded dispatches to be telegraphed to the loved ones and friends of the saved, scampered to the nearest telegraph office. Each passenger had spent the several days aboard the *Trimountain* composing, editing, and re-editing messages in the most meaningful form, disciplined by telegraph economy. Why Bishop and Waite were chosen is not known, except perhaps because they were males, and they had money. Waite had managed to save some bank drafts and some cash. Bishop, through the tragedy, had held onto some seven hundred pounds in British bank notes and gold, despite repeated warnings that the ship was sinking and that the money would weigh him down.

Anna Spafford's cablegram was received in Chicago at 5:40 a.m., December 1, 1873, and delivered to Horatio's office. Unpunctuated, telegram-style, it read:

> Saved alone what shall I do. Mrs. Goodwin children
> Willie Culver lost go with Lorriaux until answer reply
> Porclain 64 Rue Aboukir Paris
> Spafford

As the story has been incorrectly told for many years, a popular reference in countless sermons, Mrs. Spafford supposedly sent only a two-word cable: "Saved alone." Though that version became family lore—perpetuated even by the Spafford's daughter—the actual cablegram, which Sankey said Horatio kept framed on his office wall for a number of years, is now in the American Colony in Jerusalem Collection of the Library of Congress and is evidence to the contrary. At the bottom of the telegram, the operator, having counted the words for the purpose of assessing the charge, penciled the number "29."

Others' messages were also in the clipped language of cable-speak. Bishop informed his office: "STEAMER WRECKED; BREEDEN LOST; DAUGHTER AND MYSELF WELL." Llado's cryptic cable was: "STEAMER SUNK. ARRIVED SAFE AND SOUND."

Waite and Bishop were busily engaged in directing the messages until 4:30 Monday morning, Waite staying with the operator to assure that every last message was, indeed, sent. Dictation of the wording, transmission, copying the impulses on the receiving end, putting the message into presentable form for local delivery, with the time differential of the United States vis-à-vis Britain, the cablegrams still must have reached most recipients on December 1. Meanwhile, the arrival of the survivors and the news they bore became the substance of a special, December 1 edition of the *South Wales Daily News.* Telegraphy then carried the story to the rest of the world, reported as "Dreadful Collision at Sea" in the December 1 issue of *The Birmingham* [England] *Daily Mail,* and similarly in the December 2 newspapers of London, all Britain, and major cities of the world.

From the telegraph office, Charles Waite hastened to welcome fellow passengers who set their feet on land at 5:00 in the morning, December 1. Only fifteen days previous, they had loaded on board the glamorous *Ville du Havre* their trunks of elegant clothing, their keepsake jewelry, their money and belongings; as they disembarked, they had nothing, nothing but the ragtag sailor's castoffs on their backs.

Despite the early hour, the welcome party included American officials and the French consul, Monsieur Rin, who abbreviated formalities so survivors could get to the Royal Hotel. Once merchants had opened their shops, Captain Bocande the local agent for the French Line, commissioned Cardiff's two principal drapers and outfitters to supply the survivors with their needs, including appropriate mourning dress, so very important in the custom of that era. Cardiff's fashion selections would have been limited, but were still a vast improvement over their emergency, seafaring salvage-wear. The *Daily Telegraph,* December 4, 1873, described the ladies situation.

> Hurried from their berths when the collision took place, in only their night dresses, or the scantest underclothing, they had to be covered with blankets and sailors' apparel, and when they disembarked at Cardiff in this sad plight, bonnetless, shoeless, and with their feet protected only by sailors' socks, they were only too glad to be able to get ashore before daylight unobserved. The change that took place in their dress, however, though it spoke much for the liberality of the agents and their principals, helped to bring out vividly

the suffering that these ladies had undergone. When the time arrived to start from Cardiff, every one was dressed in mourning, and it was understood that all, without a single exception, had suffered the loss of husband, child, or other relative.

In recounting the family's story more than seventy-five years later, Bertha Spafford claimed that as her Mother considered all the somber black dresses, veils, and bonnets, she "felt her daughters' reproof," since "heaven is a happy place . . . no sorrow . . . no tears." Her mother chose instead a simple black-and-white outfit, of which her companions did not approve. Whether such a deviation from custom occurred immediately, or whether it might have occurred later in the mourning period, such an iconoclastic gesture did not draw comment in any observer's or survivor's account, or in any known newspaper story.

Shopping and refreshing themselves occupied the group until half past noon when the train departed Cardiff for London. The officials and Captain Urquhart were there to say farewell, each survivor well-dressed, with six British pounds, and a railway ticket to Paris, compliments of the shipping company. In a kind act of consolation, the stationmaster had added to the train a special saloon carriage to make the group more comfortable; he also telegraphed ahead for berths on the ferry and for a special saloon carriage for the onward journey to Calais.

Arriving next at London's Paddington Station from Cardiff at 5:50 that afternoon, they were at once carried by taxis to the Charing Cross Hotel. Most passengers followed Charles Waite's lead and took advantage of the opportunity to sleep in their first motionless bed since November 15. Their sleep was disrupted the next morning at 6:00 by about a half-dozen anxious friends, who had dashed from Paris to express their concern and to support their friends in grief. Among early-comers to the hotel was the husband of a lady who, with her two children, perished in the accident. The husband had held out hope that his family might still be alive and was totally distraught to confirm that they were, in reality, gone. The *Standard's* reporter observed with compassion that it had been "inexpressibly painful to see the survivors meet some of their acquaintances in London, and no one could look on at the meetings without feeling, if not expressing, a prayer that God in his own good time might give the survivors the comfort they so sorely need."

After breakfast, they shopped all day, a process that diverted attention from sorrowful memories, their harrowing experience, and their loss. All London, naturally, wanted to reach out to the victims. For example, when the Waite family's London minister, Reverend George W. Weldon, called on Charles, he took him to Mr. Lincoln, his hatter. After being properly outfitted with a new hat, Mr. Lincoln insisted, "he would take it as a favor if Mr. Waite would not think of paying for it."

The manager of London's Charing Cross Hotel refused to allow Waite to pay for lodging the ladies and himself, but Waite insisted on presenting the bill to the steamship company, which had already given him money for their transport to Paris. *The Standard,* December 3, 1873, made it clear that all London did its part.

> It would seem that all the bankers with whom they came into contact yesterday opened accounts with perfect willingness; that the tradesmen to whom they applied for outfits were perfectly content to let the accounts stand until they had recovered themselves sufficiently to attend to such matters; that, in a word, everybody . . . did all that was possible . . . Yesterday London, it is pleasant to say, did its part thoroughly. The survivors, rich, or competently affluent, or poor, found heaps of friends in this our great metropolis, whether they had bankers' references, or other references, or no references at all. . . . Therefore, between the hour at which the survivors arrived at Paddington, clad in such poor weeds as they could pick up in an hour or two at Cardiff—and, what we did not think it yesterday

quite delicate to mention, none of the ladies was, on
Monday night, without more or less crape to mark her
mourning . . . all the party had, out of their actual or
their prospective resources, been able to find perfectly
proper clothing in replacement of the contents of their
"Saratoga" or other trunks which are now floating in
mid ocean, a 150 miles off the Western Islands.

Later, when the 8:45 evening train pulled away for Dover, a
reporter noted, it was "not amid cheers, but never were hats more
respectfully raised than the hats of those on the Continental
platform of the West-end Station . . . and whom all wished
bon voyage." Upon arrival at Paris, Wednesday, December 3,
everyone was met by friends, instantly relieving Charles Waite of
his informal leadership duty, his mission accomplished.

Back at Cardiff, as might be expected, the *Ville du Havre's*
Captain Surmont and crew received less preferential treatment.
Officers had been housed in hotels, while the crew stayed at
the Sailors Home. Seven injured or ill had been taken to the
Hamadryad, a locally anchored hospital ship. Together, their
circle numbered about sixty, as they left Cardiff Wednesday
morning for Bristol and Southampton, accompanied by the
shipping company's agent. From Southampton, they boarded the
steamer *Alice* of the London and South–Western Company, which
sailed at midnight for Le Havre, their long-delayed destination.

In that era, when European society's class distinctions
were sharply defined, the crew of the *Loch Earn* later had its
own problems and met with much less sympathy. Though crew
members' personal generosity and kindness to survivors had been
admirable, seven men went to the Mansion-house Police Court, in
London on December 8 to ask for assistance. They said they had
lost everything through misfortune and selfless generosity toward
the rescued, and had been sent to London by the Shipwrecked
Mariners Society of Plymouth.

> The spokesman, who was a man of colour, explained
> that since the collision they had given all their clothes
> away, except those they were now wearing, to some
> of the passengers and crew who had been rescued
> from the *Ville du Havre* and were now in a state of
> destitution. Unfortunately, the magistrate for the day,
> Sir Robert Carden, had left the court, and Mr. Oke,
> the chief clerk, did not feel himself at liberty in his
> absence to entertain the application.

One can only hope the crew's benevolence was ultimately rewarded.

As for Captain Urquhart, when his passengers had acquired proper mourning attire, they summoned him to their hotel and bade him a fond farewell. He went on to testify to the harbormaster about how his ship had first found the *Loch Earn;* thereupon, the *Trimountain* and crew continued on their way to Bristol, their original destination. The unique relationship of the survivors to the kind and helpful Captain Urquhart was to be long-remembered. Indeed, when in retirement at age sixty-seven in 1910, the Captain published his *Reminiscences: The Merchant Marine,* his dedication stated:

> Being particularly identified with the wrecked
> steamer *Ville du Havre* the most important event
> of my seafaring life, I dedicate the book to the
> survivors of the lost steamer, quite a number of
> whom are now living. W.W.U.

The telegrams sent by Waite and Bishop, and the stories originating after the *Trimountain's* arrival at Cardiff, sounded alarm around the world. The story was huge. The *Ville du Havre's* shipwreck was one of several significant disasters at sea that year, and one of the most touching because of the grandeur of the ship, the number of women and children among both fatalities and survivors, the prominence of those on board, and the seeming lack of a rational explanation for the accident. Not only via newspapers, but through announcements in churches, news of the accident spread rapidly. It was doubtless aided in Britain by the uncommon and rapidly increasing attention directed to the Americans Moody and Sankey. Beginning in the fall of 1873 in Scotland, they were drawing tremendous crowds and becoming the subject of common talk. The friendship of Moody with Horatio and Anna Spafford had been built over a number of years as Horatio had worked with Moody and his associates in YMCA endeavors, in visiting hospitals and prisons, in evangelistic services. The tenderhearted Moody, close to the Spaffords, already in Britain at the time of the accident, and having made ocean crossings previously, would have been deeply moved by the shipwreck.

Moody's awareness of the Spaffords' loss is evident from a surviving letter he wrote them, as well as other sources. According to one account, a resident of Glasgow, Robert Bremner, having heard so much about the Moody meetings, went to Edinburgh to the noon prayer meeting, December 4, 1873, just three days after the world learned of the *Ville du Havre* disaster. Intending to satisfy his curiosity about the Yankee evangelist, Bremner was astounded to find nine hundred people assembled in Free Church Assembly Hall. According to his account, Sankey led the congregation in songs, and then sang a solo, "Hold the Fort," which had been so enthusiastically received by the Scots. Moody stepped up to give a brief message on the right object of faith, his title being, "Have Faith in God." Toward the close of his homily, Bremner related, the Evangelist "made a very feeling and touching reference to the sad bereavement which a dear Christian friend and fellow laborer of his own in Chicago had sustained by the loss of his four children, who were drowned in the recent calamitous destruction at sea of the *Ville du Havre . . .*" Bremner said Moody "turned it to good account in urging upon the unsaved among the hearers the uncertainty of life and the blessedness of being in Christ, as he believed these four children were when overtaken by death."

Years later, after Horatio's death, Bertha Spafford would remember that Moody, touring the Holy Land in the 1890s, came to call on her mother. As the sentimental evangelist reflected upon her father, she saw him sob and later noticed a puddle of tears at his feet.

There was yet one more group to account for out of the disaster. Captain Robertson, a few crew members of the *Loch Earn,* the Reverends Cook and Weiss, and the fireman, Zaffiere, had been transferred to the American ship, *British Queen.* They had a new set of experiences on the strictly commercial, Philadelphia petroleum ship, hauling crude oil in open drums, oil that was frequently spilling as the ship lurched. Yet, the two clerics became such dear friends of the religiously minded Captain Marsters and his crew that the sailors urged their two chaplains to continue on with them to Antwerp. But each slow day, only quickened the longing of the French "reverends" for their homeland and home.

On the morning of December 6, Captain Marsters explained to the captain of a pilot boat that he had thirty-four survivors of a shipwreck on board and that he was bound for Antwerp. The pilot-boat captain agreed to accept the passengers and assured that he would take no payment. As they prepared to leave his ship, the French clerics learned that Captain Marsters after reaching Antwerp would likely be routed to Mobile and from there to somewhere in the Gulf of Mexico, his wife not expecting him for many months. In one final kindness, he insisted on dividing with Cook the nine pounds sterling he had in his pocket and bade his friends farewell. Once the transfer was complete, all thirty-four (Captain Robertson and *Loch Earn* crew of twenty-nine, plus Zaffiere, Weiss, and Cook) joined in three shouts of "hurrah" for Captain Marsters and the crew of the *British Queen*. So, one more transfer had them ensconced aboard the local pilot cutter Number Eight, *Isidore*, based at Plymouth.

Progress was slow due to the still winds, and all day December 6, the *Isidore* plodded forty miles toward Plymouth. Anticipating separation from the crew of the *Loch Earn*, with whom they had shared so much, Cook and Weiss gathered them for one last devotional meditation. Reading from the Captain's well-worn English Bible, Cook took his text from the Book of Acts, which tells the story of the Apostle Paul's shipwreck. The crew identified with the nautical references. Cook thanked them for their kindness. He concluded with an admonition for them to live by the lessons they had learned from their near-disastrous experience. He expressed the hope that they would meet again, in heaven, if not on earth.

At last on land at Plymouth, the evening of December 6, eight days after leaving the *Trimountain*, Weiss and Cook shook hands in a warm benediction with Captain Robertson and his crew of the *Loch Earn*, with whom they shared unspeakable bonds of sentiment known only to those who together have traversed the valley of the shadow of death. The two French pastors hastened to entrust the still invalid fireman, Zaffiere, to the official consul of France, and ran just in time to board the day's last train for London. When they arrived, tense and fatigued at London's Charing Cross station, they briefly considered overnighting in a hotel in order to rest. But Weiss, his right arm bound and useless, yielded to Cook, who, simultaneously shivering with fever and with the sheer excitement of at last being on *terra firma* and the prospect of home, insisted that they hurry on. They attracted curious glances, rushing about almost clown-like in their ragtag attire—Cook in an overcoat much too small for him, topped with a broad-brimmed gray hat and Weiss in Captain Robertson's cap, a worn overcoat, a sailor's pantaloons, and his right arm in a sling.

They reached Dover in good time, glided across a calm Channel to Calais, catching the last train to Paris on Sunday, December 7. The sun had been replaced by a dense fog, which sent Reverend Cook to the back of the train in dread of a collision. Offers of food and drink were generously made by fellow passengers wanting to hear details of the horrors the clerics had survived. Each whistle-stop brought on newcomers, who caught wind of the story and were eager to hear it from the beginning. Finally arriving at Paris, Weiss entrusted the fevery and exhausted Cook to his wife and seven children, his entire family a personal welcoming party. It was a great moment: their spirits entwined, having so much in common, having been together in such intensity, having mutually nursed each other, at last nearing the end of their journey. But the two friends surprisingly quickly exchanged blessings and went their separate ways. By this time, their roles had completely reversed. Originally, Cook had insisted on remaining with Weiss because of the latter's fragile condition. As Weiss recovered, Cook had become ill, the object of Weiss's prayers and concern.

Sadly, on January 29, 1874, Pastor Emile Cook died. Near the end, he had written his friend Weiss, "I am strongly threatened with inflammation of the lungs. I have a terrible fever—BUT ALL IS WELL."

A few months after the accident, Weiss wrote the only firsthand account of the *Ville du Havre* tragedy. It was originally published in French, but later it was translated into English as *Personal Recollections of the Wreck of the* Ville-du-Havre *and the* Loch-Earn. He dedicated the volume to "you who perished on the fatal night of November 22d." Even in his dedication, he could not fail to reference the children, noting that the pleasant conversation of the adults had been, so often interrupted and brightened by the graceful forms of children. Encasing his tender sentiment in prose, he paid especially touching tribute to his minister friend Emile Cook in one final paragraph.

> A special place here would I reserve for you, faithful and devoted friend, who, having been with me even to the end of the voyage, were snatched from me by the hand of God, when we were already within the haven. Involuntarily, unceasingly will my thoughts turn upon all that is associated with you, till, after a separation longer or shorter, I meet you again, with all those that have preceded you in eternity.
>
> Paris, April, 1874   N. Weiss

Unknown to Weiss and Cook, that same December 7, at the very time of their rush to Paris, a memorial service was being held in the great Cathedral of Notre Dame in Paris. A large crowd saw a catafalque in front of the altar, surrounded by wax candles. Survivors of the crew of the *Ville du Havre,* Captain Surmont, the directors of the Company, the mayor of Le Havre, and many local officials were on hand. The curate, Monsieur Duval, delivered the sermon, seasoned with his own profound emotion. At one point he burst into tears, turned, extending his hands toward the catafalque and exclaimed, "And we have not even the consolation of having the bodies of those for whom we mourn." It was "an extraordinary manifestation of grief," the newspaper reported, and several women fainted.

Touching reports were made all over Britain and France. One newspaper described the St. Paul's Cathedral, London, afternoon service, where Canon Liddon spoke of modern materialism and urged respect for human life. According to the newspaper summary, the Canon declared:

> The catastrophe which befel the *Ville du Havre* was of the sharpest, most piercing kind. . . . Few could have read in the morning papers the account of two

> hundred and odd men, women, and children, just like
> themselves, roused from their beds on a winter's night
> to find they had but some twelve minutes to live ere they
> sank into a grave beneath the waves, without saying,
> "Had I been there in bed in that *Ville du Havre,* how
> would it have been with me? What would have been
> the convictions on my mind in that moment of supreme
> agony? . . . Would I have said, from the depths of my
> soul, 'Into Thy hands, O Lord, I commit my spirit'?"

At Pontifical High Mass at St. George's Roman Catholic Cathedral, Southwark, London, the Rev. Monsignor Capel, preaching a series of advent sermons, spoke of the Roman Catholic priest on board the *Ville du Havre.* He went on to tell the congregation how such a melancholy catastrophe "should cause them always to be prepared for their last hour, and to live in amity and goodwill with all mankind."

December 3, at the Brevoort House Hotel in New York, services of remembrance for the passengers of the *Ville du Havre* were held in the parlors, attended largely by friends of the Waite family and by guests at the hotel. Reverend Dr. Taylor of the Broadway Tabernacle offered prayers and Reverend W. T. Eustis, of Springfield, Massachusetts, made a few remarks. Mr. Waite and his family were deeply affected during the services.

Also in New York, a relief fund was announced to assist the families of the Reverends Carrasco and Pronier, who were lost in the accident, Evangelical Alliance colleagues of Weiss, Cook, and Lorriaux. According to the *Chicago Daily Tribune,* by the time of its January 13, 1874 edition, that relief fund had grown to almost $4,600.

While public services were being held, the business side of the tragedy needed tending. Before leaving Plymouth, Captain Robertson and others of the *Loch Earn* had given their official depositions to the Collector of Customs. Proceeding to Glasgow, Captain Robertson went immediately to interview with Messrs.

Aitken, Lilburn, and Company, managing firm of the Glasgow Shipping Company, the ship's owners. Much debated was the question: Was the collision the fault of the *Ville du Havre* or the *Loch Earn*? With the news spread abroad, and with the captains, crews and survivors safely landed, controversy was sure to result. The pride of both Britain and France was at stake, to say nothing of legal liability and the careers of key personnel. An early report in a newspaper quoted some officers and crew, as well as Captain Robertson of the *Loch Earn,* concluding that the French ship was to blame.

> She [the *Loch Earn*] was on her course from Liverpool to the United States, and appears to have acted on the unquestionable rule of the sea, that a steamer is bound to give way to a sailing ship. If the *Ville du Havre* had starboarded her helm even when the bowsprit of the *Loch Earn* was over her side the awful fatality might have been reduced in its dimensions; but no attempt appears to have been made to avert the doom of one of the finest steamers that ever swam. The second officer in charge of the *Ville du Havre* has not survived the calamity; and as it may be well to leave the consideration of his conduct to a proper tribunal, we need only say here that the awful event appears, according to the *prima facie* case, to have been due to his want of presence of mind.

Later, when the *Loch Earn* crew had arrived at Plymouth, *The Standard* for December 8, 1873, published what today would be called an investigative report, wherein its reporter quoted the extremely frank opinions of *Loch Earn* crew members. In fact, *The Standard* claimed, "the following narrative may be taken as the collective statement of the officers and men of the *Loch Earn,* whose conduct appears to have been the very reverse of that displayed on the other side." Among the *Loch Earn* personnel's allegations were:

1. The *Ville du Havre* "appears to have been the sole cause of the collision."
2. The officers and men of the *Ville du Havre* "are charged with having looked after themselves, and left the passengers to perish."
3. "When the lights of the *Ville du Havre* were reported the *Loch Earn* held on her course in accordance with the accepted rule of the sea."
4. The *Loch Earn's* "bells had been going five minutes before the steamer's horn was sounded."
5. "the *Ville du Havre* did nothing to avert the collision but put on full steam to cross the *Loch Earn's* bow."
6. "Immediately after the collision, a boat manned by four men with an officer came off from the steamer to the *Loch Earn*. The first idea on the *Loch Earn* was that she had been sent to render help, but this was a complete mistake. The officer in charge of the boat asked if there were any passengers on board the ship, and understood the reply to be that there were not. . . . although it was stated that the steamer was injured," Not the slightest information of the extent of the injury was given, no distress was presented, and "the captain and crew of the *Loch Earn* were left to find out that for themselves by seeing the steamer sinking before their eyes."

Justifying their frankness, the newspaper explained: "It is only fair to state that they might not have been so outspoken had it not been for the indignation which they felt at reading some of the statements which have already appeared."

The *Daily Telegraph* of December 8, 1873, published even a harder hitting and more accusatory report, allegedly quoting passengers as well as the Captain and crew of the *Loch Earn*. Those accusations drew an angry letter of response from Captain Surmont, dated December 11, and printed verbatim in the *Glasgow Herald* (December 15, 1873). Captain Surmont was particularly offended by the charge that he had saved himself, without thinking first of his passengers, as duty required, and having appeared never to have been in the water. Even the official inquiry was somewhat inconclusive.

In all the debate about blame, the point that seemed to have most irritated surviving passengers was the claim of the purser and a few of the crew on the *Ville du Havre* that there was excessive panic and pandemonium on the deck of the ship and that such chaos impaired lifesaving efforts. For example, the purser's description drew from the well-tempered Pastor Lorriaux a quiet but firm rebuttal in the newspapers.

> In the account given by the purser of the *Ville du Havre* there is a very regrettable omission. He speaks about the Catholic priest conveying to those around him religious comfort and consolation. We all admired the noble conduct of that faithful clergyman, but the narrative adds, "while around the priest there was a terrible excitement and frenzy." That is not correct. Never have I seen people so calm and resigned as the passengers of the *Ville du Havre*. Not one shriek, not one cry, was heard from the moment the *Loch Earn* struck us to the moment we went down. Every one was composed and wonderfully calm. A young lady was pressing her mother on her breast, saying, "Courage, dear mother; it will be one minute's struggle, then we shall enter together into heaven." Four sweet little girls were surrounding their mother and two friends who were with her, saying, "Let us pray; let us ask God to keep us." About ten or twelve ladies were a little further on engaged in earnest prayer. I have never witnessed such a manifestation of the power of faith.

The "young lady" was, of course, Lallie Bulkley. The "[f]our sweet little girls" were the Spafford daughters.

Legal concepts of liability, as we know them today, were still evolving in the 1870s. A thoughtful letter from Spafford's neighbor and lawyer friend, Daniel Goodwin, who lost his wife and three children in the shipwreck, appeared in the *Chicago*

Daily Tribune, a year and a half after the accident, May 23, 1875. In it, Goodwin explained that he had made his own investigation of the accident. He had even attended the trial in London before the Admiralty Court, and interviewed officers of the French, English and American ships. He placed blame on "the French steamer," charging it with "the most inexcusable and aggravating carelessness," her owners having "collected over one million of dollars of insurance, but repudiated all liability for losses." In consequence, Goodwin "drew up an agreement to prosecute the company," in effect, to sue for damages, and, as a demonstration of goodwill, to give to St. Luke's Hospital any "avails of the suit." But after extensive consultation with legal minds, due to the state of marine law, he concluded: "[A]fter a full examination it was decided we were remediless, and principally on account of the statute limiting the liability of vessel-owners to the vessel itself or its value." Goodwin offered his own idea for a remedy: "When that law is repealed and vessel owners are made responsible in damages for loss of life and cargo, they will invent all new safeguards . . . and will perfect all possible guarantees for safety."

PART TWO
TRAGEDY AFTER THE TRAGEDY

10
THE COST OF TRUSTING

On the American side of the Atlantic, no news had been wrongly presumed to be good news, as friends and relatives unknowingly awaited confirmation of a safe arrival of the Chicago contingent on the *Ville du Havre*. Estimates of transoceanic arrival times normally varied by several days, requiring patience of family members and friends. Wind and weather played havoc with timetables on transatlantic voyages of that era, and without ship-to-shore communication, it was not possible to communicate. Only the night before the *Ville du Havre* shipwreck, November 20, a large wedding had taken place in the Lake View mansion of the Spaffords' wealthy neighbor J. B. Waller. The Waller's daughter, Lucy, married the Spaffords' minister at Chicago's Fullerton Avenue Presbyterian Church, Reverend W. C. Young. Horatio Spafford had been present, and inquiries about his family met a polite reply, that the ship bearing his family and the Lake View friends must be nearing its destination and that he would likely be receiving word soon. On the evening of November 25, he had written in his distinctive hand a warm, loving letter to his wife and children, a letter fully commensurate with the season.

> Day after tomorrow will be Thanksgiving Day. I will not say how I shall miss you and the dear children. But I will not think too much about that. Let us instead strive to profit by the separation. I think this separation

has touched me more deeply than anything else that
has ever occurred in my life. . . .

Oh, but it is a long distance across the ocean! But,
never mind, my heart. If the Lord keeps us, we hope
before many months to be all-together again, better
understanding than ever before the greatness of His
mercy in the many years of the past.

When you write, tell me about the children. How
thankful I am to God for them! May He make us faithful
parents, having an eye single to His glory. Annie and
Maggie and Bessie and Tanetta it is a sweet consolation
even to write their names. May the dear Lord keep and
sustain and strengthen you.

Unknown to Horatio, of course, as he wrote so candidly of
his anxiety over business issues, his love for his family, and his
desire to grow spiritually, he would soon be facing a far greater
challenge than distress over real estate. Almost another week
would pass before he could know that his four children had been
lost at sea three days earlier, and that his beloved wife—bruised
and battered, heartsick and on the edge of despair, dressed in
tatters and sailors' castoffs—was miraculously alive aboard the
Trimountain, enduring circumstances and conditions he would
not even know about for another week. By the time Anna's
cablegram arrived at Horatio's office, she was with the survivors
in the stores of London, vacillating between unspeakable sorrow
and the practical necessity of scavenging to replace clothes and
personal effects. Not from Le Havre, France, as expected, but
from Cardiff, Wales, came the cablegram, blaring the news of
that would wreck the Spaffords' idyllic world. Upon receiving
the news, Horatio, thoughtful lawyer with a poet's heart and
a cleric's spirit, was knotted in anguish and spent the entire
night walking the floor, searching for understanding and for
consolation. He was near; she was far. Neither was near the site
where their girls lost their battle with the ocean, disallowing a
proper mourning and interment. There were no bodies. There

were no arrangements. There was no prescribed way to grieve. His near neighbor, businessman-turned-evangelist Daniel W. Whittle, also a close friend and ministry associate of D. L. Moody, consoled him the entire night. Toward morning, accepting a Job-like testing of his faith, Horatio summed up his feelings, employing words similar to those used by his wife, as though conscious of the special privilege they had enjoyed to that point in life: "I am glad to trust the Lord when it will cost me something."

Responding to Anna with a cable of his own, in cryptic cable-speak, Horatio replied that she should proceed with Pastor Lorriaux to Paris, an instruction she was already fulfilling, even as his cable's pulsations were sent racing across the Atlantic. He promised to join her as soon as he could.

Though she had friends in Paris, Anna Spafford went directly to the Lorriaux home in the village of Bertry outside Paris. Mademoiselle Lorriaux, preoccupied with reinstalling her husband as head of the house, still gave gracious attention to the visiting American survivor during a span of two weeks, until Anna felt strong enough in body and spirit to go to Paris. There she was welcomed into the home of Bertha Madison Johnson, the special friend from school days at Dearborn Seminary, fifteen years earlier, and by the time of the accident, a Parisian resident.

Letters to Anna came first from Europe, and later from America, offering help and support in all dimensions. Consolation notwithstanding, she wrote: "Oh, how sad my heart is without my birds. How little I thought when I left my happy home that I should set my foot first upon foreign soil alone!"

As Anna grappled alone with her sudden childlessness and loss, Horatio searched his theology, his Scriptures, his life experience for explanation and help. In the space of slightly more than two years, they had suffered the tragic Chicago Fire, dissatisfaction with the practice of law, and the loss of his office and law library, as well as problems and uncertainties with investments. Then, in one terrible catastrophe, they lost their four daughters, the children's governess, Mademoiselle Nicolet, and the Lake View circle traveling with them: the Goodwins and Willie Culver. Separated by three thousand miles, neither could be consolation to the other, bound only by those invisible ties that supersede telegraph or sound waves.

Immediately, Horatio made arrangements to travel to Paris, to be with Anna. On December 3, he was on a train to New York with Daniel Goodwin, where on the fifth they would board the Cunard Line's *Abyssinia* for Europe. Horatio wrote his sister, Maggie (Margaret S. Lee), declaring the theological conviction that his troubles were not designed by God as penalty or punishment—a protestation he repeated often and with force. His sorrowing mind racing from theological intensity to practicality, he later wrote, while on board the *Abyssinia,* Anna's half sister, Rachel Frederickson, requesting that she go to their Lake View home to put away all the children's possessions in hopes of saving Anna from further anguish.

Daniel Goodwin was himself suffering the emotional pain of losing his wife and three children: Goertner, Julia, and Lulu. No record exists, but it seems likely that Horatio had been the one who first delivered the terrible news to Goodwin. Without a family member or a close friend surviving the accident of the *Ville du Havre,* and American newspapers not yet having the story, Daniel Goodwin most likely learned the news from Horatio since Anna's cablegram would have been the first word to reach Chicago. Her cablegram had explicitly confirmed that Mrs. Goodwin, her children, and Willie Culver were lost. One can only imagine a red-eyed Horatio Spafford, clutching the cablegram as hard evidence countering the natural tendency to disbelief, steeped in sorrow, his heart aching, his mind ricocheting from memory-to-memory of those dear lost faces, crunching his way across the graveled street to the silent, coifed acreage surrounding the stately gabled Gothic of the Goodwin home. Then, the telltale door knocker sounding the alarm, breaking the solemnity of the evening, bringing the anxious father to the door for Horatio to blurt out the terrible news as softly as he could imagine, through tears and staccato gaps in his composure, that Goodwin's family had perished. Some minutes of grieving together and Horatio, the harbinger of bad news, needed to move on, summoning all the inner resources at his command to tell Mr. and Mrs. Belden F. Culver of the loss of their son, Willie. The grandparents in Germany, planning to meet Willie at Le Havre, would have known the terrible news before the parents. Obituary writers would later say that the grandfather, respected clergyman and theology professor, likely never got over the sudden unusual death of his namesake. Life events sometimes distill a lifetime of spiritual experience.

Goodwin and Spafford had much in common. Both lived in fine homes in Chicago's most enviable neighborhood. Goodwin had been extremely successful in residential real estate development, in addition to his law practice. Spafford had done well in the practice of law and sought good fortune in real estate. Professionally, they had worked together most recently in the legal resistance to the de-annexation of a portion of Lake View, so that it could be annexed into Chicago. Then, unpredictably, with the tragedy of the *Ville du Havre,* they were bonded in grief and loss.

Horatio probably thought often of his visit to New York's dockside just two weeks earlier to settle his family and friends into berths on the *Ville du Havre.* On that excited November day, he could never have imagined traveling to Europe to reunite with a bereft wife, just having narrowly cheated death, being suddenly childless, and accompanied by poor Goodwin, now alone in all the world. He must have often wondered about his last-minute decision to back out of the trip, whether, had he been present, he might have been able to save one of the girls. Aboard the *Abyssinia* those December days, compassionate fellow passengers quickly became aware of the tragic aura that hovered over the two men, and reached out empathetically. One day, midvoyage, the Captain called Goodwin and Spafford to his private cabin and told them that according to his reckoning, they were passing the point where the *Loch Earn* tragically struck the *Ville du Havre,* the locus of what had become a graveyard of the sea. In Spafford's letter to Rachel he wrote:

> On Thursday last we passed over the spot where she went down, in mid-ocean, the water three miles deep. But I do not think of our dear ones there. They are safe, folded, the dear lambs, and there, before very long, shall we be too. In the meantime, thanks to God, we have an opportunity to serve and praise Him for His love and mercy to us and ours. "I will praise Him while I have my being." May we each one arise, leave all, and follow Him.

Later, Horatio and Daniel eagerly pursued every clue and detail about their families final days and moments. One evening, relaxed in a fashionable Paris parlor, Pastor Nathanael Weiss, who had copiously maintained a detailed account of the voyage and compressed his writings into a small book, carefully recounted for Goodwin all the details he could recollect of his family's final moments, drawing upon his notes.

"I am convinced," Goodwin concluded, "that my wife and children perished in their stateroom. I love to think of them thus passing all together into eternity. They were united in life; death did not separate them; and it will not be long before I rejoin them."

To Spafford, Weiss expressed his regret that he had not kept in his clutches at least one of the four Spafford girls in those last moments on deck, thinking that he might have saved at least one. Spafford recalled aloud what he said to the Captain when they passed over the area where his children were lost:

> Yes, I am sure they are there—on High—and happier far than if they were still with me. So convinced am I of this, that I would not, for the whole world, that one of my children should be given back to me.

11
SPIRITUAL UPHEAVAL

The New Year 1874 began on foreign soil and in deep sorrow for the many families impacted by the *Ville du Havre* catastrophe. For the next two months, Horatio and Anna's time was spent in France, from whence Goodwin returned to London, his lawyer mind eager to examine legal issues and to learn more about the accident and its causes. Three significant holidays— Thanksgiving, Christmas, New Year's—had been obliterated from the Spaffords' life by the tragedy of losing their children. Yet the routine day-to-day living had to resume, and the Spaffords returned to Chicago and cherished Lake View.

Back at home while gathering the special things that belonged to their children, they found a note written by Maggie. It read:

> Goodbye, dear sweet Lake View. I will never see you again. Maggie Spafford.

They assumed that she must have written it shortly before their departure for France and then, deposited it in the play post office, sheltered in a huge elm tree close to the house. They wondered, did Maggie have a strange sense of foreboding about the trip?

Up to the time of the accident (1873), individually and in their life together, Horatio and Anna were blessed with near perfect circumstances—lovely family, beautiful home, professional prestige and public recognition, rewarding volunteer work, and sufficient material wealth to enjoy a high standard of living. But circumstances changed, and on the surface, the Spaffords' postshipwreck lives may have seemed only slightly altered, but a dramatic turn was about to take place, their restlessness or malaise being as forgivable as it must have been observable to close friends and family.

Visits by Dwight L. Moody and the consolation of friends had doubtless meant a great deal during days of healing and adjustment. They were engulfed in rounds of tearful embraces, expressions of sympathy and commiseration from friends at Fullerton Avenue Presbyterian Church, as well as the Moody circle.

Oddly, after the accident, Horatio never seriously re-engaged in the practice of law. At first, he performed a few simple legal chores and maintained awareness of legal actions involving the area surrounding his real estate. Any outside observer at that point would have judged Spafford a professional man who needed no particular, visible means of support.

When he first arrived in Chicago, Spafford set up a law firm, Spafford & Tucker, with Joseph Tucker as his partner. Later, he was a partner in Borden, Spafford & McDaid, which dissolved. In 1870, he formed a new firm with Henry O. McDaid and John P. Wilson, as Spafford, McDaid & Wilson. Whether Horatio's postaccident malaise, the Great Fire, or other factors caused the dissolution of the law firm, we do not know, but in July 1874, almost three years after the Fire, but only eight months after the *Ville du Havre* disaster, an announcement appeared in the newspaper:

> The Hon. Oliver H. Picher has recently resigned the office of judge in Jasper County, Missouri to accept a partnership with McDaid & Wilson, in place of Mr. Spafford, who retires from the firm.

Unfettered by the demands of a legal partnership or practice, professionally listless, with no established business routine, Horatio spent long hours reading and reflecting in his study at home, despite having no alternative means of earning a living. He made visits to cities nearby with little explanation. While civic and volunteer work was tapering off, Horatio remained active with Moody's group. As an intelligent, studied layman, he was eminently capable of delivering a well-prepared sermon. He could also teach Sunday school lessons, and counsel people looking for spiritual encouragement. For example, when a large conference of Christian Workers was held at Farwell Hall in April of 1876, a reporter commented, "P. P. Bliss was present, looking as strong, and vigorous as ever. His singing formed one of the most agreeable features of the day." The reporter went on to note that at the noon prayer meeting, where the subject was "Prayer Meetings: How to Conduct Them," H. G. Spafford was among those who expressed their views.

In early January, 1875, Spafford was the first lecturer for a new YMCA popular "Dime Lecture" series at Farwell Hall. There, he gave his lecture on Cromwell, refined during his earlier solo trip to England (1870). An unfavorable *Chicago Tribune* writer, admitting the dryness of the subject, and noting the poor attendance, observed, "The weather and counter attractions may atone for the size of the audience, but certainly not for the inertness of the lecturer, for whom the Association, in its announcements, manifested such great pride." Later the same month he repeated "The Life and Times of Oliver Cromwell" in the chapel at Wheaton College, with a twenty-five-cent admission charge to benefit the Ladies Benevolent Association. In December 1875, he went to Philadelphia to participate in the great revival services held there by D. L. Moody and Ira Sankey, and he was the featured speaker, Sunday, December 19, 1875 at Farwell Hall.

According to the account of D. W. Whittle in 1876, when

Bliss and Spafford ministered to prisoners at the Illinois State Prison at Joliet, one of Bliss's Gospel songs, "Are Your Windows Open Toward Jerusalem?" owes its origin to a Sunday service at the prison. Bliss sang at the service, and Spafford's sermon was built around the Old Testament prophet, Daniel in Babylon, as an illustration of a captive holding onto hope, posing to hearers the question: "Are your windows open toward Jerusalem?" The theme stuck in Bliss's mind, and gave rise to words and music for a song that became much loved among church people of that time. The title remains poignant, given Spafford's evolving destiny with Jerusalem.

Are Your Windows Open Toward Jerusalem?

Do you see the Hebrew captive kneeling,
At morning, noon and night, to pray?
In his chamber he remembers Zion,
Though in exile far away.

Chorus: Are your windows open toward Jerusalem,
Though as captives here a little while we stay?
For the coming of the King in his glory,
Are you watching day by day?

Do not fear to tread the fiery furnace,
Nor shrink the lion's den to share;
For the God of Daniel will deliver
He will send His angel there.

Children of the living God, take courage;
Your great deliverance sweetly sing,
Set your faces toward the hill of Zion,
Thence to hail our coming King.

Philip Paul Bliss (1838-1876)

The Spaffords, with their natural inclination to help others, found their work with Moody to be an outlet for Anna's compassion and care. Moody entrusted his entire "women's work" (as he called it)—ministering to prostitutes, abused wives, and young women in trouble—to Anna, though it must have been for only a very short time. Anna readily relinquished it to Miss Emeline Emma Dryer, former preceptress of the Illinois State Normal School.

Spafford's involvement in such Moody endeavors was cited in the written account of Moody's wealthy Chicago friend, benefactor and coworker, John V. Farwell. The last such reference occurred March 2, 1877, when Farwell and Spafford conducted evangelistic services in the small communities of Paw Paw and Lawton, Michigan, halfway between Chicago and Detroit. Farwell noted that in the little community of twenty-five hundred, crowds had filled the churches, and more than three hundred people made decisions to follow Christ as a result of their labors. Despite such success, during that time, Spafford was gradually drifting from Moody and his associates in terms of both participation and friendship, as his theological views underwent a metamorphosis and as other life pressures came to bear.

As time passed, an increasing restlessness was showing in the Spaffords' lives, an annoying uneasiness, a fraying around the edges of the fabric of their lives. It is possible that their discomfort had arisen earlier and had been part of the original motivation for the trip abroad. Surely, no one has fully understood the Spaffords' original decision to indulge a two-year family romp around Europe, at the peak of a man's professional career, only two years after the Fire, within weeks of the economic Panic of 1873, and, as will become evident, when they did not have a sufficiently sound financial foundation. Family accounts, in the same way memory tends to adjust events to their most favorable retelling, blame the Fire for the strain and upset in the Spaffords' lives, claiming that event, even though far more catastrophic for others, still, took its emotional toll when the Spaffords opened their home to other people in crisis. That story has persisted in family tradition, despite the Spafford home being out of the Fire district and their principal loss being Horatio's law office and library. It has long been suggested that the trip was proposed by the family physician, though Anna seemed at the time to have had no particular malady. Others have believed it was merely a holiday, though it would have been an unthinkably expensive option for a family with the Spaffords' resources. In any event, if the years just before the 1873 accident were unsettling for Horatio and Anna, the years after the accident unraveled their contented circumstances in almost every way.

Three years following the loss of their four daughters, a son, Horatio Goertner Spafford, was born on November 16, 1876, taking his father's first name and a middle name from the son the Daniel Goodwins had lost on the *Ville du Havre*. His birth was a great joy, and just sixteen months later the family celebrated the birth of his sister, Bertha, born March 24, 1878. She was named for Anna's friend Bertha Madison Johnson, who, living in Paris, had been so gracious to her immediately after the *Ville du Havre* accident.

With two births restoring vitality to the family nest, just when the sounds of children were being comfortably restored to Lake View's routine, tragedy struck again. Horatio, not quite three years and three months old, died suddenly of scarlet fever, February 11, 1880. Then, ten months after the trauma of losing Horatio's namesake, daughter Grace was born, January 18, 1881.

No one can doubt that crises powerfully redirect life's course. They present unforeseen demands and draw from us unanticipated reactions, often reshaping the future and the way the past is recalled. Punctiliar events, accidents, the decisions of others, "acts of God," as they are called in the insurance industry, bring into our lives uninvited elements to which we are compelled to respond. But as so powerfully presented in

Victor Frankl's famous work, *Man's Search for Meaning,* there is the response we choose to those elements. The feelings, attitudes, and choices of our reaction to crucial events can be positive or negative, with the capacity to incite fresh ambition and goal-seeking, to arouse spiritual concern or confusion, to revitalize, or to give into depression. They can dampen the enthusiasm of life, diminish optimism, wear down one's sense of hope, and allow futility and cynicism to overwhelm—our response refining our own definitions of *self;* of *character,* of *personality* and *purpose.*

Quietly and without fanfare, two central elements of the Spaffords' lives were changing—the spiritual and the financial. Horatio had cited the conflict between the two in his Thanksgiving letter to his thought-to-be Europe-bound family, in November 1873.

> I feel more and more that the absorbing pursuit of anything earthly is not well for one's spiritual life. I scarcely know what to do about the Park [real estate] matters (brackets added). If I should withdraw altogether from taking an interest in things, it is very possible that great injury might be the result, not only to my own, but other interests, and yet I feel half inclined to do so, so harassing, so vexatious, so even dangerous to one's spiritual peace do I esteem these selfish contests about money, money, money.

Seeking balance between God and mammon, Horatio took to searching the Scriptures more aggressively. For unknown reasons—whether his theology was changing as a result of his studies and experiences, there is no evidence—Horatio was involved in a bold move to depose the Reverend W. C. Young, pastor of Fullerton Avenue Presbyterian Church, according to the *Chicago Daily Tribune,* July 8, 1876. As chairman of the Finance Committee, his hand was involved in calling a crisis-type congregational meeting, ostensibly to deal with financial exigency but, secretly, intending to terminate the pastor. When the membership assembled to hear the sad plight of financial hardship, it was revealed that the church was, in reality, in excellent financial condition. The vote on removing the pastor failed decisively, one hundred twenty-six to twenty-nine, to the complete embarrassment of the dissident group. Having been so obviously devious in creating a chimera of financial distress as an excuse to oust a popular pastor was likely the first public crack to appear in Horatio's rock-solid image as a man of impeccable Christian integrity. Press reports cited the leader of the complainers as the normally amicable and irenic Dr. Samuel P. Hedges. In an action so decisive, feelings would be intense, and the event was the first time in their church life that Horatio had been defeated and overwhelmingly.

Whereas he had been the second elder selected among the founders of Fullerton Avenue Presbyterian Church in 1864, and had been the first Sunday school superintendent who had grown the Sunday school from fifty to two hundred in one year, Horatio gradually disassociated himself from the church after this. Perhaps as a direct response to his humiliation at the church—we cannot be certain—but during that same year a small cadre of friends began to gather at the Spafford home for Bible study, as an alternative to church. Beginning as a small Sunday-school-type meeting, originally without a name, they were gradually tagged by outsiders, the "Overcomers." The Chicago "Overcomers" had ties with a similar group in Valparaiso, Indiana, not far from Chicago, about which little is known. As much as doctrinal kinship, the group appears to have shared personal compatibility, to have uniformly and willingly submitted to the Spaffords' leadership, and to have commonly sought after something different from mainline churches in their Christian religious expression. Their former

127

church, or any church, became nonessential. Perhaps evidence of the Overcomers' repudiation of Moody came, not from Spafford himself, but from a supporter in a newspaper interview about four years later in 1881. Charles Gaylord, a former Baptist, was asked if his Spafford-inspired theology was an outgrowth of Moodyism? "No, sir," was the reply. "Moody and his followers are all wrong, as well as all the churches."

Once the Spaffords ignored the church and began meetings at their residence, they modified a little outbuilding on their property into a very small chapel. In a manner of speaking, they had established their own house of worship.

No membership role was maintained, and no one ever quoted a specific number of adherents or participants. Without specific membership roles, the number of Spafford-followers cannot be known. "Membership" was informal, as a contemporary newspaper account noted: "A person desirous of being identified with the worshipers simply consecrates himself to the will of the Divine. Baptism is ignored." The same newspaper article continued, "There is quite a large number of persons of the persuasion at Valparaiso, Indiana, which, including those residing in Chicago, will aggregate several hundred." Nevertheless, the core group may have included as many as thirty or thirty-five people, rarely, if ever, assembled at one time.

The distinctive purpose of the gatherings was never explained. Meetings were held on Sundays and Thursdays, and at other times, somewhat spontaneously. People came to room and board at the Spafford home for a few days at a time to enjoy the fellowship and share in Bible studies; others came only for periodic meetings. Special sessions or series of events seem to have been held whenever it seemed useful, even including a "camp meeting."

Clearly, a major figure in his life's new paradigm was Horatio's sister, Margaret Lee, who came eagerly to be part of the

Horatio Gates Spafford was born in Albany, New York, and moved to Chicago to open a law practice. This portrait was made in 1873, the year of the shipwreck.

Anna Tubena Larson Spafford was born in Stavanger, Norway, and married Horatio Spafford, September 5, 1861, in Chicago, at the age of nineteen.

The Spafford's first home was situated on an attractive five-acre lot in the affluent residential area of Lake View township, north of Chicago. The home and acreage were bounded by Evanston Road, Halsted Street, and Graceland Avenue, outside the "burnt district" of the Chicago Fire of 1871.

Horatio Spafford practiced law with the firm Spafford, McDaid & Wilson in Chicago. Their office, located in the Republic Life Building on LaSalle Street, was completely demolished by the 1871 Chicago Fire (*right*).

H. G. Spafford.   *H. O. McDaid.*   *John P. Wilson.*

SPAFFORD, MᶜDAID & WILSON,

Attorneys & Counselors at Law,

ROOM 37 REPUBLIC LIFE BUILDING,

157 & 159 LASALLE STREET,   *CHICAGO.*

A Currier & Ives print gives a glimpse of the active Bay of New York in the 1870s during the time the Spaffords boarded the *Ville du Havre.*

Numerous depictions of the collision of the *Ville du Havre* with the *Loch Earn* were done. Stanley Rogers, a respected marine artist and authority on maritime subjects, illustrated the collision (*above*) and the *Loch Earn* (*inset below*) that were published in his book, *Barenetha Rock* (1957). The most well-known illustration is the Currier & Ives print (*below*) that shows the *Ville du Havre* shortly after the *Loch Earn* cut a hole thirty-five feet long and twelve feet deep in the side of the *Ville du Havre*. Note the missing jibs and jib-boom from the *Loch Earn* caused by the impact. It was estimated that the *Ville du Havre* sank in fifteen minutes.

Annie Spafford, age 11

Maggie Spafford, age 9

All four Spafford girls fought to survive, but their small bodies were unable to withstand the relentless force of the sea. Annie was remembered to offer counsel amidst the mayhem: "Don't be afraid. The sea is His and He made it" (Psalm 95.5).

Bessie Spafford, age 7

Tanetta Spafford, age 2

Trimountain's Captain Urquhart, known by his crew as "Old Man," dedicated himself to the care and well-being of the *Havre* passengers. He considered his involvement with that shipwreck "the most important event of my seafaring life" (Urquhart 1910).

Survivors of the *Ville du Havre* collision were rescued a second time when they were required to abandon the *Loch Earn* and board the American ship *Trimountain* (*left*). Catching favorable winds, the *Trimountain* entered the port at Cardiff on Sunday, November 30, 1873, a little more than eight days after the event.

Anna cablegrammed her husband shortly after arriving at Cardiff. Contrary to the many accounts of the content of Anna's cablegram, it contained more than the two words "Saved alone."

While a rescued passenger on the *Trimountain,* Mary Adams Bulkley wrote her mother about the events of the last twenty-hours. Her exceptional ability to rise above her emotions of that day and compose her thoughts into written words to describe her experience has served as a valuable resource to historians. Stanley Rogers, the well-known maritime artist, was no doubt influenced by her words when he illustrated her ordeal, entitled, "The Rescue of Mrs. Bulkley."

Because of her unique way of uplifting everyone's spirits on board the ship, Sarah Adams "Lallie" Bulkley (Mary Bulkley's daughter) acquired the nickname "The Good Samaritan." On Wednesday, January 21, 1874, memorial services were held at Christ's Church in Rye, New York, for Lallie Bulkley and Helen Wagstaff. A painted-glass window was installed in honor of Lallie. At another church in Augusta, Georgia, a stained-glass window (*left*) was erected in Lallie's honor at the Church of the Good Shepherd. Lallie's grandmother was a founding member of the Good Shepherd church, and her parents were members until they moved to Rye, New York in the 1860s. Inscribed on the window are the words, "He shall give His angels charge over them."

Horatio Spafford handwrote his poem "It Is Well" on stationery from the Brevoort House. The Brevoort House was an elegant hotel in Chicago where Dwight L. Moody, Philip P. Bliss, and Ira A. Sankey often gathered for meetings. Because his poem is written on hotel stationery, Horatio Spafford is believed to have attended one of their gatherings, and possibly, it is where he and Philip Bliss first discussed putting the words to music.

Horatio and Anna had three more children after the 1873 shipwreck. All were born in Lake View — Chicago.

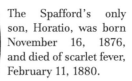

The Spafford's only son, Horatio, was born November 16, 1876, and died of scarlet fever, February 11, 1880.

Bertha Spafford was born March 24, 1878 and would live the majority of her life in Jerusalem at the colony. She was a very talented floral watercolor artist and became the leader of the colony after her mother's death.

Grace Spafford was born on January 18, 1881, less than a year after little Horatio's death. Several months later, the Spaffords went to Jerusalem, and there Grace spent the rest of her life as a member of the American Colony.

This photograph of Dwight L. Moody was found in one of the Spafford family albums. Horatio Spafford and Moody were friends for many years, though their relationship was strained at times by their difference in biblical beliefs.

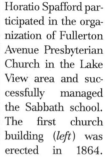

Horatio Spafford participated in the organization of Fullerton Avenue Presbyterian Church in the Lake View area and successfully managed the Sabbath school. The first church building (*left*) was erected in 1864. Reverend Dr. W. C. Young (*inset*) was pastor from 1872–1879, during the time the Spaffords were grieving the loss of their children. Dr. Young returned to his native Kentucky and served as president of Centre College until his death. He was Moderator of the General Assembly of the Presbyterian Church in the United States of America in 1892.

Dr. Samuel Hedges, family physician and friend of the Spaffords, took care of the Spafford residence when the Overcomers left for Jerusalem. He eventually purchased the residence following foreclosure proceedings initiated because Horatio had defaulted on the mortgage payments.

Upon arrival in Jerusalem, the group stayed at the Mediterranean Hotel. Anxious to settle in, the Spaffords selected a large rental house, which Bertha described "stood on a hill with its nose in the air." After the group made numerous improvements on the house, they purchased it. Rob Lawrence wrote in his diary, "Our house is on the highest point of the city and so we have delightful air and are not troubled by the terrible filth of the low portions of the city" (Vester 1950).

After his sister Eureka's death, Horatio cared for his nephew, Rob Lawrence (*right*). The likeable young man traveled with the Spaffords to Jerusalem and kept a diary of the activities of the colony. He became particularly adept at a variety of "handyman" skills. In his jovial way, he wrote in his diary, ". . . among half a dozen women there is always something that is wanted to be done, . . ." (Vester 1950). He died suddenly in September 1885, from a congenital heart defect (Geniesse 2008).

It is believed that Horatio Spafford sat for this portrait in 1885, at the Krikorian Photo Studio in Jerusalem, three years before his death.

Horatio was buried at the old American Cemetery on Mt. Zion, near the American Colony. About ten years later, the colony was told that the cemetery land needed to be sold due to overcrowding. Later (even after much political discussion), the colony unexpectedly learned that all of the graves in the American Cemetery were secretly exhumed and moved into a mass grave without coffins to the British Cemetery. Today, there is one grave site for fifteen individuals at the Jerusalem Protestant Cemetery on Mt. Zion, managed by St. George's Anglican Cathedral. The grave marker recognizes seven members of the American Colony: In Loving Memory of John C. Whiting, Horatio G. Spafford, William C. Sylvester, Herbert Drake, Margaret W. Lee, Geo A. Fuller, and John Miller. The remaining individuals died prior to the establishment of the American Colony and were most likely Christian missionaries. Around 1907 the colony purchased their own cemetery on Mt. Scopus, where Anna Spafford was buried in 1923.

The Spafford family provided attractive surroundings for colony members as seen in this 1898 photo of the upper court.

Anna devoted herself to her daughters, Bertha (*standing*) and Grace, and to the development of the colony.

One of the early enterprises of the American Colony was the establishment of a kindergarten for children of the colony (1902).

In the 1920s and the early 1930s, the American Colony opened stores, such as Dodge Brothers Motor Cars and Graham Brothers Trucks, and Vester and Company (*store with awnings around the corner*) to provide income for the colony. These stores were located at the colony's Grand Hotel.

This Spafford family photo was made at the colony around 1913–1915. (*Left to right, standing*): Jacob Spafford, Grace Spafford Whiting, John Whiting, Frederick Vester, Anna Grace Vester. (*Left to right, seated*): Anna Spafford with Jock Vester(?), Horatio Vester, Bertha Spafford Vester with baby. (*Left to right, on floor*): Tanetta Vester, Spafford Whiting, and David Whiting.

The living area of the American Colony Hotel, which Bertha related "we learned to call it a salon," was decorated by Anna. The arched windows and ornate ceiling remain part of the hotel today.

Shortly after her mother's death, Bertha Spafford Vester opened the Anna Spafford Baby Home (*right*) in her mother's honor. Today, the facility is known as the Spafford Children's Center.

Nurses of the Anna Spafford Baby Home often distributed loaves of bread to the neighborhood.

Local residents gathered outside the colony buildings to hear Bertha Vester (*center*) read the names of welfare recipients.

The American Colony grew into a multi-block community, as shown in this aerial photo, believed to have been taken in the 1950s. Though the buildings look much the same today, the interiors have been refurbished, and the area houses one of the most elegant hotels in Jerusalem (inset).

Overcomers. She moved from New York, perhaps persuaded by her brother, following the death of her husband in December 1879, Arthur T. Lee, a Civil War veteran and a federal government official. Sometime earlier, Margaret had prayed to be filled with the Holy Spirit and had seemed to be spiritually renewed. Her sudden enduement of gifts of biblical exposition and divine interpretation made a profound impression on her brother. Initially, as later written out, probably by a young Bertha from dictation by her father, it happened as follows.

> She found herself on her feet an [sic] it was as though some one else had spoken and not she, herself. She was as much astonished as Mother was at what had happened. She said it was the most astounding experience of her life. After that, she conducted Bible readings and expounded the scriptures with such simplicity an [sic] such an unassuming manner that people flocked to hear her. Father came from Chicago and during family prayers, which used to be rather formal at the Lee's [sic] house, Aunt Maggie explained passages in the Bible, which made them live. Father was much impressed.

While Margaret's gift for expounding the Scriptures was a delight to the Overcomers, they grew to respect her abilities as divine interpreter of matters other than Scripture. Almost like a divine Oracle at Delphi, questions raised in the ordinary course of life could be posed to her, and a divine response elicited. At first, during those moments when she was under the spirit's spell, confirmation that she was giving a divinely authorized response came in a strange and audible cracking of the jaw. Gradually, it became such a nuisance to her husband, especially since it often occurred during meals, that she asked for a quieter confirmation; thereafter, she developed a special look about the eyes, indicative of divine telepathy. Occasionally one or two others within the group would temporarily appear to have the "sign," their parlance for the ability to give divine leadership by interpretation.

Lacking Margaret's advantage as Scriptural interpreter, Anna Spafford in time was seen as gifted with special prophetic powers for conveying spiritual messages directly from the Lord. This ability gave enormous power and authority to the two women, who evolved into *de facto* spiritual leaders as a result. From the "Overcomers" earliest meetings, there appeared to be competition between Anna and Margaret for leadership. Not only did Horatio not object, he appeared to have stifled his natural leadership capacities, and the male chauvinism common to the times yielded to their nascent assertiveness.

Horatio was quick to affirm the authenticity and veracity of his sister's interpretations, fully defending the validity of her gifts, and her status as leader, as we learn from his letter of March 1879 to Miss Wadsworth (see Appendix B for the complete text of Spafford to Wadsworth, March 17, 1879). (As far as we know, Horatio gave no similar detailed apologia for Anna's divine connections, although he clearly acquiesced to her leadership.) In the letter, he laid out a lawyer-like brief supporting his sister's teachings and guidance, and giving the most explicit declaration available of his own new perspectives. He based his arguments for Mrs. Lee's credibility on her moral and spiritual strength; she was untrained and not seeking spiritual leadership, making her status the more believable since she had so surprisingly become an unexpected vessel. Second, while she had not been studious about the Scriptures and formerly sought interpretations and answers from him (Horatio), inasmuch as he had been a diligent Bible student, suddenly and for about the previous two-and-a-half years she had been giving isolated interpretations that in his view had gradually taken form as a harmonious system. He believed none of her comments failed to integrate with Scripture, but illuminated the Scriptures. Third, unanticipated and unsought,

Mrs. Lee was almost instantaneously given a remarkable familiarity with and insight into the Scriptures, corresponding to an even stronger spiritual life and presence. Fourth, Horatio claimed to have independently verified the correctness of Mrs. Lee's teaching concerning the final triumph of God's love in Christ over every created being. He became convinced that a person attained the status of overcomer by utter consecration and separation unto God. Only those overcomers, he averred, could become the "bride of Christ." Fifth, one could fall from the ranks of the elect, in accordance with Arminian doctrine. Sixth, "Mrs. Lee, my wife & several friends, here & elsewhere— altogether indeed but a very little company, have prayerfully, & at last heartily, received these teachings, as from the Lord." Still, he wrote Miss Wadsworth, he did not feel that such truths were for all, because "many would not receive them."

The 1879 letter attributes Horatio's dramatic change to the new insights of his sister. But later, in an 1881 interview with the *Daily Inter-Ocean,* Horatio, explaining his unorthodox beliefs, never mentioned his sister. To a reporter, he used the term, "I found," three times in just a few lines. Then, continuing, he used phrases such as: "*I* pursued *my* examination until *I* was convinced;" "If *I* had found as the result of *my* inquiry;" "*I* was glad to find. . . ." He had, even perhaps unknowingly, come to claim his sister's views as his own.

The views and practices of the Overcomers appeared curious to traditional Christian church people. Asked by a reporter in 1881 to characterize the Overcomers, Reverend Dr. Leroy Jones Halsey, distinguished Presbyterian professor at McCormick Theological Seminary and a fellow resident of Lake View, offered a cautious, respectful appraisal.

> At the head of it are a few educated, godly people, who have been members of evangelical churches and who

were at first identified with the best type of Moody evangelism. They ignore all church ordinances, and much resemble the Plymouth brethren of New England. They claim to receive direct revelations from Christ or the Holy Ghost, with outward sensible signs of his personal presence, and remind us of the book of tenets of Montanus and his followers in the early centuries; and also of the more recent Irvingites of London. Their system seems to be a species of mysticism, and it leads them to interpret the Bible by their own personal experiences and revelations made to them. . . . judging from the history of all small movements in past times, it is much to be feared that this one will lead some good people into dangerous errors. Some of the leaders of the movement claim scarcely less than divine inspiration and the spirit of prophecy.

Reverend Dr. Halsey agreed that the Spafford views resembled teachings of the then-popular Spiritists or Spirtualists but felt their views also related to Plymouthism (i.e., the doctrines of the Plymouth Brethren). He also noted their similarity to the extreme dispensationalism of J. N. Darby, which became popular in the mid-to-late 1800s. A later newspaper article claimed that two publications represented the views of the Overcomers: *Our Rest* of Chicago, and *The Restitution* of Plymouth, Indiana.

Surviving records offer no objective support for the contention, solely related by Bertha, that the Spaffords were officially expelled from the Fullerton Avenue Presbyterian Church. Bertha wrote that her parents were asked to leave the church, and that friends and associates were suggesting, cruelly, that the Spaffords' troubles were divinely dictated as retribution for sin or unfaithfulness. The final straw, as Bertha relates it, was someone's curious offer to adopt her, as though to relieve the Spaffords of responsibility. Though there is no hint of support for such an assertion, it has been made repeatedly by family members in various publications.

As recently as the March 1997 *Smithsonian* magazine article, that story was advanced by Anna Grace Vester Lind, daughter of Bertha Spafford Vester. After the Spaffords' son died, a seeming continuance of their misfortune, "instead of finding solace, they found themselves ostracized, victims of the prevailing church doctrine that judged their anguish as divine retribution for the 'sins'. " There appears to be no basis for contending that such was the prevailing church doctrine, either at Fullerton Avenue, with Presbyterians in general, or with the Moody-related folks, or that it was applied to the Spaffords: nevertheless, Anna Spafford was known later to have asserted regularly to the flock in Jerusalem that "illness was the result of sin."

To a writer for *Aramco World*, apparently unaware that the actual date of withdrawal from the Fullerton Avenue church was 1876, Bertha Spafford Vester said that "the Spaffords broke with their church in a bitter public quarrel."

> Although staunch Presbyterians the Spaffords, after what they had suffered, could neither accept the idea that their children could not have gone to Heaven—as Presbyterian dogma suggested—nor believed that their suffering was in retribution for their sins—as some of the church elders hinted. Horatio voiced his views openly, and, as a result, was expelled from the church. When some of his friends backed him they were expelled too.

Yet there is no description in the press at that time or in church records of this. Clearly, "the bitter public quarrel," "[w]hen some of his friends backed him" and "they were expelled too" can only refer to the 1876 attempt to terminate the pastor, using the trumped-up charge of failing finances.

From a number of sources, it can be understood that Bertha Spafford Vester was a loyal daughter, more concerned for her parents' reputation than for historical accuracy. In her book, *Our Jerusalem,* she sought to portray her parents in the kindest, most gentle light—even at the expense of obvious truth. The somewhat devious and manipulative manner of attempting to remove the Spaffords' pastor may well have provoked a majority of church members, but there is no evidence of a vote, no evidence of brash theological charges condemning their children, and no assertion of a retributive, God's gonna-get-you-for-that theology. It is possible that differences of opinion led the Spaffords to feel somewhat alienated from the church and friends there, but there is no confirmation of elders or church people blaming them. In fact, a transcript of a sermon by Reverend H. M. Collison, Fullerton Avenue pastor, in February 1880, a year before the Spaffords' escape to Jerusalem, evidences for that time a fairly liberal view of hell and eternal punishment, asserting that the Bible "could not mean a literal fire. . . ."

While not a member of Fullerton Avenue Presbyterian Church, an evangelical friend, Ira D. Sankey, Moody's musical associate, specifically wrote of his joy that the two older Spafford children had made professions of their Christian faith just before their fateful trip, and Sankey was confident that all the children were safely awaiting their parents in heaven. There is nothing to support the *Aramco* article's claims against the church or its members.

No evidence of an expulsion of the Spaffords survives in any direct or indirect reference, though Horatio was later viewed by some Fullerton Avenue churchgoers as an unexplainable curiosity. In *The Quiver,* the Fullerton Avenue Presbyterian Church's newsletter for November 1888, about twelve years after they became inactive in the church, and seven years after they had moved from Chicago to Jerusalem, Horatio was treated compassionately.

> After the loss of his children in the ill-fated *Ville du Havre* disaster, Mr. Spafford began to devote his whole life to the study of the one subject of 'Christ's second coming,' and his last years have been spent in accordance with his theory of the solution of this subject.

Several additional references, years after their removal to Jerusalem, illustrate the church's appreciation for the Spaffords, even while acknowledging Horatio's changing views. In February 1888, *The Quiver* had stated: "The people of the Fullerton Avenue church have especial reason to remember Mr. Spafford, as he was one of the organizers of our society, . . ." *The Quiver* then quoted from an article that appeared in the *Lake View Telephone*: "Many of our citizens will remember Horatio Spafford, one of the leaders of the overcomers, a religious sect that attracted considerable attention at one time."

In March 1889, *The Quiver* having confirmation of his death in Jerusalem (1888), called Horatio Spafford "unbalanced," and used the word "fanatic," even while paying him tribute.

> What a commentary upon the power of consecrated fidelity, was that recently furnished in the city of Jerusalem. The occasion was the funeral of Mr. Spafford, one of the founders, and for many years an elder of our church. . . . If he was a fanatic; if he was a trifle unbalanced, as he tarried in the Holy City, waiting for the coming of Christ, there was, nevertheless, such a mighty substratum of living faith beneath it all, as to convince men that he was genuine, that he was profoundly sincere, and as to drive him out, to embody his belief in words and deeds of love. Fidelity to conviction is power, and we all need more of it.

By the latter 1870s, the Spaffords had abandoned the church of their adult life. Horatio had given up evangelistic work, the social service efforts he enjoyed, and his friendship with D. L.

Moody and associates. He had withdrawn from the relationships established as a man of civic status, a former secretary of the Board of McCormick Theological Seminary, a former member of the Presbyterian Synod, a member of the board of directors of the YMCA, a director of the art museum, a life member of the Fine Arts Institute, volunteer chaplain at the U.S. Marine hospital. His standing as a professional man of the Bar had deteriorated as his interest in the legal profession had diminished.

Yet from 1876 onward this was the period of Horatio's greatest output of poetry and writing. A number of his poems appeared first in Christian periodicals, including *The Watchword*. It was probably about 1876 when Horatio, who had been regarded as an evangelist of the orthodox order, had authored a small, undated pamphlet, bearing no author's name, published by Fleming H. Revell, entitled, *Twenty Reasons for Believing that the Second Coming of the Lord is Near.* Revell was Moody's brother-in-law, and was becoming a prominent figure in evangelical publishing. About two years later, in 1878, when Revell issued Horatio's booklet of poetry, *Waiting for the Morning*, its flyleaf carried an advertisement for the earlier printed, *Twenty Reasons,* "by the same author." It was the first public acknowledgment of Spafford's authorship of *Twenty Reasons*, which became somewhat controversial, despite the description in Revell's flyleaf advertisement.

> This pamphlet bears evidence throughout of great care in preparation on the part of the author, who has avoided the questionable extremes of many writers, and gives us a careful, candid, and condensed series of arguments that are certainly well worthy of consideration.

At what point Horatio's views began to stray, we do not know, but they had likely been changing, even as Revell lauded the author of *Twenty Reasons* for having "avoided the questionable extremes." When *Twenty Reasons* had been first issued, "it was freely circulated about the city, and even handed out at the door of the Young Men's Christian Association." However, "[b]y leading men in the latter society [YMCA] it was pronounced the work of an infidel, but it was, nevertheless, read with great interest, and threatened for a time to create a wide rupture within the association. Only a few, however, accepted Mr. Spafford's theories . . . ."

Horatio's feelings seemed to ricochet between confidence in his faith, and the almost haunting possibility that their family tragedy might be a direct divine judgment—even though he occasionally protested against the latter. Aware of the privileged life he and his family had led, he struggled to accept the full grace of God. Recall his conclusive statement after news of the shipwreck, when he said to Major Whittle, "I am glad to trust the Lord when it will cost me something." He wrote that same sentiment to his sister from the Chicago-to-New York train, en route to cross the Atlantic after he received Anna's cablegram about the shipwreck. His reaction, then, was not impromptu, but a studied response. Though he may have meant it as an affirmation amidst pressing trials, yet his statement does not credit the grace of God—almost as though the Lord gives extra credit, favor or merit for enduring suffering, affliction, or difficulty.

12
FINANCIAL DURESS

The financial difficulties in the Spaffords' lives following the 1873 shipwreck tragedy were as real as the spiritual ones. The source of the Spafford wealth had always been obscure. Horatio was a lawyer in an era when almost no one became wealthy practicing law. In 1873, when he was not yet forty-five years old, an age when an attorney would normally be arcing toward the apogee of his professional career, he and his family planned a two-year trip to Europe. They would be foregoing two years' income, the expense of traveling first class, and the ongoing expense of maintaining the Chicago household, as well as the family's livelihood abroad. They were to pay living expenses and compensation for a governess for the two younger children and pay tuition expenses for the two older children in a Swiss boarding school. Then, Anna and Horatio planned to travel about Europe on "a sort of second honeymoon." All of this came just two years after the loss of his law offices in the Republic Life Building, which was part of the "burnt district" of the Great Chicago Fire of 1871, and amidst the financial crunch known as "the Panic of 1873," which sent shivers through the financial markets of Chicago and the nation in mid-September. The entire European venture was the type of holiday planned by the superrich.

Bank records from 1872 show that Horatio Spafford dealt in large sums of money for that day. Details are obscure, but the American Colony in Jerusalem Collection of the Library of Congress shows the account of H. G. Spafford at Merchants National Bank of Chicago to have balances of: $11,840 in June; $17,927 in July; and $24,440 in October. The sources of those particular funds cannot be identified with certainty. It is possible that they could have been funds held for others for matters in legal process, or they could have related to funds entrusted to him for management, or they might have been proceeds of his loan from Connecticut Mutual Life Insurance Company.

On February 23, 1872, Horatio and Anna conveyed a mortgage of a "large amount of real estate" to the Connecticut Mutual Life Insurance Company to secure an indebtedness of $30,000. It seems these funds supported a real estate purchase, a little more than four months *after* the Fire of October 8–9, 1871, and a year and a half before the family's departure for the intended European trip. And, it appears that borrowing yielded the funds necessary for their planned two-year sojourn in Europe. In addition to the mortgage, as an added security, they had conveyed a bond, or promissory note, to Connecticut Mutual, making them personally responsible for repayment, even beyond the value of the real estate.

The real estate, used as collateral, was consistently referred to as a large tract of real estate, but it was rarely fully identified. In family and public lore, the impression was created that the land purchase was made *before* the Great Chicago Fire of 1871, and that somehow the Fire was responsible for the "loss" of the real estate. The family continued to imply that they had somehow "lost everything" in the Fire, an uncontrollable calamity, not anyone's fault. Bertha Spafford Vester, in her book, blamed the Fire when she wrote:

> To Father and his associates in the real estate venture,
> it [the Great Fire] was a calamity. Who at such a time
> could think of enlarging parks or expanding the city?

Even Horatio's obituary in the *New York Times,* October 22, 1888, stated, "He acquired wealth in his profession, but the great fire of 1871 made him comparatively poor."

Anna's name and signature were on the deeds, and the elements of the transaction had been specifically explained to her, according to a signed statement. Yet on more than one occasion, she was unconvincingly vague about the location of the real estate, even in subsequent court appearances. In fact, deed records indicate that Horatio G. and Annie T. Spafford held title to nineteen lots in the Wrightwood subdivision, not far from their residence. In addition, together they owned an undivided one-third interest in five additional lots with Horatio's law partner, John P. Wilson, and one with Carl Marlow (Deed between Martin Andrews and Caroline W. Andrews and the City of Chicago and Horatio G. Spafford of County of Cook, State of Illinois, February 23, 1872). Apparently, Horatio's investment group had hoped for an immediate resale, likely for the much-discussed expansion of Lincoln Park, which did not happen. About that time, serious disagreement erupted over whether a portion of Lake View should be incorporated into the City of Chicago, and that issue may have influenced possible resale. A primary concern was the need for a water supply sufficient to deal with fire, should it occur, and the cost to taxpayers.

The Spaffords proceeded to default on semiannual mortgage payments for the lots. After several years, the Connecticut Mutual Life Insurance Company foreclosed in 1879, (Bill of Complaint, Case 72688, Superior Court of Cook County, State of Illinois, February 25, 1879). (It appears that Connecticut Mutual was very slow to take action, since the defaults had accumulated over several years, and the company had the right to foreclose after a default of thirty days.) All the Wrightwood lots, including the five with an undivided one-third interest, were auctioned off at the Chamber of Commerce Building in Chicago on the afternoon of June 23, 1879 (Public Notice of Land Sale, June 23, 1879, Superior Court of the State of Illinois County of Cook).

On February 26, 1878, Horatio borrowed $2,000 from his former law partner, Henry O. McDaid. He offered Lot 22 in Wrightwood as collateral for the loan. The loan was apparently never repaid, and it would appear from correspondence after the Spaffords moved to Jerusalem that Dr. Hedges may have delivered a deed to Mr. McDaid at Horatio's direction, perhaps in an attempt to compensate.

One tract of land, representing the lower half of the residential lot at Lake View, was the subject of a foreclosure, May 31, 1879, in Superior Court of Cook County (Connecticut Mutual Life Insurance Company v. Horatio Gates Spafford, Annie Spafford, his wife, Carl Marlow, and John P. Wilson). Connecticut Mutual foreclosed on and then sold the lower half of Lot 9, one section of the acreage related to the Spafford home at Lake View (Public Notice of Land Sale June 23, 1879). Public awareness of such action would have had to be an acute embarrassment.

The Spafford name was publicly linked to at least one corporate business failure. The April 5, 1873 *Chicago Daily Tribune* reported the bankruptcy declaration of the Union Screw and Bolt Company. The bankruptcy action was petitioned by H. Weller, H. G. Spafford, Edward C. Waller, Peter Page, and J. Young Scammon, the latter being president of the Marine Company and president of the Mechanics' National Bank of Chicago. The company had apparently issued two hundred bonds at five hundred dollars each, which were subscribed March 1871.

The interest on the bonds fell due February 1873, and was not paid. The company was bankrupt. All the property, material, real estate, patents, and other assets were to be sold April 21, 1873, and applied toward the debt. So far as is known, that is the only formal bankruptcy in which Horatio was involved.

Following the shipwreck, the Spaffords financial circumstances became increasingly dire. Though there is no record of it, there is no doubt that Anna carried substantial cash that would have been lost in the shipwreck. Somehow, they had managed to live well above their means, but the financial tourniquet was tightening.

Although Horatio did almost no legal work after the *Ville du Havre* accident, he kept a prestigious downtown office, the arrearage on his rent growing, month-to-month. In the *Chicago Daily Tribune,* it was reported that as the city rebuilt following the Fire, a "commodious and attractive structure recently finished at Nos. 99 and 101 Washington Street," was at an "unrivaled location," and had already secured occupants of the highest business position and character. Among those occupants, it specifically noted, not as a firm, but individually, H. G. Spafford, "well-known gentleman and legal counselor," H. O. McDaid, "attorney and counselor at law", and John P. Wilson, "a well-known member of the legal brotherhood." Whereas, according to a newspaper story, Horatio was retiring and being replaced by Oliver H. Picher of Missouri. Later, court testimony shown that Horatio was significantly behind on his rent for the "commodious" office—though why he needed such an office, when he had quit the practice of law and was dealing only slightly in real estate, is unknown.

In an 1876 letter to the Spaffords from Moody's home in Northfield, Massachusetts, where she was visiting, Emma Dryer wrote:

Mr. and Mrs. Moody talk of you affectionately. He, I think, has a deep interest in your financial troubles. In talking about them one evening he said that he thought Mr. Spafford would do well to resume his practice of law until this hard time is passed. He spoke of Mr. S's success in the past and that he was in a fair position to succeed again. . . .

Daniel W. Whittle, businessman-turned-evangelist, Moody associate and neighbor of the Spaffords, the one who had walked the floor with Horatio the night he received the cable reporting the deaths of his children, and whom Horatio accompanied on evangelistic missions, was also aware of their financial plight. He told a court in the 1890s that coldness arose in his relationship to Spafford about 1877 when he (Whittle) refused Horatio's request to intercede with Moody to get him several thousand dollars of the hymnbook money. (Moody associates, Sankey and Bliss, had published a hymnbook that enjoyed phenomenal sales in Britain and America. Both men generously gave up their royalties to a fund that Moody established, and that functioned somewhat like a modern charitable foundation. Ultimately, it was hymnbook money that financed the building of Moody's Christian schools, Northfield for girls and Mount Hermon for boys in northwest Massachusetts. Spafford was for a time a trustee of those funds and, thus, would have had special knowledge of them.) Horatio thought Whittle had done him wrong in refusing to present to Moody his petition for financial help. Whittle testified that down to the time they left Chicago (1881), Spafford told him, "he was probably bankrupt and that he had no means of raising any money even to the extent of $5." Further, Whittle told the court that Horatio Spafford "frequently came to have me pray with him that God might send him one hundred thousand dollars, along that time, those two or three years [approximately 1874–1877], that that was needed to pay his pressing debts" (brackets added).

143

Such financial stress is confirmed by Anna's confidences shared in her diary from July 1878 to May 7, 1879. She described their difficult financial straits that she had no money with which to provide even family meals, and her general worries about their support. For example, her entry of August 7, 1878, when she had only thirty cents and the fortunate repayment of a personal loan Horatio had earlier made brought $2, and temporary salvation.

On August 23, she wrote, "Satan tried to frighten me" concerning their lack of money, but "Mr. Sankey sent us $10.00." For Ira D. Sankey, D. L. Moody's musical associate, hardly a man of wealth, to rescue the Spaffords with a charitable gift of $10, means news of their plight had reached him. On September 10, 1878, Anna was disturbed because Horatio was so depressed, there being no money, and things were looking very dark. The Spaffords may have been able to harvest some benefit from equity real estate investments, which had been excluded from mortgage. In September of 1878, Horatio apparently sold off two lots in the Wrightwood subdivision. A newspaper report indicates that the purchaser, Susan Gridley, bought the lots from Spafford for the sum of $10,000, the sale recorded later, March 25, 1879.

Anna Spafford confirmed, during her testimony in Murphy v. Hedges 1896, that Horatio had given up real estate involvement a few years before 1881. When asked what means Horatio had of maintaining a livelihood, Anna admitted that he had none during that time.

By the early 1880s, with friends aware of his indebtedness, with his attempts to procure $100,000, Horatio was becoming in many respects a tragic figure. Writing Dr. Hedges, in 1886, Mrs. Amelia Gould, one of the most ardent followers of the Spaffords, reminded Dr. Hedges: "As you know Mr. Spafford stood before the noon-prayer meeting some years ago [in Chicago] & declared that the Lord would pay all his debts."

In the Circuit Court judgment (January 29, 1900), after hearing testimony and reviewing the facts, the Judge concluded concerning Horatio's financial situation as far back as June, 1874: "That he was in desperate straits for money is shown by his paying off one mortgage for $5,000 on his homestead and raising one for $10,000 without making any improvements on the homestead, . . ."

Despite the personal and business debts cited above, what brought the Spaffords' financial plight to the status of outright emergency appears to have been the convergence of several legal actions. First was the judgment of Cook County Superior Court that the Spaffords were to pay Connecticut Mutual $13,674.49 in damages as a consequence of the 1879 foreclosure and subsequent Sheriff's sale. Not having satisfied the judgment, the sheriff of Cook County was authorized to seize the "Lands and Tenements, Goods and Chattels of Horatio G. Spafford," if the judgement was not paid within ninety days of June 30, 1880.

Yet another legal action was on the horizon, carrying with it eviction from their home, loss of the small chapel used by the Overcomers, the likelihood of personal bankruptcy, and public humiliation. Though pending, and certainly on Horatio's mind and in his sphere of awareness, it did not come to light until December 1881, within four months after the Spaffords had left Chicago for Jerusalem. Dr. Hedges, who, with his family, was temporarily given charge of the Spafford residence at Lake View by a last-minute rental agreement, received a great surprise. He was notified by H. R. Chandler that rent payments should be directed to him as agent for Mrs. Hetty H. R. Green. She held a mortgage on the Spafford residence in the amount of $15,000 at nine percent interest, payable five years after date, June 15,

1874. Horatio, likely in desperate need of cash, had mortgaged his personal residence and allowed the mortgage agreement to be heavily weighted in favor of the lender. The agreement allowed Mrs. Green to foreclose (i.e., "to sell and dispose the property"), if the mortgage payment was overdue by thirty days. By the time Dr. Hedges learned of the mortgage, it was in default more than two years. Reputedly one of the richest women in the world at that time, Mrs. Green was internationally famous, extremely frugal, and known to be utterly ruthless in demanding payment of debts. (For another foreclosure by Mrs. Green, one that went to the U.S. Supreme Court, see the 1896 case, Cornell v. Green, 163 U.S. 75.) Dr. Hedges told a Court years later that Horatio Spafford had never informed him of any mortgage, though Mrs. Hedges had intimated to him that the Spaffords had been concerned about losing the property to a mortgage foreclosure. In early 1882, with Mrs. Green having instigated foreclosure proceedings, Dr. Hedges had moved to buy the house, lot, and furnishings for $20,000. This paid off the mortgage to Mrs. Green, and officially titled the property in Hedges' name.

Had the Spaffords remained in the home at the time of foreclosure, they would have been evicted, facing the embarrassment of newspapers and gossip. With the record of foreclosure and their lack of funds or cash flow, they would have had to be satisfied with a place much less spacious than their house in Lake View. They would have been fortunate to have been able to rent any housing. Horatio would have known of Mrs. Green's reputation for aggressive collection of obligations, and as one formerly highly regarded in both professional and social circles, he would have well-understood the public humiliation imminent.

Fortunately for Horatio and for his family, the Chicago newspapers did not carry the full story of Horatio Spafford's failures until a few years after his death. Court records confirm the veracity of newspaper headlines such as "Spafford's Name in Court Again."

The case in the article centered on the charge that Mrs. Mary F. Murphy, a niece of Horatio Spafford (daughter of his sister, Eureka Spafford Lawrence), had received an inheritance of $8,000 upon the death of her father, James R. Lawrence, of Syracuse, New York, in 1872. Mr. Lawrence, himself a judge, designated Horatio G. Spafford a trustee, along with J. Albert Hood, who was also an executor of Mr. Lawrence's estate. Mr. Hood declined to serve, so Spafford became the sole trustee. He was charged with managing a portion of the estate to support Mary financially.

> I direct said trustees to hold the said one-ninth share of my estate which they may receive from my executors or which may vest in them as trustees at the expiration of the said ten years from my decease and to vest the same safely and to manage and control the said real estate and receive the rents and profits thereof or to sell and convey the same and invest the proceeds thereof during the natural life of my said daughter Mary, applying the net income and profits of the said one-ninth share of my estate to the use and benefit and support of my said daughter Mary, and at the decease of my said daughter Mary to pay over and convey the principal fund and any real estate which remain unsold and which may have vested in them as such trustees to the heirs at law of my said daughter Mary.

However, as the suit alleged, Spafford, "after a time became derelict in paying interest," and mixed the funds in the trust with his own money. Then, "financially embarrassed," he left the country in 1881 without resigning his trust, or making restitution to the estate, being in arrears at least $12,000. Mrs. Murphy's suit was intended to make a claim against Dr. Hedges, who had purchased the Spaffords' former residence at Lake View following foreclosure proceedings—a purchase likely made at a resulting advantageous price. Mrs. Murphy was seeking to recover her inheritance from the equity the Spaffords had in the residence before it was sold.

Though Horatio had died seven years previously, when the suit was processed in 1895, the Spafford family did not contest the charges. At the time, Anna Spafford was in the U.S. attempting to secure the Whiting children's inheritance over the objections of their grandmother, who claimed the Colony in Jerusalem was an unfit place to raise the children. Anna actually joined Mrs. Murphy's suit against Dr. Hedges on behalf of the Spafford's daughters, Bertha and Grace. As the newspaper recorded, "the widow and heirs of Mr. Spafford are cognizant of the rights of the complainant . . . and have expressed themselves anxious that everything should be done that is possible that the complainant may have her money."

Sadder still, and surely more painful to the family, were testimony and court proceedings (1895-97) that revealed that Horatio Spafford, without permission, authorization, or even *informing* principals, had also diverted the funds of two other persons for his own unauthorized use. One such person was Mrs. J. P. Wills, a divorced woman, who was a friend of both Spafford and of D. W. Whittle. Without any supporting legal documents, Whittle said, Spafford "acted as her friend," and was made custodian of property that was sold about 1874. The $16,000 in proceeds were placed into Spafford's hands to invest on her behalf. Whittle testified that the income from that money was all the Widow Wills had to live on, and that he had regularly interceded with Spafford on her behalf so that Spafford paid her interest for four or five years. Then, interest payments ceased, because Spafford was unable to pay, despite Whittle's continued pleadings.

148

The misappropriation of funds of yet a third person was exposed during the court deliberations. These funds belonged to Miss Kopse. No one seemed to know much about her, according to the court transcript, though Anna Spafford knew that Horatio had confessed to using her funds, as well as those of the other two women. In the conclusion of the Circuit Court of Cook County, Illinois, Horatio's wrongful application of funds was:

> probably used to tide over his real estate speculations, likewise the trust funds of Mrs. Murphy, Mrs. Wills and Miss Kopse. The testimony shows that Spafford used all the trust funds to tide him over his speculations, and that he never distinguished one fund from another or the specific use he had put any one trust fund to.

What seems more likely from the current perspective is that Horatio misappropriated funds of the three women to pay for his ordinary living expenses, as well as for payment of taxes and interest on his real estate speculation.

Horatio's confession before the Overcomers group admitted his breach of trust in his use of others' funds. He confessed it as sin, and informed the group of his severe financial condition, his inability to make restitution. Mrs. George "Tryphema" (sometimes, "Tryphemia") Rounds, a devout Overcomers member and leader before her defection just after the Spaffords' 1881 departure, testified in the 1890s that at many Overcomers meetings the Spaffords need of $100,000 was openly discussed. She said, "We were asked to pray that the Lord would deliver him from those debts and from those that were persecuting him." Anna Spafford told the court he had confessed to her and before the group: "We never covered it up. We confessed it as a sin before all the people, and Dr. Hedges." And, when asked to name any other party whose money Horatio might have had at the time they went to Jerusalem, and which he had not paid back, Anna answered:

"I know that when he confessed about Mrs. Murphy, having wronged her, he confessed of having wronged Mrs. Wills and Miss Kopse; that is all I remember."

When the suit of Mrs. Murphy and the Spafford daughters against Dr. Hedges had finally coursed its way through final judgment by the Illinois State Supreme Court, the anguish of Mrs. Murphy was vented in a letter to Anna Spafford, April 16, 1908. Twenty years had passed since Horatio's death and thirty-four years since the death of Mrs. Murphy's father, who established Horatio as trustee.

> But alas. It was of no avail. All is lost!!!!!! The courts have decided against us & allowed Dr. Hedges to hold $150,000 worth of real estate for $20,000.
>
> This long fight has nearly ruined me. Has placed me deeply in debt but I had the sure hope to the last that you & yours could have your lovely valuable house once more & that I could be paid through a mortgage. Oh what a pity poor dear Uncle Horatio did not invest well, tell me the truth & allow me to save him & myself at the same time as I could have done!!!!!
>
> A man of his fame as a lawyer—His good name to protect: His wife & children to protect, & provide for. This young niece left in his care. Why! Why!! didn't he trust me, who loved & honered [sic] him above this bad, bad, pretender! This falsifier, this hypocrit [sic]!
>
> Don't be angry dear Aunt & Cousins. I have needed & suffered for this increase all these years since 1874.

Sadly, all three victims of Horatio's breach of integrity were women. Two of them, are known to have been dependent upon the funds he oversaw for their very livelihood. Is it any wonder, whatever else might have plagued him that he seemed never quite able to taste full forgiveness? Though of little consequence to those he owed, even after removal to Jerusalem, Horatio's conscience seemed not to rest, tormented by his indebtedness. He noted in his Jerusalem diary, Saturday, July 8, 1882, "Prayed with Mr. Page for the payment of all debts."

13
RESITUATED IN THE HOLY CITY

Of all aspects of the Spaffords' spiritual journey, the most bizarre to the modern observer is the consistent prophesying or interpreting of supposed direct divine instructions by Margaret Spafford Lee and Anna Spafford, a subject carefully avoided by the Spaffords' daughter Bertha in her book *Our Jerusalem*. After 1876, it appears to have been a regular and routine centerpiece of worship and life among the Overcomers, for the five years that centered around Lake View and, afterward, in Jerusalem until both Margaret (August 12, 1891) and Anna (April 17, 1923) died. Margaret Lee may have been the group's original leader, but throughout Anna Spafford's years as the unquestioned leader of the American Colony in Jerusalem after 1881, and with varying degrees of emphasis until her death, she relied upon a supposed ability to relay divine messages, verbatim and infallibly. Important as it was, it is not in Bertha Spafford Vester's book.

According to sworn testimony in U.S. courts in the early 1890s, describing the interpreting or mediumship of Anna Spafford, some of the divine directions "consisted in a single sign for the affirmative made by a sort of epileptic sniffle or grimace. To communicate with the deity it was only necessary to put to one of these prophetesses a series of questions requiring a negative or affirmative answer. If there was no sniffle that meant 'No;' and if, on the other hand, the sniffle was given, that meant 'Yes.' " Court testimony further confirmed that the Colony's official records actually referred to Anna Spafford as "prophetess" and acknowledged her role in interpreting truth from falsehood and right from wrong. Anna Spafford was asked by lawyers: "Did you ever claim to be a prophet?" Hesitating for a moment, she replied: "Only a prophet as Christ expects me to be. That is when the Holy Ghost speaks to me, but in no other way." The questioner continued, "And did you hear those voices—I mean did—that is—did the Spirit speak to you?" "Yes, the Spirit has spoken to me," Anna responded. Finally asked to explain, Anna Spafford could only answer, "It would be utterly impossible to explain these things to the ordinary, uninitiated mortal . . ." Clearly, their status as the Lord's oracles, beginning with the Overcomers in Chicago and extending to the American Colony in Jerusalem, allowed the two women to assert dictatorial power over their followers, as though God-ordained, and they used it.

The latter half of the nineteenth century was a time of exceptional curiosity about the spirit world, séances, communication with spirits, etc. Famous personages, such as Sir Arthur Conan Doyle, creator of Sherlock Holmes, were identified with attempts to cross the boundaries of the physical and spiritual worlds, giving cache to such attempts. It was a time of prosperity for the formal Spiritualist Church, and the concept of mediumship seemed to gain a measure of acceptance. Psychic research societies were formed, and attempts to relate the spiritual and physical worlds often took on a somewhat simplistic veneer of science. Whatever the explanation, the interpretations of Mrs. Lee and Mrs. Spafford were extremely useful in allowing the two women to justify and maintain strong control over what transpired among the Overcomers, right down to choosing the most significant day of the Spaffords' future.

That special day came to them in Chicago in August 1881, when suddenly, the stage was set for a crucial decision. A revelation came to the group "through Mrs. Spafford that the second coming of Christ was only a month or two off, that he [Christ] would descend on Mount Zion near Jerusalem, that a large part of the 'Overcomers' should go to Jerusalem at once to meet him, and that Dr. Samuel P. Hedges should bear their expenses." Anna Spafford later attributed the departure decision to her sister-in-law, Margaret Lee, but the evidence favors Anna as source of the Jerusalem directive. Without attempt at similar authority based on biblical quotations and interpretations, Anna seems gradually to have asserted claim to similar divine interpretations and influence on that basis.

Anna had charisma, to be sure. Dr. Hedges wrote in the spring of 1881, just several months before their leaving, when Anna Spafford was sporadically absent from the group's meetings, nursing ill baby Grace. It was during a time when Horatio was away from Chicago visiting in Philadelphia, and doubt, dissension and threats of pulling away were beguiling the Overcomers. Tending the flock as best he could in the absence of the Spaffords, Dr. Hedges emphasized how much all was coming to depend upon Anna:

> From every side, as by concerted agreement, everybody came to Mrs. Spafford with their trials, doubts, fears, etc., etc. The dear precious soul of mighty faith stood like a rock, the Lord being ever with her, and so the tested ones stood, the doubtful ones took higher ground in faith and the fearful ones were strengthened.

Perhaps it was a combination of compassion and charisma, coupled with the ability to prophesy and to supposedly give divine answers to human questions that permitted Anna Spafford to hold almost absolute control over the group's members.

In obedience to the ladies' perception of divine directives, seventeen passages were arranged, and sixteen "Overcomers" set out from Chicago, August 17, 1881. The group included Horatio, Anna, Bertha, and Grace Spafford and Horatio's nephew, Rob Lawrence; Margaret Lee; William H. Rudy and his foster mother, Mrs. Caroline Merriman; Mr. and Mrs. John Whiting and their baby, Ruth; Mr. and Mrs. John B. Adamson, Mrs. Amelia Gould, and Annie Aiken. For undisclosed reasons, they deliberately chose to go by way of Quebec (strange, since it is not the normal or most direct route). Traveling by way of Quebec added a segment to the journey, but as critics later pointed out, if one wanted to get out of the United States as quickly as possible, Canada was the nearest exit. They sailed for Liverpool and went by train to London where they stayed several days, perhaps waiting for money to be sent from the U.S. From London they went by rail to Brindisi, Italy. From whence they sailed for Jaffa, and then passed over land to Jerusalem.

The Overcomers later agreed that before their departure, in the spring and summer of 1881, they had heard about a need for the Spaffords to travel abroad, though an exact destination had not been specified. So, motivated solely by Mrs. Spafford's divine mandate, a travel party, a destination, and date of departure were suddenly made specific. The travel party had no return tickets or reservations, and while their friends left behind expected them back about December 1, their return was open-ended.

Apparently, at some appointed time never specified in their writings or corporate memory, but soon after their arrival, the group had ascended Mount Zion, dressed in white in anticipation that Jesus Christ would appear, though nothing happened save for a dispute between Anna and Margaret. Members would have had to be embarrassed and somewhat defensive, having openly promised friends and even the Chicago media before their departure, "the Lord would come at his second coming, and put his foot on Mount Zion visibly," "there would be wonderful things take place—an acknowledgment of them [the Overcomers] by Divine revelation," a powerful vindication of their hopes and predictions. They had even avowed to the Overcomers left behind in the States that the second coming would be a happening of such magnitude that they would not need to write or cable because "the whole world would know it by electricity."

Absent a plan of what to do, once in Jerusalem, perhaps deflated by the failed prediction of the Second Coming of Christ, it is quite amazing that the group managed to stay together, eking out an existence, and surviving in that tumultuous land.

Back in Chicago, the remaining party of Overcomers had waited patiently but heard no announcement from the public media of any exceptional happening, despite the prediction that a worldwide event (the Second Coming) would be known without messages passing between them. Disappointed and discouraged by the failure of prophecies made by those whom they thought to be the Lord's spokespersons, the Chicago remnant very soon disbanded.

Mrs. George Rounds, Dr. and Mrs. Hedges, and Mr. Charles Gaylord were members of the group of Overcomers who stayed in Chicago. Others included Mr. and Mrs. V. Mumford Moore; Mr. Moore was a hardware manufacturer, who had lived in Milwaukee and in the 1890s was moving his business to Cleveland, Ohio. Dr. W. A. Bonniwell was a forty-five-year-old dentist, who by 1896 lived in Kansas City, Missouri, along with Jennie F. (Edwards) Bonniwell, fifty-five, also of Kansas City. Mrs. Matilda Parker (E. P.) McElnen (sometimes referred to as McElnay), was a fifty-five-year-old housekeeper, residing in the 1890s in Oakland,

California. Mrs. Rachel Frederickson, fifty-nine years of age in 1895, lived in Chicago and was the half sister of Anna Spafford. C. H. Adams was a Lake View real estate agent. Martin Aslaksen, a tinner by trade, for a time during 1881 lived with his family on the grounds of the Spafford home at Lake View, somewhat as a caretaker and participant in worship and Bible study.

In Jerusalem, the seventeen seemed unfazed by the nonreappearance of the Lord. They interacted with the local community, performed acts of charity and kindness, and established themselves among locals, coming to be known as "The American Colony," from their arrival until about 1930. Apparently, some of the people had brought substantial sums of money that provided sustenance for their first weeks. Gradually, they relied heavily upon borrowing and sought to obtain money from relatives. Barely getting by in those early years, the group settled into a disciplined routine, with Margaret and Anna making most decisions.

Even in their earliest days in Chicago, Horatio had seemed content to allow the two prominent ladies in his life to take charge. During the early months in Jerusalem, he appears to have acted somewhat as a senior advisor, his influence and authority diminishing as he gave himself to his studies, curiosities, and rambles. In a grandfatherly way, he appears to have been respected and generally left alone. He wandered about Jerusalem and its environs, investigating local flowers and shrubs, and teaching English in a boy's school. He had plenty of time for studying his well-marked polyglot Bible, a Christmas gift from his wife in 1872. With his study and reflection, he worked with his poems. He also kept up an avid correspondence, as we may see from a journal he kept haphazardly through 1882.

In the American Colony in Jerusalem Collection at the Library of Congress is a set of uniform, galley-like papers. They contain individual pages of Horatio's poems, some pasted from his little booklet, *Waiting for the Morning,* and others clipped from periodicals in which they had been randomly published. Many have editing marks and refinements as though he were preparing a new and complete edition of his poetry, though as far as we know, none was ever published.

"Simple people," Anna sometimes called her followers. God-fearing and biblically centered, they could be cowed into submission by authoritative-sounding claims of divine direction and a desire not to conflict with the divine will. The discipline of the group's strange spiritual methods and theological beliefs tended to resolve into a core of common beliefs. Obviously, living in a foreign land where they did not speak the language or know the customs made individuals cautious and dependent upon others. Having forfeited their personal possessions, so that all was held in a common treasury, no member of the group was able to make independent plans or choices involving money. Predominantly Anna fashioned the rules for this new community, but she often acted with Margaret. They meted out harsh physical punishment for doubters and questioners and noncompliance. They claimed all actions were consistent with Divine direction, and in the early days, contended that Christ would soon appear, making such matters of no importance.

Just how significant and sincere was the group's expectation of the imminent return of the Lord is difficult to judge. Once it was clear that the second coming of Christ was not going to occur at the time and place predicted, the group's members appeared always ready to deny that their original purpose in traveling was to witness the second coming. Instead, they made vague claims of how they went to Jerusalem to show the world how to live together in harmony, or to avoid the hurry and crush of the secular world, etc. Reference to the imminent return of

Christ was avoided after the failure of their early prophecy.

The Spaffords' daughter Bertha admits that the move was supposed to be temporary, according to letters written about that time, and she expresses the belief that, if her father had lived, he would have returned to Chicago. Making no reference to the Second Coming, she stated somewhat disingenuously,

> He was seeking peace and solace for mind and soul. He was leaving the center of a controversy he was tired of, and hoped to be able to see things plainly and more in perspective. In a letter to a friend he explained: "Jerusalem is where my Lord lived, suffered, and conquered, and I wish to learn how to live, suffer, and especially to conquer."

In 1888, Horatio was sixty-years-old, having lived the communal life almost seven years in Jerusalem. He had no noticeable health ailments, although some believe, he was showing signs of dementia. Early on, at Anna's suggestion, they had agreed to give up their conjugal bed as an act of purity and devotion, a practice that she made a Colony requirement. Anna gradually developed an attitude of negligence toward Horatio, perhaps due to his declining clarity of mind, but also because he was so clearly nonessential. By some estimates, she was cruel to him. When he became ill, he received no treatment and began a fairly rapid decline. While Anna and the Colony would later build a reputation for nursing and caring for others, regardless of their religion or ethnic background, Horatio appears to have been left with much less attention.

During his last days of waning health, by his request he was transferred to the home of a Mrs. Alice Davis, in the hope that her house in one of the elevated sections of Jerusalem with an attractive garden, would prove salubrious. One day in 1888, in the mental haze of his illness, according to a letter of Mrs. Davis, quoted by Jane Fletcher Geniesse in *American Priestess,* Horatio mused in barely audible words:

> What does it mean? What is it all coming to? Is it a
> phase of Spiritism or what? What will come of it all?
> I cannot believe that this is the work of Spiritism. . . .
> What does it mean?

Equally strange is the account of Horatio's dying, as rendered by Bertha. On September 25, 1888, she was ten-years-old, and her Mother was forty-six. Upon her father's return on a sickbed from Mrs. Davis' house, they noticed the exceptional heaviness of his breathing. Bertha wrote that while she was at her father's bedside, her mother went outside and danced vigorously. Finally, wet with perspiration, she returned to his bedside to hear him say, "Annie, I have experienced a great joy; I have seen wonderful things." He mumbled on, his waning strength unable to support his desire to tell what he had seen. Anna told Bertha, "Stay with Father to the end. I must go away," and departed the room. Not long after, Bertha went to tell her mother that her father had stopped breathing. Anna's response was: "He knows it all now. He has seen Him face to face. We must not sorrow like those who have not hope."

Anna went into seclusion and did not attend the funeral. An eclectic, informally ecumenical memorial service was held. There is no record that anyone chose to sing or to recite "It Is Well with My Soul." Horatio Spafford was buried in the nearby cemetery, without a marker of any kind. Sometime later a grave marker was placed to recognize seven members of the American Colony: *In Loving Memory of John C. Whiting, Horatio G. Spafford, William C. Sylvester, Herbert Drake, Margaret W. Lee, Geo A. Fuller, and John Miller.*

14
A NEW LIFE IN THE HOLY CITY

Horatio's kindly presence and gentle spirit were surely missed by many Colony members, but we have almost no surviving testimony to that effect. The group was passing through difficult years, with scant means of financial support, and with unrelenting needs. The quest for sustaining revenue for food and the necessities of life was its greatest challenge.

Over the years, two separate infusions of new life were injected into the *American* Colony, even though its greater population was to come from Sweden, and it more accurately could have been called "The Swedish-American Colony." It is likely that the group could not have survived without the Swedes. One coterie of Swedish immigrants came from Chicago in 1895, subjected to the powerful persuasion of Anna, who recognized them as a possible source of revenue, and who appreciated their simple, uncomplaining work ethic, their easy penchant to be led. Anna and her daughters, with a few others, had returned to Chicago for the first time since leaving in 1881, to deal with a lawsuit involving the Whiting children's inheritance, so very important to the Colony. Anna also oversaw the pressing of a suit of her own. The Spaffords and the colonists identified with the Swedish immigrant group and stayed in a house rented from one Swede. When the Colony delegation was ready to return to

Jerusalem, the Swedish group asked to accompany them, and Anna, who likely planted the idea, seemed very ready to welcome them. Without hesitation, the Swedes abruptly left their adoptive home in America, bringing their workplace skills, their cash, their spiritual hunger, and their willingness to work. Once settled in Jerusalem, and writing to friends in Sweden of the unique situation they had found in the Holy City, the Swedes learned that their friends decided to sell their homes and farms and travel to Jerusalem to be a part of the American Colony. Blending in with the few longer-term adherents, the largely uneducated Swedes, with less emphasis upon independent Bible study and individual interpretations, without strong feelings of dissent or independence, seemed readily to subordinate themselves to Anna's authoritarian form of governance. Strangely, as is often the case, certain extreme views probably helped build a sort of boot-camp cohesiveness among colony members—extremes such as a ban on conjugal contact between husbands and wives, while encouraging periodic togetherness between the sexes, even other than one's married partner, as a means of "testing" one's faithfulness; forbidding marriage; banning individual ownership in favor of maintaining a common treasury; allowing Anna Spafford to resolve virtually all disputes and to decide where any money was spent.

Perhaps one of many evidences of what might be seen as Bertha Spafford Vester's embarrassment over her parents' views, is that her book (*Our Jerusalem*) is totally silent about her mother's prophesying, her harsh demands, her abusive physical punishments, and dictatorial rule. Somewhat apologetic and searching for words to describe her parents' departure from the traditional church and evangelical perspectives, Bertha wrote:

> I find it difficult to interpret to this modern generation Father's and Mother's attitude toward life at this

time and throughout the following years without making them seem impractical, fanatical, narrow, and visionary. They were none of these things.

But even from the perspectives of their evangelical friends, the Spaffords' strange views did seem fanatical, impractical, narrow, slowly alienating their friends, even more by theology than distance. Moody and Sankey, Whittle, Hannah Whitall Smith, Frances Willard, and W. E. Blackstone are just a few who appear to have been baffled or alienated by the Spaffords' beliefs and practices. While there appears to be no record of Moody's judgment about the Spaffords, for two or three years before, and after their removal to Jerusalem, the lack of contact between them is surprising, given their earlier close association. Horatio's diary indicated in 1882 that he sporadically sent letters to Sankey, as well as to Moody's close friend and associate, Emma Dryer, and other evangelical leaders, including A. T. Pierson, Major J. H. Cole, Blackstone and a few others. There is little evidence of response.

The Overcomers' abandonment of traditional evangelical views can be seen in one incident. Horatio had been absent from Chicago on an unexplained journey to Philadelphia. Dr. Hedges wrote him (May 25, 1881) of apparent disturbances among the Overcomers. He explained, "Mrs. Young and Miss Carter . . . were so shaken by Mr. Erdman's visit," adding, "are again all right, especially Mrs. Young." Reverend W. J. Erdman was pastor of the Moody Church, the Illinois Avenue Church, a nationally known and respected evangelical leader, and it appears that he had made a call on two ladies—perhaps formerly members of his church—with the effect of temporarily unsettling the confidence of the women in the Overcomers.

Theodore Monod, well-known French pastor and evangelical leader, had been among the first to reach out to Anna immediately

162

after the tragedy while she was in his native France. He first wrote to Anna, December 6, 1873, expressing his sorrow and disbelief at the accident. Later, on Christmas Eve and Christmas day, he wrote Horatio and Anna, united in Paris, thanking them for Christmas gifts received for the Monod children, and regretting that he could not "go and shake hands with you today." But there appears to be no subsequent, continuing correspondence.

An exchange of letters crossed between the Spaffords and Hannah Whitall Smith, practical Quaker writer, and author of the highly successful Christian classic, *The Christian's Secret of a Happy Life.* One newspaper report—*Daily Inter-Ocean,* August 17, 1881—claimed in obvious error that Hannah Whitall Smith of Philadelphia, is "among the noticeable followers" of the Spaffords. Horatio's diary, November 1, 1882, noted, "wrote Mr. Bell enclosing copy letter to Mrs. H. W. Smith. . . ." Surviving among the papers in the Hannah Whitall Smith Collection at Asbury Theological Seminary, Wilmore, Kentucky, is a subfile labeled, "Spaffordites," which Hannah maintained under the general file heading, "Fanaticism." The file contains about a dozen newspaper articles Hannah collected on the Spaffords and their American Colony. Some, apparently, were clipped and sent to her, by others, who knew of her interest.

One letter with a clipping in the Smith "Spaffordites" file was apparently supplied by Frances E. Willard, longtime president of the Women's Christian Temperance Union, and friend of the Spaffords and of Hannah Whitall Smith. The letter covers a variety of subjects; however, it began:

> Dearest Hannah: I know you were interested in the Spafford phenomena [sic] and so send you these painful developments. I do not believe Mrs. S. is bad. They now are making out that she was a Swedish [sic] servant girl.

The clipping enclosed was apparently from the *Chicago Daily News,* December 15, 1897, which stated that Anna Spafford was "said to have been once a Norwegian servant girl, . . ."

January 25, 1883, Hannah Whitall Smith had written the Spaffords, opposing aspects of their belief and work, Mrs. Lee's acting as intermediary or interpreter, the concept of Horatio as "The Branch," etc., and contending against the Spaffords' notion that the Lord's Supper (Holy Communion) was no longer necessary. In reply, Anna expressed the thought that someday Hannah and others would realize they had condemned a holy work. In responding, February 7, 1883, Anna regretted that Mrs. Smith could not understand and accept some of their teachings, and Anna concluded somewhat rudely that, until they saw eye-to-eye, it was best that Hannah not reply.

In another letter published in *A Religious Rebel: The Letters of H.W.S.,* Hannah summarized her view of the Spaffords.

> We have met lately some travelers who have given us news of the "Chicago party" at Jerusalem. You will remember that Mrs. Lee and her brother and his wife, Mr. and Mrs. Spafford, and a little band of followers started a fanatical mystical form of religion some years ago in Chicago, guided thereto, as they most fervently believed, by the Lord Himself, through a series of most remarkable signs. Mrs. Lee was the "Moses" of the New Dispensation, and Mrs. Spafford was "The Righteous Branch," and others of their members were equally exalted personages! Their fanaticism was simply unbounded, but strange to say they were all of them people of education and intelligence, and of undoubted and unusual piety; and moreover they were all middle-aged! . . . They had a great many remarkable "leadings," and finally were called, as they believed, to Jerusalem there to await the manifestation of the "Branch," (when) the Star of Bethlehem would come and rest on Mrs. Spafford's head. . . . Of course, nothing of the kind took place, but nothing daunted they have gone on.

The intelligent, practical Quaker wisdom of Hannah Whitall Smith, whose writings were so widely appreciated in the Victorian religious world, as they are today, could only classify the Spaffords as "religious fanatics." In a footnote in *A Religious Rebel* (fn. 1, p. 82), the editor (her son) summarized in his own words Hannah's description of the Spaffords and company, drawn from Chapter VI of the volume based on Hannah's papers.

> The original leader . . . was a Mrs. Lee, "a charming lady, whose husband had held some official position in Washington." After praying for some tangible sign, by which she might recognize the will of the Lord, Mrs. Lee was given, so she believed, such a sign, namely that "her lower jaw was cracked against her upper jaw with a loud crack," whenever she was properly carrying out the Lord's will. Later, "as the cracking was very loud, it became unpleasant to her husband, especially as it would often take place in the very middle of a meal, so she prayed that the Lord would please give her a quieter sign" and it was graciously transferred "to her eyes," which were drawn back into her head, as if by strings fastened behind and pulled by an invisible hand.
>
> With such and other evidence of infallible direction, she had no difficulty in leading a number of disciples to Jerusalem, where they were disappointed of every promised and expected sign, a fact, it seems, by which they were not in the least disconcerted. Later Mrs. Lee was deposed, and another leader appointed in her place.

William E. Blackstone, well-known Christian Zionist, likely to be very positive toward Horatio Spafford, found the "Overcomers" a group curious. In a letter from Dr. Hedges to Horatio, November 3, 1881, only a couple of months after their arrival in Jerusalem, the doctor wrote from Chicago:

> Mr. Blackstone has been in to my office to inquire about you & your party & of the news. He comes in nearly every week to inquire and seems to have great interest. He evidently has heard that we were expecting great & world startling announcements from the Holy

City. He asks all sorts of questions as to why you took
such a step, etc., etc.

We cannot know whether the spiritual havoc of the Spaffords'
postaccident lives left them open to the bizarre, or whether the
spiritual trauma of such an event as the loss of their four children
propelled them to search more aggressively and to even examine
the fringes of theological thought for life's ultimate answers.
How a bankrupt couple was able to transition a small Chicago
Bible study network into a citadel of strangers in a foreign land,
gradually becoming self-sustaining entrepreneurs who became
prominent in civic, social, and political affairs, to be known for
social service and, ultimately, owners of a major hotel—that is a
remarkable feat that has been chronicled in *The American Colony*
by Helga Dudman and Ruth Kark (1998), and recently in Jane
Fletcher Geniesse's *American Priestess: The Extraordinary Story
of Anna Spafford and the American Colony in Jerusalem* (2008).

15
THE JOURNEY ENDS IN JERUSALEM

The story of the Spaffords' struggle and its consequences is not complete without raising the question: Whatever became of the American Colony in Jerusalem? Articles over the years have described the inhabitants, their beliefs and practices, and their life together. The most complete answer is addressed in relatively recent writings of Dudman and Kark, and of Jane Fletcher Geniesse. The Colony had been formed almost by accident—the Spaffords apparently seeing no way out of their financial plight than just leaving to start over in another country. Thus, not knowing what to do after they got to Jerusalem, they seemed to have operated on a day-to-day serendipity, rather than any long-range plan or intent.

Less attention has been paid the remainder of the Overcomers, those left behind in Chicago when the sixteen departed for Jerusalem in 1881. Though they tried to carry on as usual, doubt and dissidence set in only a couple of months after their departure, and according to a November 3, 1881 letter from Dr. Hedges to Horatio, Dr. Hedges worried, "No one here at this blessed house has the sign & you don't know how strange it seems." ("The sign" being the phrase they used to designate the ability and authority to deliver divine messages.) Still, he confided, "everything seems dark & many are shaken out of the sign & some out of the truths." And on the Jerusalem side, clearly, prophetic expectations were not being realized, as Dr. Hedges complained, "So many say that what the sign says does not come to pass, etc., etc."

When writing just three weeks later, November 23, 1881, Dr. Hedges informed Horatio that "Mrs. Rounds & Susie Pierce have led the whole assembly at Val'o [Valparaiso, Indiana] to denounce the whole thing as satanic, excepting Mrs. Doyle, and Mr. Clancy is barely holding on to some of the teachings (brackets added)." Just three months earlier, Mrs. Rounds's strong endorsement had been publicly quoted in the *Inter-Ocean* newspaper. The Chicago remainder group had been absent the personal charisma of Horatio, Anna, and Margaret Lee only a short time; but, without the startling news of the dramatic Second Coming of Christ that was predicted to have gripped the world, twelve or thirteen weeks were sufficient to break their confidence of faith.

Dr. Hedges testified in court in 1895 that the remnant of Overcomers never did formally disband. It simply disintegrated within four or five months of the group's departure, largely because "the teachings had been a failure"—i.e., predictions and foretellings of Anna Spafford were not fulfilled. Asked if such feelings were universal, Dr. Hedges replied, "Quite universal, I think."

In response to further questioning as to why the group fell apart, he explained, "It was an absolute failure of Mrs. Spafford's prophecy of what would happen when they got to Jerusalem. She prophesied when they got there, there would be wonderful things take place, —an acknowledgment of them by Divine revelation, and that we would not need to write or cable, because the whole world would know it by electricity. Nothing happened when they got there. They expected the Lord would come at his second coming, and put his feet on Mount Zion visibly, but it didn't take place."

The attorney then asked, "And that is what shattered your faith?"

Without expressing an opinion as to whether the Spaffords may have convinced themselves to trust their predictions, or whether their predictions were merely serving their own ends, Dr. Hedges replied, "Yes, that had been a positive revelation by Mrs. Spafford."

Holding everything in common, and using up their immediate resources, the group borrowed and begged funds in various ways and managed to survive while developing a reputation as a group of caring and capable foreigners. They were open to the region's Jews and Arabs, alike and seemed to take delight in (a) providing assistance to people in need as a justification for their presence; (b) serving as a way station or refreshment contact for Americans and other "foreigners" who came to town; (c) allowing the leadership (i.e., the Spafford family) to enter into the social life of the city's upper echelons.

Horatio Spafford's death in 1888 had little effect. His passing was more the sadness of losing an amicable, grandfatherly presence not essential to the operation.

After fourteen years of struggling and scraping to barely hold the group together—a remarkable feat on Anna Spafford's part—the Colonists received a couple of significant financial boosts. The Chicago trial of 1895 centered on the guardianship of the Whiting children, and the case ultimately brought their inheritance to the Colony treasury. The court dismissed the 1895 case, because it found nothing peculiar in their mother's theology at the American Colony, and therefore, the children could remain with their mother. Later in the early 1900s when John Whiting was nearly an adult, an appeal was made for at least part of his inheritance. A settlement was reached, and he and his sister began receiving a hundred dollars per month, and a lump sum payment of five thousand dollars with which to acquire a business. The funds were a huge help to the Colony's operations.

Even more significant was the decision of the Swedish groups (described earlier) to join the Spafford colony in 1895. The addition of the Swedes was the single most helpful happening to assure the continuity of the Colony. About thirty adults plus seven children, including younger adults and older folks, were in the 1895 group, many of whom had mingled with the Spaffordites during the year or two they were in Chicago. No sooner had the Chicago Swedes arrived and adjusted in Jerusalem than friends and relatives from Sweden who had been in contact, expressed their desire to come to the Holy Land. So, in 1896, thirty-eight additional, devout Swedes sold their farms in and around Nas, Sweden, and arrived in Jerusalem, pooling their resources and casting their lot with the Colony. Along with their commitment to hardwork, the Swedes, fundamentalist Christians called by Bertha Vester "simple folks," were also, quietly and uncomplainingly, willing to be led. The farmers among them went to work growing usable crops; others baked bread; some got hold of looms and knitting machines to make cloth. Even Bertha Spafford Vester acknowledged, both the Colony's former dire straits as well as the contribution of the Swedes, concluding, "Other industries were started, and little by little, with diligence, the Colony emerged from poverty."

Looking back, the Swedes appear to have been extremely docile, to have worked hard with no promise of recompense, as though sold on the spiritual and religious justification of the community, without regard for personal wages or prosperity. They seem never to have looked back with doubts or concerns about their considerable capital contributed to the Colony's treasury. From our modern vantage point, it is almost hard to believe that people could be so dedicated as to accept such a modest existence, while supplying the funds and support for Bertha Spafford Vester, her husband, and children. In effect, the Vesters had household servants, they traveled first-class between the U.S. and Jerusalem, and their children were enrolled in expensive private schools in the U.S. At the same time, as Dudman and Kark (1998) point out, the average member of the colony had to beg from Frederick Vester, Bertha's husband, even for the money for a pair of shoes.

Yet, thanks to the Swedes, by 1906, Bertha Vester could observe, "The American Colony was a prosperous and respected force in Jerusalem." Only a decade or so earlier, debts had become so great, and fund-raising had become so aggressive, that negative rumors reached the Chicago newspapers. An October, 1894 *Chicago Daily* headline read, "Is on Its Last Legs. Spafford's Jerusalem Colony Apparently Going to Pieces." The article referenced former Chicagoan, Mrs. Amelia Gould, who appeared to have been desperately writing letters to her Chicago relatives, making offers to sell personal items, and seeking funds to resolve Jerusalem debts.

With Anna Spafford's remarkable courage, strong-will, and diplomacy, the American Colony made it through World War I, endearing itself to the Turks who controlled Jerusalem, as well as the Jerusalem citizenry. In the absence of medical personnel, Bertha and the Colony agreed to nurse the wounded, both British and Turks, who had been unattended, gradually taking over three or four hospitals. The Turks, impressed with the quality of service, even turned over the feeding operations of their soup kitchen to the Colony. The shifting sands of regional and provincial governments and the horrors of war failed to diminish the group, and actually added to its standing, locally and internationally.

The prophetess, Anna, then in her early seventies, had once told colonists, "I am not going to die. The resurrection is near, when we will have the dead back with us." But in July of 1923, only a couple of months after Anna Spafford's death, which came peacefully, April 17, 1923, dissension arose among the colonists. Informally, Anna's leadership mantle had been passed to Bertha, whose less spiritual, more businesslike approach was both a stark contrast and an irritant. Members of the Colony seemed less willing to honor the managerial directives of Bertha, who made no claims to spiritual motivation. Bertha unilaterally installed an "Expulsion Policy," suggesting that for certain reasons, persons could be excluded from the group with only a travel ticket and a minimum of pocket cash. Eleven members left for good. Frederick Vester had sent a letter to the registrar of companies in Jerusalem requesting that the Colony's business firm be registered as a partnership *exclusively* between Frederick Vester and John Whiting, claiming the partnership had begun in 1903. When announcement of the registration was first reported to the general assembly of the American Colony in 1923, it evoked shock and dismay. That all the "equals" in the Colony were not offered equal shares set in motion a gradual demoralization, a slow destruction of the bonds of commonality, a gradual disintegration that lasted about seven years. The Colony's "haves" and the "have-nots" became embroiled in the complexities of unraveling an organization to which so many had uncomplainingly given their acquiescence, their cash, their skill and labor, and the productive years of their lives.

When, in the 1920s, full incorporation documents were first presented to Colony members, *fait accompli*, with ribbons and seals, in expectation of the approbation and signatures of the members, explicit legal provisions excluded all the hard workers who had devoted their sweat equity to the Colony. The documents provided for a headquarters in New York City, for the forfeiture of all property rights by anyone who was expelled from the Colony, and designated the five corporate directors to be the Vesters, Nils Lind (married at the time to Anna Grace Vester, but later divorced), and an unknown American.

The uproar among colonists made agreement appear impossible; so Bertha enlisted an arbiter, a lawyer from Cairo, to arrive at some reasonable solution. In the end, each member was given $5,326.10, though the arbiter later said "never had a trial left him with such a bad taste." It later became known that Bertha and Frederick Vester had paid the arbiter one hundred thousand dollars.

The group had seemed to change character somewhat after Horatio's death in 1888 and after Margaret Lee's death, becoming less biblically and spiritually oriented. It changed even more extensively with Anna's death in 1923, when its members were simply inclined to make the most of what they had and were less theologically vested.

Despite all the internal difficulties, in 1925, the Spafford Baby Home had been formed out of the need for training in childcare and nutrition. The social prominence of the Spafford descendants continued to rise, and the Colony continued to provide many charitable services—some, short-lived in response to specific exigencies, and some more enduring—as the Colony had through World War I. Similarly, the Colony was vitally involved on both sides of the Middle East dilemma in World War II. And after the war, having operated almost as a hostel for a number of years, and with that hospitality instinct nourished among Arab cultures strongly felt in the Colony, the idea arose of operating the property as a hotel. Bertha's daughter, Anna Grace, returned from the United States to lead in the remodeling and transforming of the property into a first-rate hotel, beginning in 1952. Her job was handed over to her brother, Horatio Vester, a London solicitor, who came back to Jerusalem in 1962. Bertha died June 27, 1968, just after her ninetieth birthday. Bertha's son, Horatio Vester, retired in 1980, handing over hotel management to Gauer Hotels of Switzerland, which still operates The American Colony Hotel, one of the most attractive residences for travelers in Jerusalem. Horatio Vester died in 1985, survived by his elegant wife, Valentine Vester, who daily conversed with Hotel visitors until her death in the spring of 2008. It was Valentine Vester who took the lead in placing the files and memorabilia of the Spafford Family and the Hotel in the U.S. Library of Congress.

The Spafford Children's Center still operates from a base in the old city, dependent upon voluntary contributions. The Center focuses on physical and mental health for the disadvantaged children of Jerusalem and the West Bank.

16
CHRISTIAN FAITH:
SENTIMENTALITY AND REALITY

In light of conflicting evidence, when the more detailed Spafford story is reviewed, a modern observer is left to ponder several major issues: (1) Did Horatio Spafford actually buy and sell real estate, or did his real estate *intentions* go largely unfulfilled? (2) Did the Spaffords leave Chicago for Jerusalem out of financial exigency, fear of public humiliation, or to escape prosecution? (3) Was the Spaffords' interest in the Second Coming of Christ genuine, and their sense of Christ's imminent reappearance authentic? (4) Had the Spaffords planned to return to Chicago or to remain in Jerusalem in order to avoid facing their failures?

Did Horatio Spafford actually buy and
sell real estate, or did his real estate intentions
go largely unfulfilled?

Horatio Spafford originally wanted to disengage from the practice of law with its constraints and time demands—what modern lawyers refer to as the tyranny of "billable hours"—in order to be freer to give his time to religious and volunteer pursuits. An illustration of a lawyer finding success in real estate was ever before him in the person of his neighbor Daniel Goodwin. Goodwin had developed a hugely successful subdivision.

Chicago was rife with real estate speculators at the time, and great fortunes were made in quick turnarounds of property. The area around Lake View may have been especially enticing in the days after the Great Chicago Fire of 1871, when Chicago's new ordinance required a higher (and thus, more expensive) level of residential construction, but the ordinance pertained only to the city proper, whose northern boundary was Fullerton Avenue. Thus, Lake View, beyond the boundary of Chicago with its stricter construction code, already very attractive because of its distance from the city, its lush, park-like environs, was made even more appealing as a residential area after the Fire. Yet, following the accident of 1873, while Horatio Spafford continued to maintain an office, he did not seriously engage in the practice of law, nor was he active in buying and selling, or developing real estate.

One principal real estate investment of Horatio and Anna Spafford was their personal residence, which they occupied from the time of their marriage, September 5, 1861, until they chose to depart for Jerusalem in August 1881. Anna told the court in 1895 that they had moved into that residence when they were first married, renting it for the first year or so. They then bought it, July 1, 1863, for the grand sum of three thousand dollars. It was a handsome, cottage-style residence, located on a triangular lot containing five acres, in one of the most attractive spots in Lake View. The lot is bounded by Evanston road on the West; Halstead street East; and Graceland Avenue on the South. Just across Halstead Street is the site of the U.S. Marine Hospital. In 1873, Chamberlin thought the Spafford property, including the five-acre lot on which the house was located and the additional five-acre lot, was worth $75,000. The opinion of William J. Haerther, a property expert, was quoted in court testimony to the effect that the Spafford home and grounds (only the northern half of Lot 9 remained) were worth fifty thousand dollars in the

1890s. A Chicago lawyer, C. B. Elliott, wrote December 18, 1896, that Dr. Hedges' property (the former Spafford residence) "was worth $80,000 to $100,000. . ." Specifically, the property was described as follows:

> The North half of Lot Nine (9) in Hundley's Subdivision of the East half of the South East quarter of Section Seventeen (17), Township Forty (40), Range Fourteen (14) East of the Third Principal Meridian, Cook County, Illinois. The South half of the property was approximately an additional five acres.

We know that Horatio came to have mortgages on both halves of the property, North and South, the residence having been built upon the North half. By their departure date in 1881, he had progressively accumulated a total of seventeen thousand five hundred dollars in mortgages on the house and lot on the North half, and he had received ten thousand dollars in exchange for a mortgage on the South half. The only other property Spafford was known to own were the lots in Wrightwood, often referenced as "a large amount of real estate," but never precisely identified, which secured an indebtedness of thirty thousand dollars to Connecticut Mutual Life Insurance Company. In one sense, then, following the wreck of the *Ville du Havre* and the loss of their children in 1873, the claim that he was "dealing in real estate"— was largely a respectable cover for his being unemployed, as he shuffled revenue from mortgage loans to provide sufficient cash flow to support the family and to make periodic payments to Mrs. Murphy, Mrs. Wills, and Miss Kopse. All the while, the three ladies' funds had apparently been consumed in supporting the real estate, as well as the Spaffords' household and day-to-day living. There is no evidence to support a claim that he "dealt" in real estate, except for his position as an investor, holding the residential lots he had held for some years.

However, claims have been made and impressions left by the family upon history, to the effect that Horatio suffered serious financial losses in real estate as a direct result of the Great Chicago Fire of 1871. Obfuscating that claim, the date of purchase of that property, the acreage or amount of such property and its location, the identity of partners, if any, the limitations or obstacles to profitable sale—all such details have seemed intentionally to remain undisclosed by the family.

Largely the "spin" provided by Bertha and Anna, the general public's perception of the Spaffords' misfortune was, as stated as recently as 1967: "It began with the Great Chicago Fire of 1871, seven years before Bertha was born. In the Fire Horatio Spafford, her father, a prominent lawyer and father of four daughters, lost his law offices, a valuable library, and most of the money he had invested in real estate just before the disaster."

Even in an interview with Dr. Barbara Bair, historian at the Library of Congress, as late as January 12, 2005, Valentine Vester, granddaughter-in-law of Horatio and Anna Spafford, married to Bertha's son, Horatio Vester, was asked about the impact of the Fire on the Spaffords. She answered, "Well, a very big impact. He was into real estate amongst other things. And he was just about to embark on some big project when everything was burnt to the ground. And, of course, there was terrible distress. And after the Fire was over, she . . . they were very philanthropic and good, wholly religious people. . . ."

Of course, raw land would not be rendered worthless by fire; yet, no explicit connection between the Fire and the consistently, vaguely described "loss" of real estate has ever been established. The only known loss of the Spaffords' personal property involved in the Great Chicago Fire of 1871 appears to have been Horatio's law office, which occupied rented space. His residence was undamaged. The area of his residence and real estate investment, Wrightwood or Wright's Grove, were both outside the "burnt district." Property values and the appeal of the area north of Fullerton Avenue—with the possible exception of the first few weeks following the Fire—appear actually to have been enhanced by the Fire, rather than negatively impacted.

Chamberlin, in his book published in 1874, noted the "mountains of litigation" that surrounded the possible expansion of Lincoln Park—the struggle over de-annexation of part of Lake View so that it could be annexed into the city of Chicago. It seems likely that litigation related to Lincoln Park issues was the actual reason that Horatio Spafford felt he needed to remain in Chicago and send his family onward to Europe in November 1873. Tradition has been that a last minute telegram informing Horatio of the sudden death of a prospective buyer of his property was the cause of his deferring the European journey. We have no record of such story from either Horatio or Anna, or a contemporary source.

In court testimony, in 1895, seven years after Horatio's death, even though her name and signature were on deeds, Anna was forgetful, disingenuous, or intentionally protective of Horatio's legacy by providing only extremely vague testimony about real estate investments. The mortgage document, copy of which survives to this day, required that she be cosigner, and the required bond even had a rider, signed by Anna, confirming that the Notary had, independent of her husband, explained to her the entire matter before asking her to attest with her signature. Yet, her answers were of little value, as she told the court in very pliable language:

> Mr. Culver and Mr. Stark I *think* and Mr. Spafford bought *a large block* [sic] of real estate around Wright's Grove, in Lincoln Park. I don't know exactly, I just have *a general impression* and it was just before the Chicago Fire and they met the Friday before the Chicago Fire to

> lay it out, expecting to sell directly and pay that debt. On Sunday or Monday the Chicago *fire came and swept it away* and this was *left on their hands* and what with the taxes and interest and different things he had a very heavy load to carry and things got worse instead of better . . . (italics added)

Anna's cloudy recollection provided almost no substantive information. She did not say *who* were the partners (she was wrong about Culver and Stark) and what happened to them, whether they dropped out or continued to participate. She did not state exactly *where* the property was located, even a street address. She did not describe *how* land could "be swept" away by a fire. She did not make clear exactly *what* was "left on their hands," its value, required maintenance, etc. While the attorneys did not pursue greater specificity, Anna continued her testimony with undefined, disingenuous answers.

> Q. By reason of that speculation, Mrs. Spafford, your husband was very deeply involved financially?
> A. I should imagine he was.
>
> Q. Far beyond his available means?
> A. I could not say anything about his business affairs because I don't know, but I know that he was in great trouble.
>
> Q. And that continued up to the very time that he left Chicago?
> A. He had as far as I know—he has [*sic*] given up the land except the homestead, but I don't know, I think so.

Clearly, Anna did not know, declined to say, or was coached not to share impressions and feelings about family business. In responding to an attorney's specific questions in court, Anna's answers were never direct.

Q. He owned considerable amount of land in Chicago at that time?

A. At one time, yes.

Q. Can you recollect any pieces of property that he owned, besides the homestead on which you lived at the time?

A. I don't know how much he owned when he went away.

Q. Can you recollect where your husband had any pieces of property (real estate) at the time he made that confession to you?

A. No, I could not say.

Q. Cannot describe any one piece?

A. No, I don't know how much he had when he made that confession.

Q. Do you know he had considerable?

A. At one time.

Q. When you say at one time, what time do you refer to?

A. About the time of the fire—just before the fire I know he had bought a great deal of real estate.

Q. Where was that, Mrs. Spafford?

A. I think it was about the Parks, somewhere about Lincoln Park.

Q. Didn't he in anticipation of the extension of the Park buy a very considerable quantity of land in the vicinity of Diversey Ave. and Clark St. south of Diversey Ave.?

A. I know that he bought with others a large tract of land.

Q. You don't remember the location of it?

A. No.

181

Q. What I am trying to get at, Mrs. Spafford, is
whether it created in your mind any impression or
idea as to the character and extent of his property
and where situated?

A. No, I knew that at one time he had a lot on the Lake
Shore north of the homestead on the Lake Shore
and I knew that in the vicinity of the Park he had
land and the homestead. I don't know anything
more than that, and when he made that confession
I was under the impression that everything was
so mortgaged that it was all gone, that there was
nothing at all left.

It seems almost inconceivable that with the tract of land so
near their family residence, so important to the family's fortunes,
reputation, and goodwill, that Anna could possibly be so unaware.
With the leadership that Anna subsequently demonstrated in
seeing the group to Jerusalem and to survive there under difficult
circumstances, it is almost unbelievable that at some point she
would not have been driven past the property. According to the
deed, as one of the owners, she executed a formal signature on
a number of documents, and it seems that in conversation about
signing, about their subsequent financial crises, about prospects
for the future, she could not have escaped awareness of the
location of the land, its prospects, and possibilities. Her hazy
assertion that the Fire "swept away" subdivided building lots,
and that real estate lots were "left on their hands" seems almost
too nebulous to have any ring of truth.

Whittle had frequent conversations with Spafford, urging
him to pay Mrs. Wills her interest, and responding to Spafford's
request that he pray with him. Whittle was expected to be alert
to financial matters as a former businessman and treasurer of
a watch company; yet, Whittle told the court "the property he
was carrying that he called the Wright's Grove property, I

cannot definitely state whether it was twenty or thirty acres, it was a large block [sic] of land north of Lincoln Park, that had swallowed up everything that had been in his hands of his own and of his friends." (It appears that even Whittle had a more accurate understanding than Anna had.) Then, in a bizarre twist, Whittle stated, "He [Horatio] hoped by silver legislation, back in the time of gold resumption, that if he could carry it that he would get out of it."

In reality, it appears that Horatio—probably not with malice of forethought—backed into a form of Ponzi scheme. He used money intended by the will of Mr. Lawrence to be held in trust for the benefit of Mrs. Murphy, and he used the funds of Mrs. Wills and Miss Kopse, as well as the proceeds of his mortgages, for living expenses and to make periodic payments to Mrs. Murphy, Mrs. Wills, and Miss Kopse. Without additional income or borrowing, when funds ran out, Horatio could no longer make such payments.

Did the Spaffords leave Chicago for Jerusalem out of financial exigency, fear of public humiliation, or to escape prosecution?

The Spaffords' extreme financial condition provokes another musing that probably can never be resolved: Did the Spaffords hastily leave Chicago for Jerusalem out of financial exigency, fear of public humiliation, and to escape prosecution, or were they drawn to Jerusalem, sincerely expecting the return of the Lord? Testimony from almost everyone except Anna and Mr. William Rudy supports the claim that, while the possibility of leaving the country had been discussed with the Overcomers, the signal to depart was given in response to some directive, prophecy, or interpretation from either Horatio's sister, Margaret (Mrs. Lee), or from his wife, Anna. There are indications of competition between

Mrs. Lee and Mrs. Spafford in their prophetic deliverances, and it may be that both brought the same directive about leaving the country—particularly, after Horatio had shared with them word of the oncoming crisis. Dr. Hedges and Mrs. Rounds testified that the directive to go came from Anna Spafford. By the time of the trial (1895), both Horatio Spafford and Margaret Lee were deceased, so they could not confirm testimony.

Certainly, claims of divine perception or messages, as well as less divine messages, can be influenced in behalf of someone you love. In any event numerous factors support the claim that they departed suddenly. (1) When asked in court in 1895, why the Spafford party had left as suddenly as they did, Mrs. Rounds testified, "Mr. Spafford was afraid of being arrested." She went on to explain that even Anna and Horatio Spafford did not know they were going for certain until the very morning of their departure. Dr. Hedges made similar statements, accusing Horatio of having "sneaked off to Canada." In the 1890s, Anna Spafford and William Rudy claimed the trip had been planned and passage booked two months prior to the date of departure, though that assertion is not supported by eyewitness accounts of Rudy's conversation with Horatio and others the night before their departure. (2) The choice of the route via Canada—the most immediate way to get out of the United States, but a far more complicated and less direct way to get to Europe—seems to confirm the urgent need to leave American jurisdiction. (3) The slight preparations regarding their personal residence, business obligations, and debts support the idea that the departure crucible came suddenly. Horatio actually wrote from Canada, the first stop on their journey, informing Dr. Hedges of what to do about papers in his office, about disposing of his office furniture and applying proceeds to his delinquent office rent, and about fulfilling a commitment to the Murphy family, requesting that Dr. Hedges would treat them without charge. (4) Despite strenuous financial hardship, and the expectation of family and friends that they would return to the United States, Horatio never returned, and no Spafford family member returned until after Horatio had died. (5) Press reports took note of the caution and secrecy surrounding the possible trip and a published interview may have added to the necessity to depart speedily. A *Daily Inter-Ocean* reporter had a fairly extensive interview with Horatio concerning his theological beliefs, just prior to their leaving. Toward the close of the article, the interview having gone well, and Horatio having discoursed freely on tenets of his beliefs, the reporter ended his article with this unexplained personal vignette.

> Prior to his visiting Mr. Spafford, the reporter learned that that gentleman contemplated a trip to Jerusalem in a very short time, and pointedly put the question:
> "Mr. Spafford, are you going to Jerusalem?"
> "I hope to, sometime," was the prompt reply.
> "But are you going this week?"
>
> Hereupon the gentleman [Spafford] quickly arose from the chair, and, as he hurried across the room, said, "I decline to be interviewed."
> "You will not answer my question then?"
> "I tell you I decline to be interviewed."
>
> From another source it was learned that Mr. Spafford, in company with a number of the lady disciples, intends to start to-day for Jerusalem. . . . There is an evident desire to keep the fact of this intended pilgrimage hidden from the public, but it leaked out through some of the believers, and it is not unlikely that the pilgrims will have started before this article sees the light.

When the reporter's story appeared the next day, the Spaffords and party were already en route to Quebec. The report was headlined: "A Singular Sect. A Band of Male and Female

Pilgrims to Start To-Day—On for Jerusalem" (August 17, 1881).

Also supporting the idea that the Spaffords removed themselves from the United States for very practical considerations is the fact that they seemed never to have looked back. From all the correspondence and records, there is no stated justification for their remaining in Jerusalem, no explanation for not considering returning, no pining for home, and no expression of compassion or concern for those left behind. Dr. Hedges, in a Chicago-to-Jerusalem letter, expressed surprise that Horatio had made no mention of returning about December 1, 1881, as they had apparently indicated, but we have no response.

Was the Spaffords' interest in the Second Coming of Christ genuine, and their sense of Christ's imminent reappearance authentic?

If leaving Chicago for foreign soil alleviated impending legal action, it seems right to weigh the evidence concerning the Spaffords' newfound interest in Jerusalem and the Second Coming of Christ. Horatio had been a fairly devoted student of the Bible, a Sunday school teacher and lay preacher. Whatever his previous interest in prophetic themes and the afterlife, it seems consonant with having lost four children that he find greater interest in the future, the consolation that might be found in religious teaching concerning Christ's return. Heaven and hell and afterlife were tenets of D. L. Moody's belief, though not points he dealt with excessively. According to Horatio's 1879 letter to Miss Wadsworth (see Appendix B), Margaret Lee played the major role in his own theological pirouette.

Additionally, somewhere, Spafford came into contact with William E. Blackstone, a wealthy businessman, who had written a small book, *Jesus Is Coming,* which espouses a standard, dispensational-premillennial view. Many people would say that it takes a particularly positive view of Israel as holding a preferred status, and represents something of a doctrine of Christian Zionism. Of course, many still affirm premillenial views of the Scriptures, without feeling particular affinity for the modern state of Israel, and Jerusalem, and certainly without feeling the need to rush to Jerusalem, either now or in the future, to be present for the return of Christ.

Clearly, friends and other evangelicals interpreted the Spaffords sudden longing for Jerusalem as an expectation of Christ's imminent return. Horatio was, after all, the author of *Twenty Reasons for Believing that the Coming of the Lord is Near,* a millennial booklet that caused considerable controversy. His hymns and poems reference a literal return of Christ.

Originally, Horatio, Anna, and Margaret left the impression of an almost divine summons or directive for a group of Overcomers to go to Jerusalem. The sense of close friends was that the Spaffords were merely following their ardent premillennial leanings. As Ira D. Sankey remembered it, for example, "While still living in Chicago Mr. and Mrs. Spafford became much interested in the Second Coming of Christ. So zealous did Mr. Spafford become that he decided to go to Jerusalem with his wife and the one remaining daughter, and there await the coming of the Lord. Mr. Spafford died there not long afterward."

A letter, dated April 13, 1886, was written by Horatio Spafford to a Chicago friend, a Mr. Chandler, and was later published in the *Daily Inter-Ocean* and in a Mormon youth magazine, *Autumn Leaves*, evidencing his continuing fascination with the Second Coming. His letter first described the beauty of flowers and the surround, and stated:

> It would seem that a sight of it, without other proofs,
> would be sufficient to suggest to one whether the
> curse which had so long lain upon this land had not
> begun to pass away, and whether the set time to favor
> Zion had not come.

After noting how Jews were returning to Jerusalem, so that
they numbered more than half the city's population, he concluded:

> The busy world has taken little notice of it—but it has
> come. Does it not look as if that time of the treading
> down of Jerusalem by the Gentiles—upon which so
> many of God's purposes respecting the Jews and the
> whole world are in the Scriptures made to depend—was
> about fulfilled [sic].

Two important points seem to indicate that, however strong
prophetic beliefs may have been concerning the return of Christ,
practical considerations related to the indebtedness and breaches
of trust were stronger factors in the decision. First, it was said
in the meetings of the Overcomers, that several different venues
had been discussed as places to which the Spaffords might have
to flee, once it seemed to be coming clear that they might have to
depart the United States. If, originally, a choice was to be made
from among several world cities, any one of which would suffice,
it would appear that emphasis was upon getting *away from* the
U.S., rather than being *drawn to* Jerusalem. Annie Aiken, the
daughter of the Spaffords' Chicago cook, went with the Spaffords
to Jerusalem to help with the children. Her mother testified in
court in the 1890s that she never would have allowed Annie to
go with them, if she had known they were going to Jerusalem.
She had thought they were only going to London.

Secondly, once on the scene in Jerusalem, and more-or-less
having decided to remain, the group persistently disavowed the
notion that its purpose in traveling to Jerusalem had been to
witness the Second Coming of Christ. Horatio continued his

explorations with Professor Piazza Smyth (astronomer royal for Scotland), about the bizarre possibility of measurements of the pyramids holding a clue to the date of the Messiah's return, inasmuch as the pyramids were built by Hebrew slaves. The rest of the group seemed almost programmed to speak generally in terms of being present to watch the flowering of the land of Israel, getting away from the fast pace of American life, and seeking to learn how to live together. In 1895, Mrs. John Whiting's ethereal explanation of their purpose in coming to Jerusalem was equally unusual: they came because there was nothing in the world that was not corrupted and that is why we went apart from the world, so that we might endeavor to get the wrong out of ourselves as much as possible and find out what it is.

Asked to explain during the 1895 judicial proceedings what occasioned the group's going to Jerusalem, Anna Spafford's best effort was a rambling reference to Scripture, a vague plea for unity, and a claim of helping both Jews and Arabs.

> We felt that God was going to fulfill in Jerusalem concerning the Jews and the building again, and we went to witness it, and we felt that there was a great lack in the world and that God wished us, according to his Word in the 17th Chapter of John, to be made one and that His people should live in harmony and in unity and be made one as He was one with His Father in perfect harmony with His Father, that we would benefit the world and we aimed to be made God's will as much as we could in order to benefit the world, and when we went to Jerusalem we fed about 250 Gaddites for many months and we worked for the people and did anything that we could for the people there, Mohammedans and Jews. We fed the Jews and we cared for the Jews and we do until this present day.

When William Rudy was asked why the group left Chicago for Jerusalem, he answered that they "believed it to be God's plan for us." Again, asked for what purpose they had gone and what they were to do after arriving, Rudy responded, "That, we had not previously determined."

Had the Spaffords planned to return to Chicago or to remain in Jerusalem in order to avoid facing their failures?

Without a plan of any kind, even a plan to form a commune, and with vague intent from the outset, it is fair to ask whether the Spaffords ever intended to return to the United States. Relatives, such as Mrs. Spafford's half sister, Rachel Frederickson, believed the intention was to return some day. Even Bertha Spafford Vester believed that had her father lived, he would have wanted to return. However, Horatio would have been cognizant of statutes of limitation and would have realized the necessary passage of time required for resolution of circumstances he left behind. (For example, the suit of Mrs. Murphy, and Bertha and Grace Spafford against Dr. Hedges was not fully resolved until action of the Supreme Court of the State of Illinois, in 1908.) Thus, even if they later desired to return to the United States, it might have been too risky, legally, to have returned during Horatio's lifetime.

In a letter from Dr. Hedges to Horatio Spafford (November 3, 1881), less than three months after their departure for Jerusalem, Dr. Hedges expressed concern about the persistence of a local lawyer seeking some deeds and papers Spafford held. After asking for instructions, Dr. Hedges went on to write, "I told him also that *we were expecting you about the 1st of Dec.* But as *your letter says nothing* of your starting, I judge you may not leave so soon as you thought (italics added)." Then, as the Overcomers disbanded, the subject of the Jerusalem group's return seems superfluous, to both those stateside and those abroad. As the *de facto* leader of the group left behind, the one charged with various errands and responsibilities in behalf of the Spaffords, and as the occupant of their home, it would seem that Dr. Hedges should have known of any intention or plan. However, his impression of a near-term return was left unfulfilled.

One other note of sadness surrounds the small band of Overcomers. They were the "True–Believers," the followers, the ones who had left churches and long-term connections to be part of something they considered very special. Apparently persuaded by the lofty goals, the apparent status and charm of the Spaffords, they accepted the interpretations and oracular leadership of the two women leaders. Confident that great things were to happen once they arrived in Jerusalem, their hopes were dashed, and their confidences proven to be misplaced. They had been duped. Yet, almost no concern was expressed by the Jerusalem group for those left behind in America. As the stateside group fell away, little anxiety was expressed from the other side, and little attempt was made to keep the group intact. It was almost as though, by mutual agreement, each individual understanding his personal as well as collective disappointment, they disintegrated.

There is no evidence to support the claim of Bertha Spafford Vester that the remainder group disbanded after a failed plea for divine healing of a baby; or, that the group fell apart over internal bickering, as Anna Spafford, according to Bertha, had predicted. No mention of such incidents is corroborated by any testimony offered by adherents in the court proceedings of 1895 and following, nor in surviving letters or news reports.

Genuine sympathy can be felt for the sad article that appeared in the *Chicago Daily Tribune,* August 31, 1902, "Old Homestead Is Sold." It told the story of the Lake View home, so dear to the Spaffords—the house and grounds with the tree, in which little Maggie in 1873 deposited the farewell note, fearing she would never see it again.

> The homestead of Dr. Samuel P. Hedges at Buena
> Park has been sold during the last week by Knott,
> Chandler & Co.
> Referring to this transaction, Luther Laflin Mills,
> whose home is in Buena Park, said: "The sale in a
> subdivision of the greater portion of the homestead
> of Dr. Samuel P. Hedges in Buena Park is an event
> of peculiar interest, especially to the citizens of
> that community, for it marks the yielding of one of
> the historic places of Lake View to the inevitable
> modern advance. It was originally the residence of
> Mr. H. G. Spafford, who died in Jerusalem and who
> is remembered as a leading lawyer of Chicago, and
> was purchased by Dr. Hedges nearly a quarter of a
> century ago. To this home, back in the '70s, first
> came the news of the drowning at sea, while they
> were on a voyage to Europe, of the Spafford children
> and others of the neighborhood, after which terrible
> event Mr. and Mrs. Spafford journeyed to the holy
> land and there began their permanent abode. Dr.
> Hedges' homestead, with its picturesque, widely
> extended house, broad lawns, and tall old trees, was
> a beautiful place, and with delightful associations
> of hospitality and friendship will long abide in the
> memory of his neighbors."

From the vantage point of more than one hundred years after
the Spaffords' and Overcomers' migration to Jerusalem, it can
be seen that the Spaffords certainly benefitted from the move.
Horatio avoided criminal prosecution, which likely would have
occurred had he remained in the United States. The humiliating
publicity and loss of face would have been difficult to bear.
Horatio would likely have been imprisoned, and the family left
with no financial means of establishing a new residence and
maintaining a livelihood. The family had no income nor prospect
of income. By going to Jerusalem, though bankrupt and in deep
financial trouble, the Spaffords were able, not only to start over
again, but to do so maintaining a high quality of life—essentially
a life with servants and support, and eventually with social

station. Their children and descendants ultimately received excellent educations, enjoyed a reasonable standard of living, and appeared to have prospered. Deciding to go to Jerusalem, Anna Spafford's sense of divine guidance—whether authentic, or influenced by personal need—probably saved the family from total disgrace and a very meager future existence.

At the same time, Horatio took with him a great deal of baggage. The awareness that (a) he had withdrawn from his profession as a lawyer, at which he was highly competent; (b) he had been unsuccessful in real estate; (c) he had betrayed confidence and trust invested in him, his having been the sole instrument of depriving three vulnerable, dependent women of their livelihood; (d) he did not make restitution for wrong, as evangelicals believe the Scripture requires; (e) he misled people—his and his wife's endorsement of his sister's predictions about the second coming of Christ, being at worst, a fraud, at best, a well-intentioned failure; (f) by taking advantage of other persons, he solved his personal problems at the expense of others whom he abandoned; (g) consciously or subconsciously, he manipulated his religion and others to meet personal needs; (i) his livelihood in Jerusalem was maintained at the expense of others.

Horatio Spafford in Jerusalem was a broken man. His journal illustrates his personal spiritual angst and his seeming inability to find forgiveness.

> Friday, June 9, 1882,
> Anna showed me text which she got a day awhile [*sic*] ago: They shall '"make" "you" "fall into a pit" "that they might destroy him [*sic*]." "Trust" "and stand."

> Saturday, June 10, 1882,
> Prayed that if it be possible all suffering because of my evil doing might in future pass away from me. Yet nevertheless not as I will but as thou wilt, O God!

Tuesday, June 27, 1882,
Thanked God that He had been so faithful to me &
prayed that I might have such a testable and perfectly
humble spirit that it would be forever unnecessary
after for God to punish me as an evil doer & that He
might [unintelligible word] "lift me up."

However damaged was his sense of personal integrity, he yet had
enough remaining to torture his conscience.

17
IT IS WELL

Great as the Spafford family contributions have been to the people of the Middle East, it seems likely that its *greatest* gift to all humankind was Horatio's words to "It Is Well with My Soul." Few hymns have had such universal acceptance, across all Christian denominational and international boundaries, and few have been so unfailingly consoling. Likewise, the family's experience—of survival, of grace under pressure, of real world faith in the arena of life—is one of the great illustrations of the indomitable human spirit, and of the validity of true faith. In sermons and speeches around the world, and likely on most any Sunday of the year, the Spafford family's story of resilience, persistence, and trust has been told and retold.

Lacking a full account of the Spafford family, its trials and ordeals, perhaps it is no wonder that the story, as told, has usually been inaccurate and incomplete. Until the descendant's recent contributions to the U.S. Library of Congress, vital information was not available. Of course, many references have been made in summary, in haste and were not made by historians or for historical purposes. The inspiration mined from the Spaffords' experience is that of persistent faith despite "bad things happening to good people."

The story popularly perpetuated over the years asserts that

Horatio Spafford wrote the poem, "It Is Well with My Soul," as the ship passed over the exact site of the wreck of the *Ville du Havre* and the *Loch Earn*, when, just after the accident, he was on his way to be reunited with his wife. Most storytellers usually claim that it was a two-word telegram that Anna sent Horatio as soon as she reached land. The myth usually claims that the Spaffords were wealthy and lost their wealth in the Great Fire of 1871. It makes a dramatic saga, which became part of family lore, serving well the intent of the Spaffords' daughter, Bertha to enhance her parents' perception by history. From countless pulpits over the years, and in many books, versions of that story have been told, modified and confused.

However, Spafford, himself, was silent about how and when the poem was written. Even in the letter he drafted for Anna's half sister, Rachel, in December 1873, aboard the *Abyssinia* en route to be reunited with his beloved Anna, he mentioned passing the geographical fix of the shipwreck the previous evening and confessed to intense feelings. But he made no reference to a poem, nor to the sentiments expressed in the poem.

Nor did he mention writing a poem, a couple of weeks later, after having joined Anna in Paris, when he and Daniel Goodwin sat in a Paris café, mining dialogue with The Reverend Nathanael Weiss for every detail Weiss could possibly recall about their children and the tragedy. Spafford related to Weiss his story of the Captain's calling them to his cabin to tell them they were at the approximate site where the *Ville du Havre* went down, and Horatio confessed to having been "deeply agitated" that night in the Captain's quarters—not exactly the mood for poetry writing. In neither account did he mention a poem, a phrase, or the experience of having been inspired to write. In the letter to Anna's half sister, he quoted a passage from the Psalms, "I will praise Him while

I have my being (paraphrased Psalms 146:2b)," but he did not refer to a poem, or quote any phrase from it. Nor was the poem published as a poem, as were many of Horatio's creations.

Ira D. Sankey, the musical associate of Moody, knew the Spaffords well, had been their houseguest, once sent them money when they were in desperate straits, and is the only known contemporary to provide an account of how the song, "It Is Well with My Soul," came to be. He was also present at Farwell Hall, Chicago, in November 1876, the night P. P. Bliss, composer of the music, first sang the song as a solo. Bliss, a tall, handsome man of thirty-eight, was already known around the world for his hymns and gospel songs, and as a compiler of religious music. At that very time, October–November 1876, Sankey and Bliss had spent days compiling hymns for a new songbook. The two musicians had their antennae out for good prospective material. For example, they included several other Bliss songs, several published for the first time in the new book.

It happened that Moody and associates came from their various distant evangelistic efforts to reunite in Chicago for one of their periodic team meetings in November 1876. Moody's group gathered in a hotel, or in homes from time to time to share results of their efforts and relay greetings from mutual friends. It was a time of rest and inspiration, a few days to enjoy warm camaraderie, and to recoup spiritual and physical strength from the ardors of travel, the constant meeting of people, speaking to crowds, and responding to questions. For example, in his biography of Bliss, Whittle noted, "Needham and Stebbins, Moorhouse, Charles Inglis, Rockwell, Morton, Jacobs, Farwell, Spafford, Dean and others were frequently together . . . dining with Moody, and discussing Gospel truth or plans of work, or in Bliss's room listening to some new song."

According to Sankey, it was out of this sort of team

meeting that the hymn of testimony, "It Is Well with My Soul," came about.

> In 1876, when we returned to Chicago to work, I was entertained at the home of Mr. and Mrs. Spafford for a number of weeks. *During that time* Mr. Spafford wrote the hymn, "It is well with my soul," in commemoration of the death of his children (italics added). P. P. Bliss composed the music and sang it for the first time at a meeting in Farwell Hall.

That account is somewhat corroborated by Whittle.

> October 1st [1876] Mr. Bliss arrived in Chicago, and was present at Moody and Sankey's opening service. He was the guest, at this time, of Mr. H. M. Thompson, of the Brevoort House, and here completed several of the songs that appeared in *Gospel Hymns No. 2.* He did not participate in any of the Chicago meetings in a public way, but for three weeks was a constant attendant, and was greatly blessed in the remarkable services that opened Mr. Moody's work in Chicago, and in the personal contact with Mr. Moody and Mr. Sankey, with the latter of whom he spent most of his time, removing for a couple of weeks to Mr. Sankey's hotel, that they might be uninterruptedly together. Until this time they had never been much together in the work, but had arranged for their hymn books mostly by correspondence.

Two points seem especially important: (1) The surviving copy of "It Is Well with My Soul," now in the Library of Congress Collection, written in Horatio G. Spafford's own hand, is on Brevoort House stationery, the place to which Bliss had retreated in order to focus on the demands of their proposed new songbook. (2) So far as we know, the earliest printing of "It Is Well with My Soul" came in *Gospel Hymns No. 2*, copyright 1876, and released in printed form to the public in 1877.

R. C. Morgan, British publisher of the periodical, *The Christian,* friend of Moody and highly regarded by evangelicals on both sides of the Atlantic, related the story as he had heard it.

While not concurring in all respects, he did not report that "It Is Well" had been written at sea. In an 1891 article, he remembered:

> The shock and sorrow of this sudden and terrible bereavement, I need not say, affected the parents very deeply; yet they were comforted of God, *and a few months later* Mr. Spafford composed the hymn (No. 210 in *Sacred Songs and Solos* 1877)—When peace like a river attendeth my way, . . . (italics added).

Sankey and Moody had been in Edinburgh when the *Ville du Havre* sank, and Moody had rushed to Liverpool to meet the Spaffords and to stand by them in their anguish. Sankey later recalled that Spafford had kept framed on his office wall the cablegram from his wife announcing the loss of their children and friends. It was apparently that framed cable that inspired the writing of a poem to commemorate loss of the children in the accident. Interestingly, Sankey, having seen the framed telegram hanging on Spafford's wall, noted that it did read "Saved alone," but he did not perpetuate the myth of a "two-word cablegram." (The original cablegram of twenty-nine words is now in the American Colony in Jerusalem Collection of the Library of Congress.)

As a hymn, by Spafford and Bliss, "It Is Well with My Soul," was copyrighted in 1876 and, so far as can be determined, first appeared in print as number 76, of *Gospel Hymns No. 2,* by P. P. Bliss and Ira D. Sankey, 1876. That songbook must have been released to the public in early 1877, since Bliss had sent a letter to his coworker Whittle, only a few days before the end of the year, 1876, and only a few days before Bliss's tragic death, stating, "On my table lie the proof-sheets of *Gospel Hymns No. 2* . . ." Without music, and as a poem, "It Is Well with My Soul" was not published until it appeared in Horatio Spafford's paperback pamphlet of poems, *Waiting for the Morning and Other Poems,* the author identified only as "the Author of *Twenty Reasons for Believing that the Coming of the Lord is Nigh,*" published by F. H. Revell in 1878.

Accepting Sankey's account, Bliss was likely the first to use the word Gospel as a modifier to describe a new genre of religious music—"Gospel song," or "Gospel hymn." The world was familiar with traditional hymns, addressed to God. In more formal churches, the Psalter was relied upon, essentially the setting of passages of Scripture to music. Over the years the term has come to refer to more recent religious music (1850s to present), related to one's personal testimony or commentary about a Scriptural theme, or declaration of one's own personal faith, belief, and trust. While Sankey lived longer, and ultimately became much better known, having traveled with D. L. Moody and having been part of the great Moody mass meetings both in the U.S. and abroad, in 1876 Bliss probably had more copyrights than Sankey and at the time of Bliss's death, was probably better known. For example, the song, "Hold the Fort," which in 1870 Bliss crafted out of a Civil War story told by his friend and coworker Whittle, who had been a major in the Union Army, became wildly popular in the early 1870s and was sung around the world. The song gave rise to a phrase that became common parlance in numerous languages; "hold the fort" is still a popular colloquial expression today.

Bliss, a deeply spiritual man of high character, had sprung from humble origins and was largely self-taught as a musician—short-term, rural "singing schools" as close as he ever came to formal music training. He was known to have a strong solo voice, sometimes sang duets with his wife, and sang with considerable passion and feeling that often deeply moved his audience. Bliss and his wife died tragically a little over a month after he first publicly presented "It Is Well with My Soul," in Chicago. They were traveling by train to Chicago from a holiday break at his home in Rome, Pennsylvania, when a train-bridge collapsed in a disaster that claimed almost one hundred lives at Ashtabula, Ohio, December 29, 1876. Upon receiving news of the tragedy, the deeply sensitive Moody immediately dispatched three people to Ashtabula to search for the Bliss's remains and possessions. The disaster has been called almost the perfect disaster, because it included strong winds and blinding snow; it involved the train falling from a height of some seventy feet; water and ice were present in the shallow river beneath the trestle where the passengers and cars landed; fire broke out from the stoves heating the railcars and was fed by the wood and varnish of the railcar construction; and the town was too small to have much fire and rescue or emergency medical equipment. Not a trace of Bliss or his wife, Lucy, was ever found. Two young sons, left in the care of Bliss's sister in Rome, survived.

One might say that the hymn, "It Is Well with My Soul," was tested by water and by fire. The Spaffords endured the loss of their four little girls in the cold waters of the North Atlantic without a trace. Similarly, nothing was ever found of Philip Paul Bliss, thirty-eight, and his wife, Lucy, thirty-six, who were essentially cremated, their belongings incinerated, in the railway-bridge disaster. It is almost inconceivable that one song could relate to such unspeakable tragedy, impacting two different families, the loss of six lives, all within the span of little more than three years—the Spaffords before the words were written; the Blisses after the music was written, and the song had been publicly presented.

As musical consolation, "It Is Well with My Soul" is without equal in the modern world, used by a variety of denominations and faith traditions. Indeed, it seems not to have been as widely published or utilized, nor as well accepted in its earliest days, as it has been in the twentieth and twenty-first centuries. While it is the primary claim Horatio Spafford has to being remembered today, he did not give the poem or the hymn any particular attention, or place of honor among his memories or memorabilia. It is not singled out in any way from other writings, nor does it receive special mention. In Bliss's case, he received far more contemporary praise for "Hold the Fort!" and for the Easter hymn, "Hallelujah! What a Saviour," than for "It Is Well with My Soul."

To music-minded individuals, much of the song's success relates to the excellent manner in which the words are supported by the tune. It begins softly and comfortingly, seeming somewhat tentative or mournful, and swells to a crescendo of affirmation. The early lines of the first stanza may take root from a biblical phrase, "peace like a river," which is then linked both in Scripture and in the hymn to the more majestic waves of the sea.

> O that thou hadst hearkened to my commandments!
> then had thy peace been as a river, and thy righteousness
> as the waves of the sea Isaiah 48:18.

The alliteration of "sorrows like sea-billows" is cleverly matched by the repetition and rhyming of "sorrows" and "billows," the last three letters of the final syllable of each word, ending in "-o-w-s."

It Is Well

When peace, like a river, attendeth my way,
  When sorrows like sea billows roll;
Whatever my lot, Thou has taught me to say [know],
  It is well, it is well, with my soul.

Refrain
It is well, it is well,
With my soul, with my soul,
It is well, it is well, with my soul.

Though Satan should buffet, though trials should come,
  Let this blest assurance control,
That Christ hath regarded my helpless estate,
  And hath shed His own blood for my soul.

My sin, oh, the bliss of this glorious [peace-giving] thought!
  My sin, not in part but the whole,
Is nailed to the [His] cross, and I bear it no more,
  Praise the Lord, praise the Lord, O my soul!

*For me, be it Christ, be it Christ hence to live:
  If Jordan above me shall roll,
No pang shall be mine, for in death as in life
  Thou wilt whisper Thy peace to my soul.

*But, Lord, 'tis for Thee, for Thy coming we wait,
  The sky, not the grave, is our goal;
Oh trump of the angel! Oh voice of the Lord!
  Blessèd hope, blessèd rest of my soul!

And Lord, haste the day when my [the] faith shall be sight,
  The clouds be rolled back as a scroll;
The trump shall resound, and the Lord shall descend
  [and Thy kingdom shall come!],
Even so, it is well with my soul.

*The asterisked stanzas are not included in Spafford's booklet of poems,
  Waiting for the Morning and Other Poems, 1878, p 44.

In expressing the idea that despite difficulty, he has learned to find contentment, Spafford may have drawn from the Apostle Paul, who in II Corinthians 11 recited a long litany of difficulties. The Apostle also stated in Philippians 4.12, "I know both how to be abased, and I know how to abound: everywhere and in all things I am instructed both to be full and to be hungry, both to abound and to suffer need." It also has echoes of the Apostle Paul's statement in Philippians 4. 7, "And the peace of God, which passeth all understanding. . . ."

These same thoughts then carry over to the second stanza, which references the maintenance of confidence, even though "Satan should buffet" and "trials should come." The concept of confident belief in the midst of difficulty is a common virtue in the Bible and in Christian history. In Spafford's case, he and Anna both expressed the concept that they were happy to maintain their profession of Christian faith, despite their great loss. When Horatio wrote "I am glad to trust the Lord when it will cost me something," he may have been responding to thoughts planted by "Aunty Sims," the unusual character who inserted herself into the Spaffords' lives and household after the Fire. She periodically chided that it was comfortable for Anna to believe, since she had a husband, a nice family, a lovely home, assistance around the house, and no particular needs. Perhaps Aunty Sims's taunts stimulated Horatio and Anna to posit the loss of their children as "the cost." But, it is unclear what they saw as "the cost." Was it the lives of their four children? Or, were they expressing the confidence and loyalty they felt in their faith, despite their unexplainable loss? (see page 137).

One wonders if the phrase "blest assurance" might have been drawn from the testimonial song written by Fanny Crosby, "Blessed Assurance." Crosby's song had been written and first published in a magazine in 1873, three years before Spafford appears to have written "It Is Well."

The third stanza, with its confession of sin and appropriation of the death of Christ as sufficient for expiation, seems especially pertinent for Horatio Spafford. By 1876, his law practice had atrophied, his real estate ideas were not productive, and he must have been realizing that his less-than-honorable financial dealings had less and less chance of remaining unexposed, or of being remedied. The personalized phrase, "My sin," is used twice in the stanza.

The words of the fourth and fifth stanzas are expressive of the millennial theology, which Spafford seemed to view traditionally, up until about 1878 and, perhaps, even afterward. Until that time, he appears to have been close to Moody, Whittle, Blackstone, and others who espoused a traditional premillennial view of the Second Coming of Christ, as the final stanza describes:

> And Lord, haste the day when my faith shall be sight
> > The clouds be rolled back as a scroll;
> The trump shall resound and the Lord shall descend,
> > *Thy kingdom shall come!
> Even so, it is well with my soul.
>
> (One alternate was, The trump shall resound and
> Thy kingdom shall come!)

Each line relates to a biblical convention. The New Testament letter of the Apostle Paul employs the expression, We walk by faith, not by sight (II Corinthians 5.7), as in the first line. The second line blends two concepts: the Second Coming of Christ, when He is expected to appear as though "riding on the clouds" (Matthew 24:30); and, the oft used concept of sudden judgment "rolling the heavens together as a scroll" (Isaiah 34.4). The third line employs the figure of the last judgment, "in a moment, in the twinkling of an eye, at the last trumpet; for the trumpet will sound and the dead will be raised imperishable . . ." (I Corinthians 15:52).

By the time of his departure for Jerusalem, Spafford's eschatology seems to have become muddled; yet, the final stanza is one of anticipation, "And Lord, haste the day. . . ." The stated justification for going to Jerusalem a few years after the hymn was written was to witness the imminent return of Christ. And, even tinkering with the theories of Professor Piazza Smyth on the bizarre possibility that the dimensions of a room in The Great Pyramid might render a clue as to the date of Christ's reappearance, evidences Spafford's strong expectation of a soon Second Coming.

The origin of the "well with the soul" concept is unknown. The Reverend Emile Cook, the French evangelical pastor who survived the sinking of the *Ville du Havre* but took sick during the rescue and died shortly thereafter, wrote his last letter to his minister friend The Reverend Nathanael Weiss only a few days before his death. In that letter, Cook stated: "I am strongly threatened with inflammation of the lungs. I have a terrible fever—but all is well."

Greeting Horatio and Anna Spafford in England for the first time after the shipwreck, according to Sankey, Moody comforted them and was greatly pleased to find that they were able to say, "It is well; the will of God be done." Phrases such as "all is well," "it is well," and "are you well?" seem to have been commonplace at the time. The tradition of the New England Town Crier had been to call the hour, with such words, as, for example: "Eight o'clock and all is well."

John Greenleaf Whittier, then one of the nation's greatest living poets, wrote a poem just weeks after the Great Fire in praise of Chicago and its people. First known as "A Poet's Tribute," it is often cited in more modern compendia with the title, "Chicago."

Whittier opened his work with, "All is well!" attributing that statement of contentment to the people of Chicago just before the fire broke out. Whittier's line could be seen as a direct influence upon Spafford, or simply as an indication of the popularity of the phrase in common parlance.

> Men said at vespers: "All is well!"
> In one wild night the city fell;
> Fell shrines of prayer and marts of gain
> Before the fiery hurricane.

Little known in modern times, but, perhaps, the greatest influence on Spafford and Bliss was likely another song, written a few years earlier by George F. Root. Bliss had first met Root in the 1860s, and was later hired as part of a quartet Root had in mind to base in Chicago and travel, advertising the songs and music available through Root & Cady, publishers. The quartet did not work out, but Root hired Bliss to travel the Midwest, giving music lessons, meeting at music conventions and singing schools fashionable among church people of that time. Tall, handsome, always cheerful, with an impressive countenance, it is easy to imagine that Bliss would be an effective public relations advocate. Root had published Bliss's very first musical composition in sheet music in 1864. Considered something of a musical patriarch, Root combined a rich knowledge of music and talent with practical business sense. As a viable mass market, Christian music was in its early, formative stage.

In 1873, a little songbook, edited by P. P. Bliss, was published by George F. Root & Sons, entitled, *Sunshine For Sunday Schools: A New Collection of Original and Selected Music.* Included in that anthology was a little Sunday school song, written and composed by George F. Root, which had earlier appeared in print. With an interrogatory title, "Is It Well?" and with a chorus asking, repeatedly, "Is it well, is it well? O my soul, O my soul?," it appeared the song was intended to evoke a response from both singer and listener. Spafford, Sunday school superintendent at Fullerton Avenue Presbyterian Church, and a Sunday school convention leader, would very likely be familiar with such a song. Following the tragic loss of his children, it is possible that the Spafford–Bliss hymn of consolation might have been intended, whether directly or subconsciously, as a resounding affirmation to the Sunday school song's question:

> Question (Root 1873): "Is it well, is it well? O my soul, O my soul?"
> Answer (Spafford, 1876): "It is well, it is well, with my soul; with my soul!"

Since the language is so similar, and even the tune has certain commonalities, it may be that Spafford and Bliss deliberately intended to answer, declaratively and with conviction, the interrogative Root had earlier posed.

Few hymns have been more pervasively used across denominational lines. "It Is Well" has appeared in hymnbooks of the major denominations and in anthologies of consolation. Instrumental arrangements are regularly advertised on the Internet, and it is one of the all-time favorites for funeral and memorial services. At the present writing, Google lists over ten million references to "It Is Well with My Soul."

His great hymn, as well as other poetry and insight, had come to Horatio even before his fiftieth birthday, and during the time he was still active with the Moody network of friends and workers. Just a few days after his sixtieth birthday, he died in Jerusalem. From the time of the *Ville du Havre* accident (November 1873), Horatio Spafford was a different man. While, perhaps, it was well with his own soul in 1876, and he may still have been at peace in his own soul by 1881; yet, realistically, he was faced with defeat or resignation. By the time he left for Jerusalem in 1881, he had: (a) given up his law practice; (b) failed in his attempts at real estate; (c) been brought face-to-face with financial ruin and bankruptcy; (d) left the church he had helped found; (e) become alienated from his spiritual brothers and sisters in the Moody–evangelical realm; (f) dropped from prominence in local and metro Chicago civic life; (g) compromised his own reputation for integrity and honesty; (h) yielded spiritual leadership to his sister, Margaret. The torment expressed in his little diary for 1882 demonstrates that peace like a river had become a bit harder to enjoy.

As the prophets of old had their weaknesses, they remind us that the Lord's work has always been accomplished by imperfect vessels, broken men and women. Very few have been able to channel their "brokenness" into durable comfort and consolation for millions of others. Aided by Philip Paul Bliss, such is the legacy of one man, Horatio Spafford.

APPENDIX A

Several curiosities about the Spaffords and the sinking of the *Ville du Havre* remain open to conjecture. Though they may not be resolved, they are worthy of notice and reflection.

I

Captain Urquhart noted that Mrs. Spafford, "the only one saved of this family, tells of a most remarkable experience she had while struggling in the water, which I cannot relate here." Whether he felt it would be an inappropriate infringement of Anna Spafford's privacy, a violation of her trust in him, if he were to reveal her almost ineffable experience—we will never know. Later, various claims were made in behalf of Anna Spafford to the effect that she had supernatural experiences that November night in 1873, when the ship sank, and she was in the water, battling the elements for survival. However, her daughter, Bertha Spafford Vester, later wrote that she once found a scrap of paper on which her Mother had written:

> I had no vision during the struggle in the water at the time of the shipwreck, only the conviction that any earnest soul, brought face to face with its maker, must have; I realized that my Christianity must be real. There was no room here for self-pity, or for the practice of that Christianity that always favours and condones itself and its own, rendering innocuous the sharp two-edged sword of the Word which was intended to

> separate soul from spirit and the desires and thoughts
> and intents of the heart. This soft religion was as far
> removed from Chris's practice of Christianity as east
> from west. Nothing but a robust Christianity could
> save me then and now.

Somewhat in conflict with those statements, Anna had related to Dr. Selma Lagerlöf, winner of the Nobel Prize in Literature, her experience the night the *Ville du Havre* sank. Dr. Lagerlöf related Anna Spafford's story in an address before The Stockholm Conference 1925 (The Universal Christian Conference on Life and Work), admitting that it had taken place about "fifty years ago." Anna had told her a great struggle for survival had erupted on deck of the sinking ship and horrible cries and curses assailed the air, as people pushed and elbowed their way to get a lifeboat.

> But from all these scenes of cruelty and chaos, of
> merciless savagery and pitiful terror of death, she
> [Anna] released her soul to uplift it to God.
> And her soul rose up like a released captive. She
> felt how it rejoiced in casting off the heavy fetters of
> human life, how with exultation it prepared to soar to
> its rightful home.
> "Is it so easy to die?" she thought.
> Then she heard a mighty voice, a voice from
> the other world, that filled her ears with a
> thundering reply.
> "It is true that it is easy to die. That which is difficult
> is to live."
> It seemed to her that this was the greatest of truths,
> and she assented joyfully: "Yes, yes, it is true that it is
> difficult to live."
> And with a feeling of pity for those who still
> continued to live, she thought: "Why need it be so?
> Could not life on earth be so arranged that it could
> become as easy to live as it now is to die?"
> Then she again heard the mighty voice, which
> answered her: "That which is required in order
> that it may become easy to live on the earth is
> unity, unity, unity."

Memory plays a beneficial role in our lives and remembering a horrifying experience or tragedy can leave one vulnerable to confabulation, layering accumulated impressions and feelings onto the actual memory of the event, until memory is less accurate. It appears that Dr. Lagerlöf probably first heard Anna's survival story upon her visit to the American Colony in 1899, about twenty-six years after the incident. Dr. Lagerlöf's report to the conference was made an additional twenty-five years later, or fifty years after the actual incident. We can never know the accuracy of Anna Spafford's explanation, nor of Dr. Lagerlöf's retelling. There is no other record that Anna used the word unity in describing any aspect of her ordeal—not as she talked with Pastor Weiss, who told her story in some detail in his account published soon after the tragedy. There is no record that unity was a word used in her account to Captain Urquhart (although such could have been entangled in the remarkable experiences Captain Urquhart said she had related to him, but which he did not repeat).

II.

When Captain Urquhart summarized the entire experience of the shipwreck, the rescue aboard the *Trimountain,* and the off-loading of the rescued passengers, he outlined six particular ironies, coincidences or acts of providence.

1. He recounted an experience five years previous when, trading gossip with other ship captains, one had told him of a fabled, mysterious rock, Barenetha Rock, in the middle of the North Atlantic. The tale seemed farfetched and unverifiable—a sort of legend of the sea—and the other three compatriots declined to believe it, though it lodged unexplainably in Captain Urquhart's mind.

2. Captain Urquhart was not sure why, but he felt

inclined to mark the supposed location of the Barenetha Rock, pricking the latitude and longitude points on his map.

3. Captain Urquhart was transferred from his prior ship to the *Trimountain.*

4. As Captain of the *Trimountain,* his owners wanted him to set sail for Europe on Sunday, but Captain Urquhart, a man of serious religious faith, declined a Sunday departure. As he noted, had he left on Sunday, he would have been two hundred miles farther across the Atlantic and unavailable to rescue the survivors of the *Ville du Havre.*

5. Once at sea, Captain Urquhart discovered that officials in charge of loading the ship had miscalculated and left empty a large space in the cargo hold. Before encountering the *Ville du Havre,* he had even remarked to his assistant that, should they encounter a wrecked steamer in trouble, they would have room to accommodate one hundred fifty persons.

6. For the first time in Captain Urquhart's life, he decided to take the more northern route as an experiment. Had he stayed on the normal southern route, he never would have crossed trails with the *Ville du Havre.*

7. About eleven o'clock, unable to sleep, the Captain went on deck, took a stellar observation, found he was close to the location of the supposed Barenetha Rock, and unable to shake off the sense that there might just be a rock there—if, in fact, it existed—ordered the course altered two points until daylight, points that put him exactly in the path of the *Ville du Havre.*

Interestingly, the *Trimountain* was itself abandoned and lost at sea, almost seven years after its rescue of survivors of the *Ville du Havre* and *Loch Earn* collision. The *New York Times* of

February 22, 1880 carried this small item.

Loss of the Ship Trimountain

Jonas Smith & Co., of No. 66 South-street, the owners of the ship *Trimountain,* which sailed from this port for Bremen, with a general cargo, on Jan 28, received a dispatch yesterday announcing the loss of that vessel. The steam-ship *Othello,* of the Wilson Line, which sailed from this port on the 4th landed Capt. Davis and the crew of the *Trimountain* at Hull, England, on Friday last. The lost ship was built at Milford, Mass., in 1850, but was thoroughly repaired three years since. She measured 1,301 tons, was 175 feet long, 35 feet across her beam, and 29 feet deep.

III

Looking back after the accident, it was clear that several people had genuine concern about the proposed trip, if not premonitions. There was Maggie's letter in the play post office of the Spafford children's favorite tree, bearing Maggie's note saying good-bye to Lake View, and that she would never see Lake View again.

Anna Spafford had been reluctant to take the 1873 trip, and was even more dubious about going without Horatio after he backed out. On board the ship one night, she had confided to Pastor Weiss her apprehension, realizing that only a few boards were all that separated all those on the *Ville du Havre* from a watery grave.

Horatio Spafford was also guided by some unknown, unidentified instinct. Before departure from New York, he had his family and their small Chicago tribe safely aboard the *Ville du Havre,* having earlier chosen their compartment on the ship with care. But a strange conviction came over Horatio that he must change the two staterooms reserved for Anna, the children, and Mademoiselle Nicolet. He went to the purser and moved them from the center of the ship closer to the bow. He had deliberately chosen the original rooms himself, but at the last minute he could not throw off the sense that he must change the rooms. Had he not changed their rooms, it is likely that the children and Anna would have been instantly lost in the initial collision.

The ship's physician, Dr. Ouadint, a veteran of numerous sea voyages and no stranger to the sea, could not conceal from passengers a fearful fascination with the possibility of trouble. He first imagined that the ship was lower in the water than it should be, and though disproved, he continued in the assumption that something was not right. Once the collision occurred, he performed his duties heroically, but his sense of certain trouble seemed never to have left him.

Before departing New York, The Rev. Pronier had spoken of his misgivings about the voyage and indicated that, if he survived, he would not travel by sea again. The father of six children, he was lost without any trace. His colleague, Rev. Carrasco, victim of terrible seasickness, had vowed, also, that he would never again take to the sea.

IV

With prominent families involved in the *Ville du Havre* tragedy, impressive memorials and commemorations came about after the shipwreck. Princeton University received the proceeds of young Hamilton Murray's estate. Murray had been graduated from Princeton the previous June and had signed his Last Will and Testament only the night before the ship departed. After his death in the sinking of the *Ville du Havre,* his bequest financed construction of Murray Hall on the Princeton campus in 1879. Originally used for weekday chapel services, and still in use today, it has since the 1920s been the home of Theatre Intime. A large picture of Hamilton Murray hangs in an interior hallway outside the theater, and over the years, a mythical aura has developed around the structure. Generations of students have reported strange phenomena, such as the picture glowing when lights are out, tools disappearing from one spot on the stage during set construction, only to reappear at another spot. During dress rehearsals, groups have reportedly observed a young man in a top hat and heavy overcoat watching the play intently, but upon second glance, he seemed to have disappeared.

In the Episcopal Church in Rye, New York, a magnificent window is dedicated to young Sarah Adams Bulkley, Lallie, as she was called, who charmed young and old alike, and seemed the very presence of an angel. Arching over the window is the inscription, "He shall give His angels charge over thee . . . " (Psalm 91.11). In stained glass, a female figure is portrayed as borne from the sea to heavenly portals above by an assisting angel. A central panel quotes, "The sea shall give up its dead" (Revelation 20.13). The inscription in stained glass below the picture reads:

In tribute from many friends to Sarah Adams Bulkley,
Born Sept. 20th 1853. Lost at Sea Nov. 22 1873.

A similar window is in the Episcopal Church in Augusta, Georgia, where the Bulkleys also had a residence as well as timber, pulp, and paper business interests.

APPENDIX B

Horatio G. Spafford's letter to Miss Wadsworth of Brooklyn, New York, March 17, 1879, is valuable as evidence of his dramatically revised theological views. It represents the most thorough explication of beliefs after his recognition of the leadership of his sister, Margaret Lee.

> *99 Washington St.*
> *Chicago*
> *February 21st [is lined out]*
> *Mch. 17, 1879*

Dear Friend,

It has certainly been most uncivil (to put a mild designation upon it-) to let your letter remain so long unanswered;— but the incivility pardoned,—for which I do here & now apologize—it is perhaps as well that the answer has been deferred. The enquiries of your letter go to the foundation of things, & I can answer them more nearly to my own satisfaction certainly, now, than when your letter was received. Should I wait another month, I doubt not the answer would be stronger yet.

You say you "want some expression from me about Mrs. Lee's remarkable Christian experience and career." I answer, in a word, that I have no other opinion about it than that it is of the Lord—that it is a work which is nothing less than a fulfillment of prophecy and a proof of the near approach of the latter days.

As you know, it is now nearly three years since this experience of Mrs. L. began. Though that of a sister, I am not aware that that fact has had either a concluding, or any undue influence with me in reaching the conclusions I have, either as to the character of that experience as a whole,—or to the various points of interpretation and doctrine entering into it. I have sought to deal with the whole matter carefully & prayerfully,—asking God continually for wisdom and protection:—asking Him to keep me by His spirit & His word, from error, —and I fully believe He has done so;—I will here say that before Mrs. L. had this experience I was a firm believer in the truth of the personal, premillenial coming of the Lord; —believing that the Bible clearly taught that His spirit would be manifested in wonderful ways shortly before such coming, discernable to such as were watching—and that there were great and accumulating evidences,—moral, social, political, etc.— that such coming was now near;—that it was hastening greatly. Before believing thus, in such experiences as of the Lord, I had no incredulity as to the possibility or even probability of God's manifesting His power in wonderful ways, in these days, to overcome.—If any one should say that this fact lessens the weight of my testimony, I can only say, I don't think it should. I think it should give increased weight to this testimony. Not all things would be as the prophets had a foreseen, but the morning paper came withal furnishing proof that the drama was lunging to its close. But, however this may be, the fact was that I was looking for new and unusual evidence. I fully expected it. It seemed clear to me that the "fig tree was putting forth its leaves." It seemed clear that the predicted last things had begun to come to pass. I could not interpret the condition of Europe, of the Mohammedans and Papal churches, of the Jewish people, the financial state of the world, by any other key:—and while I was not looking for such evidence as that through Mrs. L., I was yet looking for evidence;— and when this came, I subjected it to the same tests as all the rest. To repeat, I examined it with prayer, jealous as I was then, and still think, for the honor of the Lord—I examined it in the light of the word;—compared it, in many points with the opinions and renderings of such scholars and commentators as experience had led me to respect as not only learned, but taught of the spirit; and now again I say that I believe that this work through Mrs. Lee is a mighty work of God. Before going further, a word about "signs"—God nowhere tells us to be indifferent to signs. His teaching is just the reverse. The wicked generation is one which will not believe without exacting signs as a conditional precedent. But Christ's own work was, in fact, proved by "signs." He followed that of the apostles by signs. His own second coming will have signs as its forerunners, and woe to those, be they shepherds or sheep, whose teaching lends to discredit or detract attention from the mercifully accredited warning. And now I will give somewhat more specifically, the grounds for this belief I have above expressed.

First, One of these grounds was and is the character of Mrs. Lee—an experienced, sound-minded, practical wife, mother & friend; knowing the world and respected by all knowing her;—no enthusiast, a fanatic; a good house keeper, steadily faithful for forty years in every homely duty; —a true, brave, noble genuine Christian woman. It seemed to me that if there were a Hannah or a Deborah to be chosen now, there was no one I know more fit for the trust—Mrs. Lee did not seem to me to be one whom the Lord would permit Satan to make a prolonged and systematic use of as an instrument of his wishes. I know of no living person who, so far as I can judge lives nearer to God than Mrs. Lee. All this had weight with me.

Second. Mrs. L., when this work began, while an intelligent ✝tian woman with a clear apprehension of the plan of salvation through Christ, was no "theologian" in the normal sense of that word. She was not at all learned in

220

bible things. The grace of the Lord was in her heart; —very deeply and wonderfully in her heart. She had been hungry for the truth from that wondering meeting at Shelter Island in July 1876; —but she had little biblical <u>learning</u>, knew little or nothing of the prophetic scriptures;—knew, in other words, —outside of the gospels and epistles, and the fundamental saving birth they contain, neither more or less of the scriptures, probably, than the average American Christian woman. —On the other hand, I had been for many years rather an unusually industrious bible student. Accordingly, Mrs. Lee had been in the habit for a long time of applying to me for information about such things —Judge then, what was my surprise to see her, about two years & a half ago—abruptly and almost unconsciously, begin a series of bible instruction and interpretations— often entirely new to me,—occasionally distasteful,— sometimes, as far as I could see, wholly disconnected with anything which had preceded it in her teachings,—and only understood through subsequent, and sometimes long subsequent, interpretations of other scriptures;—this going on for a year or more, in the form of isolated & apparently arbitrary interpretations,—& then all gradually taking form as a harmonious system.—And, here let me say, if in that system there is any error, —anything which, so far as I can discern, combats any scripture, I have yet to discover it—On the other hand, I state it as my conviction, that these interpretations seem wonderfully to light up the word, —to reconcile passages of difficulty & to harmonize all with the actual state of the church & the world today,— in a way, which alone would make it impossible for me to believe that it is not of the Lord. This constitutes a second ground of belief.

<u>Third</u>. All Mrs. Lee's teaching was through the word. I found that she had suddenly become gifted with a familiarity with,—or rather with an ability, in the line of her teaching, to use the word, utterly beyond my former, or ordinary grounds to account for: There was

no change in the word, but there rested upon her the gift of a mighty insight into that word. I found that all her teaching exalted Christ;—that no interpretation I had ever heard of, seemed so vividly to represent Him as a living, personal Saviour; that the Holy Spirit was throughout honored as a living Comforter;—that the love of the Father was magnified;—& that Mrs. Lee herself, while being constantly used as the means through whom these teachings were obtained, seemed steadily growing & strengthening in ✝tian character, & her walk & conversation daily becoming more beautiful & influential for good on those around her. This constituted a third ground of belief.

Fourth. Her announcement of the truth of the final triumph of God's love in Christ over every created being,—made in a letter from her to me, I think, about two years ago, came like a thunder-clap upon me;—& I here say, that of the proofs which preceded the announcement, that it was the Lord Himself who was working in & through Mrs. Lee, had been in any respect less complete than they were, I should then & there, probably, have committed the error of putting it all, in fear & trembling aside as wrong teaching;—so loyal was I inclined to be to the theology in which I had been educated;—and which I had never once questioned, in respect to this point, as I recollect, from the day I had become a ✝tian, more than twenty years before. But I had seen by this time too much to dare so to dispose of anything which came through Mrs. Lee,—& I accordingly began a systematic examination of the subject. This was before Canon Farrar had preached his two sermons on future punishment & before the recent renewed discussion of the general question. I had not gone far in the study before I was compelled to admit that points in the orthodox fabric of argument which I had never questioned, were at least of doubtful strength;—nor much further before seeing clearly that all the theological pressure which could be brought to bear, could not much longer avail to postpone a free & thorough investigation of the whole subject, from its foundations—I was in the first instance, surprised to find how many devout & learned men, in every age, had believed in the final universal triumph of God's love; but still I made no easy surrender. I studied the word for myself. I read the best & strongest matter I could find on both sides of the question;—and I now say to you, that the conclusion I have come to, is that Mrs. Lee's teaching is correct. I have no longer any doubt on the subject. I believe that aionon [aeons?] means age-abiding, not eternal;—that all the aions, & aions upon aions referred to in the bible, are divisions of time,—and all combined tread not one hour upon Eternity,—at the beginning of which Christ renders up the Kingdom of the Father (I Cor. 15.28);—I further believe that I Peter 3:18-20, shows that Christ—after death preached to imperfect spirits who had once inhabited human bodies on this earth:—I believe that "Sheol" and "Hades" designate an intermediate and temporary condition, the gates of which will not prevail against Christ the Conqueror;—& that Gehenna is used in the following places only: Mtt. 5.22, 29-30; 10:28; 18:9; 23:15-33; Mark 9:43, 45, 47; Luke 12:5,—James 3:6—and that Gehenna, where indeed the worm dieth not and the fire is not quenched,—the bible does not show will ever have an inmate—The Lake of fire (the second death Rev. 20:14) certainly cannot be an eternal punishment, for all that are not overcomers in the sense that "overcometh" is used in Rev 2:3;—are hurt of it;—(Rev. 2:11)—But clearly all Christians (i.e., all truly justified persons) are not overcomers, in the sense intended in those two chapters;— overcoming is there used not as a sign of justification, but for entire, utter consecration and separation unto God, having every thing on the altar. It is therefore impossible that the Lake of fire is an eternal punishment,—because, to repeat,—many a justified person will be hurt of the second death.—I believe that all will be utterly purged, sooner or later, of this selfish, God-defying will. Those so purged here in this life and who here, not having seen Him, love

Him as a faithful wife loves her husband,—I believe will escape all purging hereafter:—that such are the Elect,—the Bride;—they will be at the marriage supper of the Lamb: that all others go to purging:—That the Song of Solomon, the 45th Psalm, the parable of the woman the Parable of the nobleman going into a far country Rev. 2:3 (the inscriptions of the Epistles), etc. & many other passages show the great differences among truly justified persons. I believe that the ordaining, so called "orthodox teaching" on these points, is but a sedative to sing Christians to sleep and make them lose their reward.

So far as these opinions depend upon a construction of Greek original, I do not believe it to be in the power of any living "orthodox" Greek authority,—(so distinguished for scholarship are many of those, maintaining such heterodox opinions, or some of them) to prove them to be inaccurate. Mere dogmatism,—the mere ipse dixit of theologians can no longer be deemed conclusive—the appeal is to the word of God. These views I have expounded can doubtless be shown to be inconsistent with the generally received theology—with human "standards."—Articles, confessions etc.—but not, as I believe, with the word of God.

To repeat, such views cannot be shown to be inconsistent with the original Greek,—because the scholarship which asserts these views as correct is, equal in authority to any that exists in the world. See Coneybeare & Howson, Life of Paul, Volume 2, pp. 402, note 3; 404, note 3;—454, note 6; 412; 167-8; I Peter 3:15-20;

All this,—first, Mrs. Lee's declaration of what the Lord had shown her on these subjects—& then the confirmation my own examinations have afforded—found a fourth ground of belief.

Fifth. I find (as already, in fact, referred to) that Mrs. Lee's teaching on the subject of the future state, the Brideship, the *risen life, etc., tends plainly to reconcile scriptures which have been fruitful sources of controversies and division in the ✝tian church:—For instance,—while maintaining the truth of the "perseverance of the saints"—showing that the Arminian doctrine of "falling from grace" is but the application of scriptures which teach that beyond question one <u>can</u> fall from the rank of the Bride—that "Election," in a principal, & most important sense, is election to the Brideship,—the exercise of Christ's choice as to His Bride—([unk.] 15:16) & does not include the human addition of "election to perdition;"—that the marriage supper of the Lamb is an <u>event</u>, which when it has once taken place, will never be repeated; that those not ready when it takes place, will never be able thereafter to make up the loss;— they will not have been at the supper;—that in such sense, their loss will be eternal.—In these & other similar results of these teachings was founded a fifth ground of belief.*

<u>Sixth</u>. The fruits of these teachings in individual lives.— Mrs. Lee, my wife & several friends, here & elsewhere,— altogether indeed but a very little company, have prayer-fully, & at last heartily, received these teachings, as from the Lord. Each one of these persons, known to me, has declared that their heart has been searched by these truths as never before: & has expressed the belief that their reception of them has been of incalculable spiritual benefit & the beginning of a deeper Christian life. This is a sixth ground of belief. "By their fruits ye shall know them."

And now my dear friend, at the close of this long letter, I can only regret that a letter is the only way we can at present communicate on these momentous subjects. I should like to talk with you about them.—I believe the Lord is wonderfully opening the truth to us. I believe he has shown us "great & mighty things which I knew not." I praise Him for it, & for the faith which enables me to receive them. But I do not think these truths are for all, as yet. I do not think there are many who would receive them. Therefore this letter is to you personally. I do not say that it is for you alone, & to be shown to no one,—but I do say that I believe the number is very small to whom the showing would be a benefit now. As to this you will have to exercise abundant and prayerful caution. You should not move until the Lord moves you. But, thank God, the times are hastening on and sometime we shall be able to declare it all, even from housetops. May the Lord haste the day! We are all well. My wife, did she know of my writing, would have much love to send.

Yours in Him
H. G. Spafford

APPENDIX C

One possible influence on Horatio Spafford's choice of the theme, it is well with my soul, is the opening line of John Greenleaf Whittier's poem, written just after the Great Chicago Fire, of October, 1871. The first quatrain is quoted in Chapter 17.

A POET'S TRIBUTE
or
CHICAGO
John Greenleaf Whittier, 1871

Men said at vespers: "All is well!"
In one wild night the city fell;
Fell shrines of prayer and marts of gain
Before the fiery hurricane.

On threescore spires had sunset shone,
Where ghastly sunrise looked on none.
Men clasped each other's hands and said:
"The City of the West is dead!"

Brave hearts who fought, in slow retreat,
The fiends of fire from street to street,
Turned, powerless, to the blinding glare,
The dumb defiance of despair.

A sudden impulse thrilled each wire
That signalled round that sea of fire;
Swift words of cheer, warm heart-throbs came;
In tears of pity died the flame!

From East, from West, from South and North,
The messages of hope shot forth,
And, underneath the severing wave,
The world, full-handed, reached to save.

Fair seemed the old; but fairer still
The new, the dreary voice shall fill
With dearer homes than those o'erthrown,
For love shall lay each corner-stone.

Rise, stricken city!—from thee throw
The ashen sackcloth of thy woe;
And build, as to Amphion's strain,
To songs of cheer thy walls again!

How shriveled, in thy hot distress,
The primal sin of selfishness!
How instant rose, to take thy part,
The angel in the human heart!

Ah! not in vain the flames that tossed
Above thy dreadful holocaust;
The Christ again has preached through thee
The Gospel of Humanity!

Then lift once more thy towers on high,
And fret with spires the western sky,
To tell that God is yet with us,
And love is still miraculous!

NOTES

ADDENDUM TO PREFACE

xvi *Complete these dear unfinished tasks of mine, and I perchance may therein comfort you:* Mary Lee Hall, "Turn Again to Life."

PART ONE
LIFE IS A JOURNEY
CHAPTER 1

4   *she became the namesake of her home port Le Havre:* Charles E. Lee, *The Blue Riband* (London: Sampson Low, Marston Co., Ltd., 1930), 69.

4   *"lack nothing in equipment that can conduce to their safety":* "The Awful Collision in the Atlantic," *The Standard,* December 2, 1873.

5   *"wine is given with a liberal hand":* "The Collision in the Atlantic. Abandonment of the *Lochearn*," *Daily Telegraph,* December 8, 1873.

6   *Dr. Dionysius Lardner was demonstrating at the Royal Institution at Liverpool:* John Christopher, *Brunel's Kingdom: In the Footsteps of Britain's Greatest Engineer* (Great Britain: Tempus Publishing Limited, 2006), 119.

8   *"relief from labor, and to recruit his energies by temporary absence":* "The *Ville du Havre.* Action of the Court of Appeals Tribute to the Memory of Judge Peckham," *New-York Times,* December 5, 1873.

8-9 *M. Collodion, The only acknowledged instantaneous caricaturist:* There were numerous newspaper advertisements of his appearance with the Lydia Thompson burlesque troupe at the Olympic Theatre in New York. *New York Times,* August 27, 1873; *The Era,* May 11, 1873; *Reynolds's Weekly Newspaper,* January 5, 1873. He was also recognized in T. Allston Brown, *A History of the New York Stage from the First Performance in 1732 to 1901* (New York: Dodd, Mead and Company, 1903), 164-165.

9   *Madam and Monsieur Theodore Jouanique, married only two years:* "An Ocean Disaster," *New York Times,* December 2, 1873. This article gives brief narratives of the victims of the shipwreck. Stanley Rogers' book *Barenetha Rock* is an excellent source of information about the passengers aboard the *Ville du Havre.* Stanley Rogers, *Barenetha Rock* (London: WH Allen, 1957) 59 (hereafter cited as Rogers).

9   *described her as exceedingly beautiful:* Miss Caroline Turcas was one of the passengers on the *Ville du Havre* who died at sea. Her background was included in the newspaper announcement of her death: "An Ocean Disaster," *New York Times,* December 2, 1873.

9   *The stylish Mrs. Abraham Bininger: Ibid.,* and Rogers 1957, 59.

9   *Helen Wagstaff, a lovely nineteen-year-old, from an established Long Island doctor's family:* "An Ocean Disaster," *New York Times,* December 2, 1873.

10   *"This young American lady has golden hair, . . . Lorriaux chose to call her more biblically, 'The Good Samaritan'":* N. Weiss, *Personal Recollections of the Wreck of the* Ville-du-Havre *and the* Loch-Earn (New York: Anson D. F. Randolph & Company, 1875) 54, 60. Nathanael Weiss's book is much valued as the only personal eyewitness narrative to the voyage and shipwreck of the *Ville du Havre* in 1873. Many descriptions in this book were resourced from Weiss's book (hereafter cited as Weiss).

10   *Young Charles Burritt Waite, son of the owner of famous Brevoort House hotels in Manhattan and Chicago:* "An Ocean Disaster," *New York Times,* December 2, 1873; "Total Loss of an Atlantic Steamer," *Daily Telegraph,* December 2, 1873; and Rogers 1957, 59, 97, 103.

10-11   *Affable B. F. Breeden, of the firm of Breeden & Southwick, . . . Francis Howard, . . . Andrew B. McCreary, . . . William R. Swift:* "The *Ville du Havre.* Interesting Facts Relative to the Lost," *New York Times,* December 4, 1873.

10   *Lizzie Putnam was bound for Paris, intent on living in the Latin Quarter and continuing her studies:* Rogers 1957, 59, 100.

11   *designating Princeton University as primary beneficiary:* Alexander Leitch, *A Princeton Companion,* (Princeton, NJ: Princeton University Press, 1978), 326 (hereafter cited as Leitch).

11   *Mrs. John C. Kennet was traveling:* Rogers 1957, 59.

11 *first secretary of the Belgian legation to Washington, bearded Alfred Barbanson, . . . Francis Howard, . . . Andrew B. McCreary, . . . William R. Swift:* Ibid., 59, 88, 138.

11 *Captain and Mrs. Hammond were accompanied by their three children:* Ibid., 93, 99, 101, 155.

11 *Veteran traveler James Bishop . . . Seventeen-year-old McCloskey Butt . . . Francisco Llado . . . Henry Beltknap:* Information about these individuals can be found in *New York Times* articles "An Ocean Disaster," December 2, and *"Ville du Havre,"* December 4, 1873. In some articles, Mr. Butt's name was reported as McKoskey Brett. References to these passengers are also found in Rogers 1957.

11 *Captain and Mrs. Hunter, from Newport, Rhode Island, had attracted the astonishment of fellow passengers:* "An Ocean Disaster," *New York Times,* December 2, 1873.

12 *From Boston, Charles Mixter, about sixty, his wife, Mrs. Mixter's father:* Ibid.

12 *Miss Madeleine Mixter, "who unfortunately was out":* In letter from Theodore Roosevelt to his father and mother, February 11, 1877.

12 *William Barry "Willie" Culver, the extremely bright, twelve-year-old son of friends Mr. and Mrs. Belden F. Culver:* Bertha Spafford Vester, *Our Jerusalem: An American Family in the Holy City, 1881-1949* (Garden City NY: Doubleday & Company, Inc., 1950), 28 (hereafter cited as Vester).

12 *Mrs. Daniel Goodwin Jr., whose husband was also a Chicago lawyer:* Ibid., 28.

13 *delegates to the Evangelical Alliance Conference of 1873 in New York City:* Rogers 1957, 58.

13 *Weiss had made a study of Protestant Sunday schools and was intrigued with the religious tone of American society. A special soft spot in his heart was reserved for children:* Ibid., 99.

13-14 *Frank Hammond, . . . "French children had black faces":* Ibid.

14 *Dr. Pronier was a professor at the theological seminary in Geneva:* "An Ocean Disaster," *New York Times,* December 2, 1873.

14 *Spaniard, Reverend Carrasco, . . . "the most eminent of Spanish preachers":* *The Glasgow Herald,* December 5, 1873.

14   *the devout Reverend Cook became the ship's spiritual leader:* "The Age We Live In," *The Warrington Guardian,* December 6, 1873 and Weiss 1875, 30.

15   *Weiss, Lorriaux, and Cook, . . . were dubbed "The Three Musketeers":* Rogers 1957, 64.

15   *Henry Sigourney was a young, well-read Boston businessman:* "An Ocean Disaster," *New York Times,* December 2, 1873 and Rogers 1957, 103.

15   *Youthful LeGrand Cramer accompanied his middle-aged aunt from Troy, New York:* Rogers 1957, 104, 130, and 136.

15   *Ruldolf Adolph Witthaus . . . spent most of his time on board reading:* Ibid., 129.

15–16   *Roman Catholic priest was a passenger. Monsieur M.:* Weiss 1875, 83, 113.

CHAPTER 2

19   *a conference in Washington with President James Madison:* Spafford to Madison, Madison Papers (Library of Congress), December 16, 1814; Julian P. Boyd, "Horatio Gates Spafford: Inventor, Author, Promoter of Democracy," *Annals of the American Antiquarian Society,* 51:318, 1941 (hereafter cited as Boyd).

19   *"I have read it [the* Gazetteer*] with pleasure . . . much indebted to you for this fund of valuable information":* Letter from Thomas Jefferson to Horatio G. Spafford, March 17, 1814 in Albert E. Bergh, ed. *The Writings of Thomas Jefferson* (Washington, D.C.: The Thomas Jefferson Memorial Association, 1905).

19   *President James Madison ordered two copies. John Adams called it a monument of industrious research and indefatigable labor, and the volume earned similar plaudits from Josiah Quincy, as well as the presidents of Williams College, the University of Vermont, and many others:* Boyd 1941, 301–302.

20   *1,303 grocery stores and 160 taverns where spiritous liquors were sold.* Intermingled with statistical information, the author shared his editorial opinions, observing, for example, *there is hardly a street, alley, or lane, where a lad may not get drunk for a few cents, and be thanked for his custom, without any questions how he came by his money . . .:*

Horatio Gates Spafford, *A Gazetteer of the State of New York,* (Albany: H. C. Southwick, 1813), 36–37 (hereafter cited as Spafford, *Gazetteer*). More can be found in Boyd 1941.

20   *sectionalism, "likely to become merely political, and improper, because of evil tendency"*: Spafford, *Gazetteer,* 1813.

20   *"Nothing of the present age will outlive it [the crooked axle] in fame"*: Spafford in letter to Thomas Jefferson, March 30, 1814.

20   *"revolutionize the whole world of mechanics"*:   Spafford to James Madison, December 25, 1817; Boyd 1941, 321.

20   *"bladder, nearly filled with air, . . . are best calculated to meet alike the wishes and wants of philosopher, and the mere economist"*: Spafford published his ideas in an eleven-page pamphlet entitled *Some Cursory Observations on the Ordinary Construction of Wheel-Carriages,* 1815.

21   *"unrivalled capacity for turning every scheme into loss and ruin"*: Boyd 1941, 321.

21   *"America is the favorite soil of freedom"*: H. G. Spafford, "Franklin. 1815–1816. On a National School of Science and the Mechanic Arts, and on New Modelling the Patent System," *The American Magazine* 1815–1816, 317; quoted in Boyd 1941, 280.

22   *Spafford's Settlement:* Boyd 1941, 340.

22   *"certain purposes"*: Spafford to Jefferson, Jefferson Papers (Mass Hist Soc), April 12, 1817; Boyd 1941, 332.

23   *prompted the newspaper to write in his obituary years later, "In the death of Dr. Spafford, an interesting, but now deeply afflicted family have sustained an irreparable loss, and a large circle of friends will mourn his departure"*: Lansingburgh Gazette, Aug 1832.

24   The poem "Night," published in *Wellman's,* is not exactly the same as the poem "Night" published in Vester's book, and Spafford is not listed as the author. Instead, the name "Delta" appears as the author of the poem in *Wellman's*. It could not be determined if "Delta" was Spafford's pen name. *Wellman's Literary Miscellany* (Detroit: J. K. Wellman, April 1850); and Vester 1950, 11.

24   *His experience of seeing the heavens as never before was later to become a useful, personal illustration in Spafford's evangelistic work with D. L. Moody:* Vester 1950, 11.

25   *[T]he principal speaker was H. G. Spafford of Chicago, who made a telling and able address:* Ibid., 12.

25-31   *Anna Tubena Larssen:* Story of Anna's childhood is found in Vester 1950, 13-17.

27   *a distaste for Christianity:* Ibid., 15.

28   *"O God, deliver me, and I will never be discontented again":* Ibid.

29   *"had the bluest eyes, and abundant fair hair, . . . Her voice was lovely":* Ibid., 16.

30   *"I wish you were acquainted with Mr. Spafford. He is a true and noble man":* Ibid., 17.

30   *Bertha believed they had been etched with the diamond of her mother's engagement ring:* Ibid.

31   *Lake View was a distinctive place, as a contemporary writer glowingly described it:* The writer was Martha Pirkens Halsey, and her description of Lake View was quoted in Vester 1950, 2.

CHAPTER 3

33   *Bertha Spafford, Anna's daughter, believed that Aunty Sims might have been a contributing factor:* Ibid., 27.

35   *Horatio felt a special urge to have his family's cabins changed:* Ibid., 28.

35   *handed a telegram stating that the man planning to buy the Chicago real estate had suddenly died of heart failure:* Ibid.

CHAPTER 4

Two excellent books that provide valuable insight and information about the shipwreck are Nathanael Weiss's book: *Personal Recollections of the Wreck of the* Ville-du-Havre *and the* Loch-Earn (New York: Anson D. F. Randolph & Company, 1875) and Stanley Rogers' book: *Barenetha Rock* (London: WH Allen, 1957).

36-37   The story about the stowaways is found in Rogers 1957, 60-61.

38   *When he asked the children if they knew Sunday school songs, they*

called out many before settling on "I Want to Be an Angel": Weiss 1875, 26. The hymn was written by Miss Sidney P. Gill around 1854 in Julian 1892, 559.

40-41 "Such is the power of the imagination . . . they regain the charm and freshness of their early years": Weiss 1875, 54.

41 A few passengers voiced their feeling that, perhaps, it was a bad omen: Rogers 1957, 63.

42 One passenger said exaggeratively that the fog was so dense that it actually crept under the bedclothes: Ibid., 93.

43 "One than whom no nearer an angel ever lived": Charles Waite to his parents, December 5, 1873, in William B. Culver, Memorial Scrapbook of the Shipwreck of the Ville du Havre, 1873-1874, Holt-Atherton Special Collections, University of the Pacific Libraries.

43 "She is there to some purpose as usual, smiling, active, . . . sleeps cradled upon the wings of her poetical imagination": Weiss 1875, 68-69.

44 "to take delight in gilding her abundant hair": Ibid., 87-88.

44 "It has often seemed natural to me . . . It is because in the middle of the ocean the sun is the one necessity": Ibid., 86.

44 "Upon land bad weather is nothing in comparison with storms and fogs": Ibid.

44 "The vividness of our impressions while at sea . . . almost entirely on our surroundings": Pastor Weiss's remarks are found on page 86 of his book about the shipwreck, written 1875.

47-48 Pastor Weiss dutifully looked for Mrs. Spafford: The conversation between Weiss and Anna Spafford can be found in Weiss 1875, 98-101.

49-50 Monsieur Ouadint: Information on the ship's doctor and his concerns about the water line can be found in Rogers 1957, 93-94, 105.

50 "This is the boat the stowaways hid themselves in": This remark and those that followed by Henry Sigourney are in Rogers 1957, 103.

50 "They seem to be each man for himself. One feels very unsafe with them. They seem so undependable": Ibid., 104.

51   *Captain Marius Surmont,* spelled "Surmount" in some publications.

51   *"[N]othing impresses me with the idea of infinity, of the power of God and the weakness of man, as does the ocean":* Weiss 1875, 104.

51   *"Yes, that is very true, and I cannot tell you how often, since we set sail, I have felt our absolute dependence upon God alone":* Ibid.

52   "Santa Lucia" was transcribed by Teodoro Cottrau and first published in 1849.

53   *Most passengers would have agreed with Madeleine Mixter, who later recalled that the sea was calm, the heavens were covered with stars, and "all seemed to favor us":* Written in a letter from Madeleine Mixter to her uncles, Dr. Hall Curtis and Nathaniel W. Curtis, November 29, 1873. A typed copy of the letter is among family papers inherited by Oliver Wolcott Jr., from his grandmother, Helen Mixter Appleton. The letter was published in Oliver Wolcott, Jr., " 'A Sad Tale that Must be Told' Madeleine Curtis Mixter's Account of the Loss of the *Ville du Havre,*" *The American Neptune* 57(3):229–236, 1997 (hereafter cited as Wolcott).

CHAPTER 5

54–63   Conversations among the passengers and crew during the shipwreck were quoted from Rogers 1957, Vester 1950, and Weiss 1875.

CHAPTER 6

64   *"We feel ourselves whirled round and round as if in a vast funnel":* Weiss 1875, 116.

64–65   *"Some tremendous force parted us as we went down together":* Mrs. Mary Adams Bulkley to Mother, November 28, 1873.

66   *"There was a sudden surging of the water":* Mixter to her uncles, Dr. Hall Curtis and Nathaniel W. Curtis, November 29, 1873; Wolcott 1997.

66   *Helen was rescued crying aloud, "I do not wish to be drowned. I will not be drowned. . . . I didn't want to be drowned!":* Weiss 1875, 122, and Rogers 1957, 137.

66   *"Yes, but do not pull me under":* Wolcott 1997, 234.

66 *"I fear it was a cramp—oh! it is so hard to think he was almost saved and then lost again!!"*: Ibid.

67 *"Take hold of my coat"*: Rogers 1957, 137.

69 *"He's pretty far gone, but he's alive"*: Ibid., 139.

72 *When the Captain again called out, one of the seamen replied,* "Comprends pas": Ibid., 149.

CHAPTER 7

74-75 *"As I recognized faces of the passengers about me, I felt as if it were a resurrection of the dead. . . . Not a toothbrush among us; . . . the rest are in woolen stockings"*: Mrs. Mary Adams Bulkley to Mother, November 28, 1873.

75 *"Suddenly, [l]adies and gentlemen who before had never known a single privation were standing there shivering and destitute"*: Charles Waite to his parents, November 29, 1873, in William B. Culver, Memorial Scrapbook of the Shipwreck of the *Ville du Havre*, 1873-1874, Holt-Atherton Special Collections, University of the Pacific Libraries.

75-76 *Almost hysterical, she thought of jumping into the sea to die with her girls if they were not to be found:* Weiss 1875, 126.

76 *As she wept, she said, "God gave me my four little daughters; it is He who has taken them from me. He will make me understand and accept His will"*: Charles Waite to parents, November 29, 1873 and Weiss 1875, 140.

78 *would be judged to have died of a broken heart:* Frank Warren Hackett, *Reminiscences of the Geneva Tribunal of Arbitration 1872. The Alabama Claims* (Boston: Houghton Mifflin Company, 1911), 11.

80 *Captain Robertson sent out a small boat from the* Loch Earn: Rogers 1957, 160.

82 *"He is gravely hurt":* Lorriaux and Cook faithfully tended to their friend Weiss. Ibid., 161.

82 *"He who arrives first will send word to the wife of the other"*: Rogers 1957, 162 and Weiss 1875, 139.

83 *Mrs. Mary Bulkley . . . pleading with the Captain to remain a little longer:* Weiss 1875, 141.

84 *Lucky Urquhart:* Rogers 1957, 188.

84 *"No words can render the meek and submissive attitude of the ladies after the catastrophe. . . . I will submit to His will":* The Scotsman, December 4, 1873.

85 *"I have a pair of gentleman's slippers":* Mrs. Bulkley to Mother, November 28, 1873.

85-86 *"We all escaped with a few bruises":* Mixter to Uncles 1873 and published in Wolcott 1997.

86 *"It is mysterious to think why have I been saved, when with Lallie my life's work is done":* Mrs. Bulkley to Mother, November 28, 1873.

86 *"Finally, when the last boat came, I gave up all hope of ever seeing Julia [his sister] again":* Waite to parents 1873.

86 *"My greatest sorrow":* Ibid.

87 *hold a Thanksgiving service the next day:* Rogers 1957, 197-198.

87 *"I believe that the chain of circumstances that led the* Trimountain *to the scene of the shipwreck was not chance, but part of a preordained scheme":* Rogers 1957, 198-200. See Appendix A for complete remarks. Captain Urquhart memoirs: *Reminiscences. The Merchant Marine Ocean Travel in the Sixties and Now* (New York: Knickerbocker Press, 1910) (hereafter cited as Urquhart).

CHAPTER 8

88 *"No." Then, he explained what had happened:* Rogers 1957, 165.

89 *"I am scarcely thirty years old, and I have been shipwrecked three times in my short life,":* Rogers 1957, 170 and Weiss 1875, 153.

89 *"Certainly but all that I could understand of what he said to me in French was that he did not think the* Ville du Havre *was badly injured":* Weiss 1875, 153.

92 British Queen's *Captain Marsters:* In Rogers' book the *British Queen's* Captain name is "Masters." In Weiss's book, it is "Marsters."

92 *"Thanks to your prayers, we are saved. God has heard our prayers":* Weiss 1875, 180-181.

93   *"The wind had changed, bringing them nearer the track of ships"*:   *The Christian,* December 18, 1873, 5.

CHAPTER 9

95   *"Saved alone"* The two-word version of the telegram became family lore—perpetuated even by the Spafford's daughter Bertha in her book. Vester 1950, 40.

96   The articles were: "Dreadful Collision at Sea," *The Birmingham* [England] *Daily Mail,* December 1, 1873; "Total Loss of an Atlantic Steamer," London's *Daily Telegraph,* December 2, 1873; "The Awful Collision in the Atlantic," *The Standard,* December 2, 1873.

96-97   *Hurried from their berths:* "Collision in the Atlantic," *Daily Telegraph,* December 4, 1873.

97   *"felt her daughters' reproof"*: Vester 1950, 41–42.

98   *"inexpressibly painful to see the survivors"*: "Awful Collision in the Atlantic," *The Standard,* December 2, 1873.

98-99   *It would seem that all the bankers:* "The Awful Calamity in the Atlantic." *The Standard,* December 3, 1873.

99   *"not amid cheers, but never were hats more respectfully raised"*: Ibid.

100   *The spokesman, who was a man of colour, explained:* Ibid.

101   *"made a very feeling and touching reference"*: *The Christian,* December 18, 1873, 6.

101-102 *"turned it to good account in urging upon the unsaved among the hearers the uncertainty of life and the blessedness of being in Christ"*: Ibid.

102   *Moody, touring the Holy Land:* Vester 1950, 157.

102   *noticed a puddle of tears at his feet:* Ibid, 48.

104   *"I am strongly threatened with inflammation of the lungs. I have a terrible fever—BUT ALL IS WELL"*: Cook to Weiss, January 1874, as published in Weiss 1875, 208.

104   *He dedicated the volume to "you who perished on the fatal night of November 22d"*: Weiss 1875.

105 *"And we have not even the consolation of having the bodies of those for whom we mourn":* "Ville du Havre," *The Birmingham Daily Mail,* December 9, 1873.

105-106 *"The catastrophe which befel the* Ville du Havre": "The Collision in the Atlantic. Abandonment of the *Lochearn," Daily Telegraph,* December 8, 1873.

106 *"should cause them always to be prepared for their last hour": Ibid.*

106 *Mr. Waite and his family were deeply affected during the services: "Ville du Havre," New York Times,* December 4, 1873.

106 *that relief fund had grown to almost $4,600:* "The *Ville du Havre* Relief Fund," *Chicago Daily Tribune,* January 13, 1874.

107 *She [the* Loch Earn*] was on her course from Liverpool to the United States:* "Awful Collision in the Atlantic," *The Standard,* December 2, 1873.

107-108 *"narrative may be taken as the collective statement of the officers and men of the* Loch Earn": "Collision in the Atlantic," *The Standard,* December 8, 1873. It is printed verbatim in the Marius Surmont, "Letter to the Editor of the *Daily Telegraph*–The *Ville du Havre* Disaster," *Glasgow Herald,* December 15, 1873.

109 *In the account given by the purser of the* Ville du Havre: "The *Ville du Havre," The Scotsman,* December 4, 1873.

110 *"[A]fter a full examination it was decided we were remediless":* D. Goodwin Sr., "Steamship Disasters. To the Editor of the *Chicago Tribune," Chicago Daily Tribune,* May 23, 1875, 16.

PART TWO
TRAGEDY AFTER THE TRAGEDY

CHAPTER 10

113-114 *"Day after tomorrow will be Thanksgiving Day":* Vester 1950, 41.

115 *"I am glad to trust the Lord when it will cost me something":* Spafford to Maggie Lee 1873 and Vester 1950, 41.

115 *"Oh, how sad my heart is without my birds":* Ibid., 44.

116   *declaring the theological conviction that his troubles were not designed by God:* Spafford to Maggie, December 3, 1873.

116   *go to their Lake View home to put away all the children's possessions:* Spafford to Frederickson, December 1873, published in Vester 1950, 45.

117   *likely never got over the sudden unusual death of his namesake:* Daniel Goodwin Jr., "Sketch of Rev. William Barry," *Magazine of American History with Notes and Queries* 13:283-24, 1885.

118   *"On Thursday last we passed over the spot where she went down":* Spafford to Frederickson, December 1873, published in Vester 1950, 45.

118   *"I am convinced that my wife and children perished in their stateroom":* Weiss 1875, 207.

119   *"Yes, I am sure they are there":* Ibid., 207-208.

CHAPTER 11

120   *Goodbye, dear sweet Lake View. I will never see you again:* Vester 1950, 29.

121   *The Hon. Oliver H. Picher has recently resigned:* Chicago Tribune, July 19, 1874.

122   *"Prayer Meetings: How to Conduct Them," H. G. Spafford was among those who expressed their views:* "Conference of Christian Workers," *Chicago Tribune,* April 22, 1876.

122   *"The weather and counter attractions may atone for the size of the audience":* Regarding the Dime Lecture, *Chicago Tribune,* January 12, 1875.

122   *"The Life and Times of Oliver Cromwell" in the chapel at Wheaton College, with a twenty-five-cent admission charge: Chicago Daily Tribune,* January 8 and January 31, 1875.

122   *he was the featured speaker, Sunday, December 19, 1875 at Farwell Hall: Chicago Tribune,* December 18, 1875.

123   *The theme stuck in Bliss's mind, and gave rise to words and music for a song that became much loved among church people of that time:*

Memoirs of Philip P. Bliss, ed. D. W. Whittle (New York: A. S. Barnes & Co., 1877), 83–84.

124 *Spafford conducted evangelistic services in the small communities of Paw Paw and Lawton, Michigan:* John V. Farwell, *Early Recollections of Dwight L. Moody* (Chicago: The Winona Publishing Company, 1907), 165–166 (hereafter cited as Farwell).

125 *It has long been suggested that the trip was proposed:* Vester 1950, 27.

126 *our response refining our own definitions of* self; *of* character, *of* personality *and* purpose: Viktor E. Frankl, *Man's Search for Meaning* (Boston: Beacon Press, 1959).

126 *"I feel more and more that the absorbing pursuit of anything earthly is not well for one's spiritual life":* Horatio to Anna, November 25, 1873.

126 *Horatio was involved in a bold move to depose the Reverend W. C. Young:* "Fullerton Avenue Church," *Chicago Daily Tribune,* July 8, 1876. This article gives insight into the feelings of the members after the vote. Dr. Hedges told members that he had no personal feeling in the matter and would have changed his vote if he could. Most of the members were thoroughly "disgusted" with the instigators of this trouble. Notable among the instigators would have been Horatio Spafford.

127 *The Chicago "Overcomers" had ties with a similar group in Valparaiso, Indiana, not far from Chicago:* "Band of Male and Female Pilgrims to Start To-Day," *Daily Inter-Ocean,* August 17, 1881.

128 *"Moody and his followers are all wrong, as well as all the churches":* Ibid.

128 *Baptism is ignored: Ibid.*

129 *"She found herself on her feet":* Draft of letter from Spafford to Wadsworth, February 21, 1879. These sentences were written in pencil and not included in the final letter to Miss Wadsworth, found in Appendix B, dated March 17, 1879. Envelope 16–10, Drawer 16, American Colony in Jerusalem Collection, Manuscript Division, Library of Congress.

131 *He had, even perhaps unknowingly, come to claim his sister's views as his own:* "Band of Male and Female Pilgrims," *Daily Inter-Ocean,* August 17, 1881.

131–132 *"At the head of it are a few educated, godly people":* Ibid.

132　*two publications represented the views of the Overcomers:* Our Rest *of Chicago, and* The Restitution *of Plymouth, Indiana:* "Curious Sect," *Chicago Daily Tribune,* April 8, 1884.

132　*officially expelled from the Fullerton Avenue Presbyterian Church:* Vester 1950, 56.

132　*was someone's curious offer to adopt her, as though to relieve the Spaffords of responsibility:* Ibid., 55.

133　*"instead of finding solace, they found themselves ostracized, victims of the prevailing church doctrine that judged their anguish as divine retribution for the 'sins'"* : This was Anna Grace's explanation for her grandparents' search for a simple religious life and why they left Chicago. Jonathan Broder, "A Family, a Colony, a Life of Good Works in the Holy City," *Smithsonian* 27:128, 1997.

133　*"the Spaffords broke with their church in a bitter public quarrel":* Elias Antar, "Out of Pain and Loss, Compassion and Love . . . The Story of Bertha Vester," *Aramco World* 18(4):26, July–August, 1967 (hereafter cited as Antar). Bertha was only three years old when the family traveled to Jerusalem. At best, the information she had about the family's departure had to be second-hand.

133　*"Although staunch Presbyterians the Spaffords":* Antar 1967, 26.

134　*a transcript of a sermon by The Reverend H. M. Collison, Fullerton Avenue pastor, in February, 1880:* H. M. Collison, "Eternal Punishment," *Chicago Tribune,* February 2, 1880.

134　*children had made professions of their Christian faith:* Vester 1950, 22.

135　*After the loss of his children:* "Sunday School Items," *The Quiver,* November 1888, 53.

135　*"The people of the Fullerton Avenue church have especial reason to remember Mr. Spafford, as he was one of the organizers of our society,"* The Quiver *then quoted from an article that appeared in the* Lake View Telephone: *"Many of our citizens will remember Horatio Spafford, one of the leaders of the overcomers, a religious sect that attracted considerable attention at one time":* Ibid., 96.

135　*What a commentary upon the power of consecrated fidelity:* "Arrows from the Study," *The Quiver,* March 1889, 84.

136   *This pamphlet bears evidence throughout of great care:* Spafford 1878.

137   *"it was pronounced the work of an infidel":*   "Curious Sect," *Chicago Daily Tribune,* April 8, 1884.

137   *"I am glad to trust the Lord when it will cost me something":* Spafford to Maggie Lee, 1873 and Vester 1950, 41 (See page 115).

CHAPTER 12

Several court cases involved the Spaffords, both directly and indirectly. Court testimonies provide interesting insights into their lives. 1)*Murphy, Mary F. and Anna Spafford v. Dr. Samuel P. Hedges et al.* Il, G–142, 175 (Circuit Court of Cook County, IL 1896); 2)*Connecticut Mutual Life Insurance Company v. Horatio G. Spafford et al.* 72.688 (Superior Court of Cook County, IL 1897); 3)*Cornell v. Green,* 163 U.S. 75. (1896).

139   *H. G. Spafford at Merchants National Bank of Chicago:* H. Spafford to E. Spafford, 1875.

139   *Horatio and Anna Spafford conveyed a mortgage of a "large amount of real estate" to the Connecticut Mutual Life Insurance Company:* Conn Mutual v. Spafford et al 1879, 171–173.

140   *"To Father and his associates in the real estate venture, it [the Great Fire] was a calamity":* Vester 1950, 9.

140   *"He acquired wealth in his profession":* "Died in Jerusalem," *New York Times,* October 22, 1888.

140   *they owned an undivided one-third interest in five additional lots with Horatio's law partner, John P. Wilson, and one with Carl Marlow:* Deed between Martin Andrews and Caroline W. Andrews and the City of Chicago and Horatio G. Spafford of County of Cook, State of Illinois, 1872.

140   *proceeded to default on semiannual mortgage payments for the lots:* Bill of Complaint, Case 72.688, Superior Court of Cook County, State of Illinois, February 25, 1879.

141   *All the Wrightwood lots, including the five with an undivided one-third interest, were auctioned off:* Public Notice of Land Sale, June 23, 1879, Superior Court of the State of Illinois County of Cook at the southeast corner of LaSalle and Washington Streets in Chicago at two o'clock the afternoon.

141 *Horatio borrowed $2,000 from his former law partner, Henry O. McDaid:* Spafford notes, 1878.

141 *bankruptcy declaration of the Union Screw and Bolt Company:* "The Courts," *Chicago Daily Tribune,* April 5, 1873.

141 *J. Young Scammon, the latter being president of the Marine Company and president of the Mechanics' National Bank of Chicago. Chicago Daily Tribune,* April 5, 1873.

142 *commodious and attractive structure:* "The Sears Building," *Chicago Daily Tribune,* March 12, 1876.

143 *"Mr. and Mrs. Moody talk of you affectionately":* Vester 1950, 52.

143 *coldness arose in his relationship to Spafford about 1877:* Murphy v. Hedges 1896, August 24, 1897 Complete Whittle testimony on pages 207–214 of the document.

144 *when she had only thirty cents. . . . Satan tried to frighten me concerning their lack of money, but Mr. Sankey sent us $10.00.:* Anna Spafford Diary, August 7 and August 23, 1878.

144 *Susan Gridley, bought the lots from Spafford for the sum of $10,000, the sale recorded later, March 25, 1879: Chicago Tribune,* March 27, 1879.

144 *Anna Spafford confirmed . . . that Horatio had given up real estate involvement a few years before 1881.: Murphy v. Hedges* 1896, 25.

144–145 *"As you know Mr. Spafford stood before the noon-prayer meeting some years ago [in Chicago] & declared that the Lord would pay all his debts":* Amelia Gould to Dr. Samuel P. Hedges from Jerusalem, June 2, 1886.

145 *"That he was in desperate straits for money is shown by his paying off one mortgage for $5,000 on his homestead and raising one for $10,000 without making any improvements on the homestead":* Taylor, January 29, 1900, 44.

145 *notified by H. R. Chandler that rent payments should be directed to him as agent for Mrs. Hetty H. R. Green:* "They Claim Title to Valuable Land," *Chicago Journal,* January 15, 1898.

146 *Dr. Hedges told a Court years later that Horatio Spafford had never informed him of any mortgage: Murphy v. Hedges* 1896, 259, 266–267.

147 *"I direct said trustees to hold the said one-ninth share of my estate":* Lawrence 1874.

148 *"the widow and heirs of Mr. Spafford are cognizant of the rights of the complainant":* "Spafford's Name in Court Again," *Chicago Daily Tribune,* April 28, 1895.

148 *Mrs. J. P. Wills, a divorced woman, . . .Spafford "acted as her friend,":* Murphy v. Hedges 1896, Whittle's complete testimony on pages 207–214 of the document, August 24, 1897.

149 *probably used to tide over his real estate speculations, likewise the trust funds of Mrs. Murphy, Mrs. Wills, and Miss Kopse:* Taylor 1900.

149 *"We were asked to pray that the Lord would deliver him from those debts and from those that were persecuting him":* Rounds testimony June 16, 1897, *Murphy v. Hedges* 1896, 146.

149 *"We never covered it up. We confessed it as a sin before all the people":* Anna Spafford testimony 1896, *Murphy v. Hedges* 1896, 19-20.

150 *"But alas. It was of no avail":* Mary Murphy to Anna Spafford, April 16, 1908.

150 *"Prayed with Mr. Page for the payment of all debts":* Horatio Spafford diary, July 8, 1882.

CHAPTER 13

152 *"If there was no sniffle that meant 'No;' and if, on the other hand, the sniffle was given, that meant 'Yes' ":* "Cash for a Colony," *Chicago Daily News,* March 9, 1894.

152 *"Yes, the Spirit has spoken to me,":* "Life in the City of Zion," *Chicago Daily News,* May 14, 1895.

152 *"It would be utterly impossible to explain these things to the ordinary, uninitiated mortal":* "Holy City Their Home," *Chicago Daily News,* May 15, 1895.

153 *"through Mrs. Spafford that the second coming of Christ was only a month or two off, . . . and that Dr. Samuel P. Hedges should bear their expenses":* "Cash for a Colony," *Chicago Daily News,* March 9, 1894.

153   *"From every side, as by concerted agreement, everybody came to Mrs. Spafford with their trials, doubts, fears, etc., etc.":* Hedges to Spafford, May 25, 1881.

155   *"there would be wonderful things take place—an acknowledgment of them [the Overcomers] by Divine revelation," . . . "the whole world would know it by electricity.":* Murphy vs. Hedges 1986, Dr. Hedges testimony, 266.

155-156   *Mrs. George Rounds, Dr. and Mrs. Hedges, and Mr. Charles Gaylord were members of the group of Overcomers who stayed in Chicago. Others included Mr. and Mrs. V. Mumford Moore, . . . Dr. W. A. Bonniwell:* Murphy vs. Hedges 1986, testimony.

157   *"Simple people," . . . Anna fashioned the rules for this new community:* Murphy vs. Hedges 1986, testimony. The description of Anna's authority is confirmed in several publications, including Ariel, 1996; *Chicago Daily,* October 18, 1894, Jane Fletcher Geniesse, *American Priestess. The Extraordinary Story of Anna Spafford* and the *American Colony in Jerusalem* (New York: Doubleday, 2008) (hereafter cited Geniesse).

158   *"He was seeking peace and solace for mind and soul":* Vester 1950, 56.

159   *"What does it mean?":* Geniesse 2008, 139.

159   *Finally, wet with perspiration, she returned to his bedside to hear him say, "Annie, I have experienced a great joy; I have seen wonderful things":* Vester 1950, 154.

159   *"He knows it all now. He has seen Him face to face. We must not sorrow like those who have not hope":* Ibid., 155.

CHAPTER 14

161-162   *"I find it difficult to interpret to this modern generation Father's and Mother's attitude":* Vester 1950, 51.

162   *There is little evidence of response:* Horatio G. Spafford diary, 1882.

162   *temporarily unsettling the confidence of the women in the Overcomers:* Hedges to Spafford, May 25, 1881.

163   *"go and shake hands with you today":* Vester 1950, 43-44, 47.

163 *claimed in obvious error that Hannah Whitall Smith of Philadelphia, is "among the noticeable followers":* "Band of Male and Female Pilgrims," *Daily Inter-Ocean,* August 17, 1881.

163 *"wrote Mr. Bell enclosing copy letter to Mrs. H. W. Smith":* Note in Spafford diary, Spafford to Bell, November 1, 1882.

163 *"Spaffordites," which Hannah maintained under the general file heading, "Fanaticism":* Papers of Hannah Whitall Smith, Fanaticism: Spaffordites, Box 8, Folder 19, 1883–1907.

163 *"Spaffordites" file was apparently supplied by Frances E. Willard, longtime president of the Women's Christian Temperance Union, and friend of the Spaffords:* Vester 1950, 22.

163 *"Dearest Hannah: I know you were interested":* Willard to Smith, December 22, 1897.

164 *"said to have been once a Norwegian servant girl, . . .":* "Still Long for the Holy Land," *Chicago Daily News,* December 15, 1897.

164 *"We have met lately . . . Of course, nothing of the kind took place, but nothing daunted they have gone on":* Hannah Whitall Smith to an unidentified recipient, 1885, quoted in *A Religious Rebel,* ed. Logan Pearsall Smith (London: Nisbet & Co. Ltd., 1949).

165 *"The original leader":* Ray Strachey, *Religious Fanaticism: Extracts from the Papers of Hannah Whitall Smith* (London: Faber & Gwyer, 1928).

165–166 *Mr. Blackstone has been in to my office:* Hedges to Spafford, November 3, 1881.

CHAPTER 15

167 *"No one here at this blessed house has the sign & you don't know how strange it seems":* Hedges to Horatio Spafford, November 3, 1881.

168 *as Satanic, excepting Mrs. Doyle, and Mr. Clancy is barely holding on to some of the teachings:* Hedges to Horatio Spafford, November 23, 1881.

168 *Mrs. Rounds's strong endorsement:* "Band of Male and Female Pilgrims," *Daily Inter-Ocean,* August 17, 1881.

168 *"Quite universal, I think":* Murphy v. Hedges 1896, 259.

169 *"Yes, that had been a positive revelation by Mrs. Spafford": Murphy v. Hedges* 1896, 266–267.

170 *he and his sister began receiving a hundred dollars per month:* Vester 1950, 191.

170 *"Other industries were started, and little by little, with diligence, the Colony emerged from poverty":* Ibid., 177.

171 *"The American Colony was a prosperous and respected force in Jerusalem":* Ibid., 205.

171 *"Is on Its Last Legs. Spafford's Jerusalem Colony Apparently Going to Pieces": Chicago Daily,* October 18, 1894.

172 *"I am not going to die. The resurrection is near, when we will have the dead back with us":* Edith Larsson, quoted in Helga Dudman and Ruth Kark, *The American Colony. Scenes from a Jerusalem Saga* (Jerusalem: The Israel Map and Publishing Co., 1998), 224 (hereafter cited as Dudman).

172 *Bertha unilaterally installed an "Expulsion Policy":* Dudman 1998, 228.

173 *It later became known that Bertha and Frederick Vester had paid the arbiter one hundred thousand dollars:* Ibid., 236.

CHAPTER 16

176 *Anna told the court in the 1895 that they had moved into that residence when they were first married, renting it for the first year or so: Murphy v. Hedges* 1896, 22.

176 *the Spafford property, including the five-acre lot on which the house was located:* Everett Chamberlin, *Chicago and Its Suburbs* (Chicago: T. A. Hungerford & Co., 1874), 351 (hereafter cited as Chamberlin).

176 *The opinion of William J. Haerther, . . . worth fifty thousand dollars in the 1890s: Murphy v. Hedges 1896,* court testimony.

177 *The North half of Lot Nine . . . the South half of the property was approximately an additional five acres:* Elliott 1896.

177 *referenced as "a large amount of real estate":* Exhibits 22, 23, 24, *Conn Mutual v. Spafford et al* 1879, 171–173.

178   *lost his law offices, a valuable library, and most of the money he had invested in real estate just before the disaster:* Antar 1967.

178   *"And after the Fire was over, she . . . they were very philanthropic and good, wholly religious people":* Bair interview with Mrs. Vester, 2005–2007.

179   *Property values and the appeal of the area north of Fullerton Avenue . . . appear actually to have been enhanced by the Fire:* Chamberlin 1874.

179   *the "mountains of litigation" that surrounded the possible expansion of Lincoln Park:* Chamberlin 1874, 339.

179–180 *"Mr. Culver and Mr. Stark I think and Mr. Spafford bought a large block [sic] of real estate":* Murphy v. Hedges, 1896.

183   *"He [Horatio] hoped by silver legislation, back in the time of gold resumption, that if he could carry it that he would get out of it":* Murphy v. Hedges 1896, Daniel W. Whittle testimony, August 24, 1897, 210.

184   *"Mr. Spafford was afraid of being arrested":* Murphy v. Hedges 1896, 144.

184   *"accusing Horatio of having "sneaked off to Canada":* Murphy v. Hedges, 1896.

184   *Anna Spafford and William Rudy claimed the trip had been planned and passage booked two months prior to the date of departure:* Murphy v. Hedges, 1896.

185   *Prior to his visiting Mr. Spafford, . . . that the pilgrims will have started before this article sees the light:* "Band of Male and Female Pilgrims," *Daily Inter-Ocean*, August 17, 1881.

186   *expressed surprise that Horatio had made no mention of returning about December 1, 1881:* Dr. Hedges to Spafford, November 3, 1881.

187   *"So zealous did Mr. Spafford become that he decided to go to Jerusalem with his wife and the one remaining daughter, and there await the coming of the Lord. Mr. Spafford died there not long afterward":* Ira D. Sankey, *Sankey's Story of the Gospel Hymns and of Sacred Songs and Solos* (Philadelphia: Sunday School Times Company, 1906), 119 (hereafter cited as Sankey).

188   *"It would seem that a sight of it, without other proofs, would be*

sufficient to suggest to one . . . the set time to favor Zion had not come": Spafford to Chandler, April 13, 1886, later published in the *Daily Inter-Ocean* and in a Mormon youth magazine, *Autumn Leaves,* January, 1888.

188 *"The busy world has taken little notice of it":* Spafford to Chandler, April 13, 1886.

188 *testified in court in the 1890s that she never would have allowed Annie to go with them, if she had known they were going to Jerusalem:* "They Claim Title," *Chicago Journal,* January 15, 1898.

189 *Messiah's return, inasmuch as the pyramids were built by Hebrew slaves:* Spafford to Smyth, 1887.

189 *endeavor to get the wrong out of ourselves as much as possible and find out what it is:* "Fight for a Fortune," *Daily Inter-Ocean,* April 18, 1895.

189 *We felt that God was going to fulfill in Jerusalem concerning the Jews and the building again:* Murphy v. Hedges 1896.

190 *"I told him also that we were expecting you about the 1ˢᵗ of Dec.":* Hedges to Spafford, November 3, 1881.

191 *claim of Bertha Spafford Vester that the remainder group disbanded after a failed plea for divine healing of a baby:* Vester 1950, 58.

192 *The homestead of Dr. Samuel P. Hedges at Buena Park:* "Old Homestead Sold," *Chicago Daily Tribune,* August 31, 1902.

CHAPTER 17

196 *It makes a dramatic saga:* Vester 1950, 45.

196 *he made no reference to a poem, nor to the sentiments expressed in the poem:* Spafford to Frederickson, 1873.

196 *Horatio confessed to having been "deeply agitated":* Weiss 1875, 207.

197 *he did not refer to a poem, or quote any phrase from it. Nor was the poem published as a poem, as were many of Horatio's creations.:* Vester 1950, 45.

197 *present at Farwell Hall, Chicago, in November 1876, the night P. P. Bliss, composer of the music, first sang the song as a solo:* Sankey 1906, 119.

197 *"discussing Gospel truth or plans of work, or in Bliss's room listening to some new song":* Whittle 1877, 76.

198 *In 1876, when we returned to Chicago . . . arranged for their hymn books mostly by correspondence:* Ibid., 75.

199 *The shock and sorrow:* R. C. Morgan, "Letters from Palestine," *The Christian,* 1891.

199 *"On my table lie the proof-sheets of* Gospel Hymns No. 2*":* Bliss to Whittle December 20, 1876, quoted in Whittle 1877.

200 *"Twenty Reasons for Believing that the Coming of the Lord is Nigh,"* also advertised *"Twenty Reasons . . .the Lord is Near."*

201 *a disaster that claimed almost one hundred lives at Ashtabula, Ohio, December 29, 1876:* Thomas E. Corts, ed., *Bliss and Tragedy* (Birmingham, AL: Samford University Press, 2003).

206 *"I am strongly threatened with inflammation of the lungs. I have a terrible fever—but all is well":* Weiss 1875, 208.

206 *It is well; the will of God be done:* Sankey 1906.

206 *First known as "A Poet's Tribute," it is often cited in more modern compendia with the title, "Chicago":* John Greenleaf Whittier, *The Complete Poetical Works of John Greenleaf Whittier* (Boston: Houghton, Osgood and Company 1878), 372.

APPENDIX A

211 *Captain Urquhart noted that Mrs. Spafford, the only one saved of this family, tells of a most remarkable experience she had while struggling in the water:* Urquhart 1910, 33.

211-212 *"I had no vision during the struggle":* Vester 1950, 36.

212 *But from all these scenes of cruelty and chaos, . . . easy to live on the earth is unity, unity, unity:* S. Lagerlöf, "Christian Love as a Power for the Reconciliation of Peoples," *The Stockholm Conference 1925. The Official Report of the Universal Christian Conference on Life and Work held in Stockholm, 19–30 August, 1925,* edited by G. K. A. Bell (London: Oxford University Press, 1926), 552.

215–216 *at the last minute he could not throw off the sense that he must change the rooms:* Vester 1950, 28.

216 *imagined that the ship was lower in the water:* Rogers 1957, 94.

216 *Pronier had spoken of his misgivings about the voyage ... Carrasco ... would never again take to the sea:* Ibid., 62.

216 *his bequest financed construction of Murray Hall on the Princeton campus in 1879:* Leitch 1978, 326.

APPENDIX B

218 Spafford to Wadsworth, March 17, 1879. This letter in Horatio's own hand is among the papers in the American Colony in Jerusalem Collection, Manuscript Division, Library of Congress. Unfortunately, Miss Wadsworth's letter to Horatio, which called forth his response, does not appear to have survived.

BIBLIOGRAPHY

"The Age We Live In," *The Warrington Guardian,* December 6, 1873.

Antar, Elias. "Out of Pain and Loss, Compassion and Love . . . The Story of Bertha Vester." *Aramco World* 18, no. 4 (July–August 1967):24–33.

Ariel, Yaakov and Ruth Kark: "Messianism, Holiness, Charisma, and Community: The American–Swedish Colony in Jerusalem, 1881–1933." In *Church History.* Edited by Jerald C. Brauer and Martin E. Marty. Ephrata, PA: Science Press, December 1996.

"Arrows from the Study," *The Quiver,* March 1889.

"The Awful Collision in the Atlantic," *The Standard,* December 2, 1873.

"The Awful Calamity in the Atlantic," *The Standard,* December 3, 1873.

"A Band of Male and Female Pilgrims to Start To-Day—On for Jerusalem," *Daily Inter-Ocean,* August 17, 1881.

Bergh, Albert E., ed. *The Writings of Thomas Jefferson.* Washington, D.C.: The Thomas Jefferson Memorial Association, 1905.

Blackstone, William E. *Jesus Is Coming.* New York: Fleming H. Revell Company, 1908.

Bliss, P. P., ed. *Sunshine for Sunday Schools: A New Collection of Original and Selected Music.* Chicago: George F. Root & Sons, 1873.

Bliss, P. P. and Ira D. Sankey. *Gospel Hymns No. 2.* Cincinnati: John Church & Co. and New York: Biglow & Main, 1876.

Boyd, Julian P. "Horatio Gates Spafford: Inventor, Author, Promoter of Democracy." *Annals of the American Antiquarian Society* 51 (1941):279–350.

 Broder, Jonathan. "A Family, a Colony, a Life of Good Works in the Holy City." *Smithsonian* 27 (1997):120–136.

Brown, T. Allston. *A History of the New York Stage from the First Performance in 1732 to 1901.* New York: Dodd, Mead and Company, 1903.

Bulkley, Mary Keiza Adams to Mother, Sarah Susannah MacMurphey Adams, November 28, 1873, American Colony in Jerusalem Collection, Manuscript Division, Library of Congress.

Burlingham, Maria-Ann [Horatio G. Spafford]. *The Mother-in-Law: or, Memoirs of Madam de Morville.* Boston: A. Bowen, 1817.

"Cash for a Colony," *Chicago Daily News,* March 9, 1894.

Chamberlin, Everett. *Chicago and Its Suburbs.* Chicago: T. A. Hungerford & Co, 1874.

Chicago City Directory Supplement. Chicago: Robert Fergus, May 1856.

Chicago Daily Tribune, January 8 and January 31, 1875.

Chicago Tribune, January 12, 1875.

Chicago Tribune, March 27, 1879.

Chicago Tribune, July 19, 1874.

Chicago Tribune, December 18, 1875.

The Christian, December 18, 1873.

Christopher, John. *Brunel's Kingdom. In the Footsteps of Britain's Greatest Engineer.* Great Britain: Tempus Publishing Limited, 2006.

"The Collision in the Atlantic," *The Daily Telegraph*, December 4, 1873.

"The Collision in the Atlantic," *The Standard,* December 9, 1873.

"The Collision in the Atlantic. Abandonment of the *Lochearn,*" *The Daily Telegraph,* December 8, 1873.

"The Collision in the Atlantic. Abandonment of the *Loch Earn.*" *The Standard,* December 8, 1873.

Collison, H. M., "Eternal Punishment." *Chicago Tribune,* February 2, 1880.

"Conference of Christian Workers," *Chicago Tribune,* April 22, 1876.

Connecticut Mutual Life Insurance Company v. Horatio G. Spafford et al. Superior Court of Cook County, IL, 72.688 (1897).

Cornell v. Green, 163 U.S. 75. (1896).

Corts, Thomas E, ed. *Bliss and Tragedy. The Ashtabula Railway-Bridge Accident of 1876 and the Loss of P. P. Bliss.* Birmingham AL: Samford University Press, 2003.

Cottrau, Theodoro (transcriber). "Santa Lucia," Naples: Cottrau, 1849.

"The Courts. The Union Screw and Bolt Company," *Chicago Daily Tribune,* April 5, 1873.

"A Curious Sect. A Sketch of the Chicago Enthusiasts Who Went to Palestine to Await Christ's Coming," *Chicago Daily Tribune,* April 8, 1884.

Currey, J. Seymour. *Chicago: Its History and Its Builders.* Volume IV. Chicago: S. J. Clarke Publishing Company, 1918.

Delta [pseud.], "Night," *Wellman's Literary Miscellany,* Detroit: J. K. Wellman, May 1856.

"Died in Jerusalem. Obituary of H. G. Spafford," *New York Times,* October 22, 1888.

"The Drama in America," *The Era,* London, May 11, 1873.

"Dreadful Collision at Sea." *The Birmingham Daily Mail,* December 1, 1873.

Dudman, Helga and Ruth Kark. *The American Colony. Scenes from a Jerusalem Saga.* Jerusalem: The Israel Map and Publishing Co., 1998.

Eliot, George. *The Mill on the Floss.* Edinburgh: William Blackwood & Sons, 1860.

Elliott, C. B., Property Report, December 18, 1896, American Colony in Jerusalem Collection, Manuscript Division, Library of Congress.

Farwell, John V. *Early Recollections of Dwight L. Moody.* Chicago: The Winona Publishing Company, 1907.

"Fight for a Fortune," *Daily Inter-Ocean,* April 18, 1895.

Frankl, Viktor E. *Man's Search for Meaning.* Boston: Beacon Press, 1959.

"The Fullerton Avenue Church," *Chicago Daily Tribune,* July 8, 1876.

Geniesse, Jane Fletcher. *American Priestess: The Extraordinary Story of Anna Spafford and the American Colony in Jerusalem.* New York: Doubleday, 2008.

Goodwin, D., Sr. "Steamship Disasters. To the Editor of *The Chicago Tribune.*" *Chicago Daily Tribune,* May 23, 1875.

Goodwin, Daniel, Jr. "Sketch of Rev. William Barry." *Magazine of American History with Notes and Queries* 13 (1885):283–284.

Gould, Amelia to Dr. Samuel P. Hedges, from Jerusalem, June 2, 1886.

Hackett, Frank Warren. *Reminiscences of the Geneva Tribunal of Arbitration 1872. The Alabama Claims.* Boston: Houghton Mifflin Company, 1911.

Hedges, S. P. to H. G. Spafford, May 25, 1881. In *Murphy, Mary F. and Anna Spafford v. Dr. Samuel P. Hedges et al.* Il, Circuit Court of Cook County, IL, G–142,175 (1896).

——, November 3, 1881. In *Murphy, Mary F. and Anna Spafford v. Dr. Samuel P. Hedges et al.* Il, Circuit Court of Cook County, IL, G–142,175 (1896).

——, November 23, 1881. In *Murphy, Mary F. and Anna Spafford v. Dr. Samuel P. Hedges et al.* Il, Circuit Court of Cook County, IL, G–142,175 (1896).

"Holy City Their Home," *Chicago Daily News,* May 15, 1895.

"Is on Its Last Legs: Spafford's Jerusalem Colony Apparently Going to Pieces," *Chicago Daily,* October 18, 1894.

Joiner, Thekla Ellen. *Sin in the City: Chicago and Revivalism, 1880–1920.* Columbia, MO: University of Missouri Press, 2007.

Julian, John (editor). *A Dictionary of Hymnology.* New York: Dover Publications, Inc, 1957.

Lagerlöf, S. "Christian Love as a Power for the Reconciliation of Peoples." In *The Stockholm Conference 1925. The Official Report of the Universal Christian Conference on Life and Work held in Stockholm, 19–30 August, 1925.* Edited by G. K. A. Bell. London: Oxford University Press, 1926.

Lawrence, James R. 1874. Will and Executorship. In Taylor, Jr., Thomas Report, January 29, 1900. *Murphy v. Hedges,* Circuit Court of Cook County, IL, G–142,175 (1896).

Lee, Charles E. *The Blue Riband. The Romance of the Atlantic Ferry.* London: Sampson Low, Marston & Co, Ltd., 1930.

Leitch, Alexander. *A Princeton Companion.* Princeton, NJ: Princeton University Press, 1978.

"Life in the City of Zion," *Chicago Daily News,* May 14, 1895.

"Loss of the Ship *Trimoutain*," *New York Times,* February 22, 1880.

"M. Collodion," *New York Times,* August 27, 1873.

"Missions," *The Quiver,* February 1888.

Mixter, M. to uncles, November 23, 1873, Oliver Wolcott's Family Papers.

Moody, Paul D. *My Father: An Intimate Portrait of Dwight Moody.* Boston: Little, Brown, 1938.

Morgan, R. C., "Letters from Palestine. Jerusalem—'The Americans,' " *The Christian,* 1891.

Murphy, Mary to Anna Spafford, April 16, 1908, American Colony in Jerusalem Collection, Manuscript Division, Library of Congress.

Murphy, Mary F. and Anna Spafford v. Dr. Samuel P. Hedges et al. Circuit Court of Cook County, IL, G–142,175 (1896).

"An Ocean Disaster," *New York Times,* December 2, 1873.

"Old Homestead Is Sold," *Chicago Daily Tribune,* August 31, 1902.

Proceedings of the Illinois State Bar Association, Springfield, IL: H. W. Rokker's Publishing House, January 10 and 11, 1888.

Reynolds's Weekly Newspaper, London, January 5, 1873.

Rogers, Stanley. *Barenetha Rock. A True Drama of the Sea.* London: W. H. Allen, 1957.

Roosevelt, Theodore to Theodore Roosevelt Sr. and Martha Bulloch Roosevelt, February 11, 1877. In *The Selected Letters of Theodore Roosevelt.* Edited by H. W. Brands. New York: Cooper Square Press, 2001, 12.

Sankey, Ira D. *Sankey's Story of the Gospel Hymns and of Sacred Songs and Solos.* Philadelphia: Sunday School Times Company, 1906.

——. *Sacred Songs and Solos.* London: Morgan & Scott, Ltd., 1877.

"The Sears Building," *Chicago Daily Tribune,* March 12, 1876..

Smith, Hannah Whitall, Papers. Asbury Theological Seminary Library, Information Services, Special Collections, Wilmore, KY, 1847–1960.

——. *A Religious Rebel: The Letters of H.W.S. (Mrs. Pearsall Smith).* Logan Pearsall Smith, editor. London: Nisbet & Co. Ltd., 1949.

Spafford, Anna. August 23, 1878, Diary. Our Jerusalem, Drawer 19. American Colony in Jerusalem Collection, Manuscript Division, Library of Congress.

Spafford, Anna to Horatio Spafford, December 1, 1873, Cable Message, American Colony in Jerusalem Collection, Manuscript Division, Library of Congress.

Spafford, H. G. (the elder) to James Madison, December 25, 1815, *Madison Papers,* Library of Congress.

Spafford, H. G., 1882 Diary. American Colony in Jerusalem Collection, Manuscript Division, Library of Congress.

——. *Twenty Reasons for Believing that the Second coming of the Lord is Near.* Chicago: F. H. Revell, 1870s.

—— [by the author of "Twenty Reasons for Believing that the Coming of the Lord is Nigh"]. *Waiting for the Morning and Other Poems.* Chicago: F. H. Revell, 1878.

Spafford, H. G. to Mr. Chandler, April 13, 1886. In *Autumn Leaves.* Edited by M. Walker. Lamoni, Iowa: M. Walker Publisher (January 1888) Vol. 1, 11.

Spafford, H. G. to Rachel Frederickson, 1873, American Colony in Jerusalem Collection, Manuscript Division, Library of Congress.

Spafford, H. G. to Prof. Piazza Smyth, May 27, 1887, American Colony in Jerusalem Collection, Manuscript Division, Library of Congress.

Spafford, H. G. to Edgar Spafford, 1875 Financial Records. Our Jerusalem 1850-1919. Drawer 19. American Colony in Jerusalem Collection, Manuscript Division, Library of Congress.

Spafford, H. G. draft letter to Miss T. M. Wadsworth, February 21, 1879 and final letter, March 17, 1879. Envelope 16-10. American Colony in Jerusalem Collection, Manuscript Division, Library of Congress.

Spafford, Horatio G. (the elder). "Franklin. On A National School of Science and the Mechanic Arts, and on New Modelling the Patent System." *The American Magazine* 1 (1815–1816):317.

——. *General Geography, and Rudiments of Useful Knowledge. Digested on a New Plan, and Designed for the Use of Schools.* Hudson: Croswell & Frary, 1809.

——. Obituary. *Lansingburgh Gazette,* August 1832.

——. *Some Cursory Observations on the Ordinary Construction of Wheel-Carriages: with an Attempt to point out their defects, and to show how they may be improved; Whereby a saving may be made in the power applied, the motion be rendered more uniform and easy, and the danger of upsetting most effectually prevented,* [pamphlet] 1815.

Spafford, Horatio G. (the elder) to James Madison, December 16, 1814, *Madison Papers,* Library of Congress.

Spafford, Horatio G. (the elder) to Thomas Jefferson, March 30, 1814, Jefferson Papers. Boston, MA: Massachusetts Historical Society.

——, April 12, 1817, Jefferson Papers. Boston, MA: Massachusetts Historical Society.

Spafford, Horatio G., Grantor to Connecticut Mutual Life Insurance Company (dated 23 February 1872; filed 26 February 1872) document #15128, microfiche book 20, pp. 186–190; Cook County Recorder of Deeds (118 N. Clark St. Room 120, County Bldg.; Chicago, IL 60602–1307).

——, 1878 Notes regarding loan from McDaid. American Colony in Jerusalem Collection, Manuscript Division, Library of Congress.

Spafford, Horatio G. to Anna Spafford, November 25, 1873, American Colony in Jerusalem Collection, Manuscript Division, Library of Congress.

Spafford, Horatio G. and Annie T. Spafford, his wife, and Martin Andrews, quit claim (dated 23 February 1872, filed 26 February 1872) document #15129, microfiche book 24, p. 359; Cook

County Recorder of Deeds (118 N. Clark St. Room 120, County Bldg.; Chicago, IL 60602-1307).

Spafford, Horatio G. to Maggie (sister), December 3, 1873, American Colony in Jerusalem Collection, Manuscript Division, Library of Congress.

Spafford, Horatio Gates (the elder). *A Gazetteer of the State of New-York; Carefully Written from Original and Authentic Materials, Arranged on a New Plan, in Three Parts . . . with an Accurate Map of the State.* Albany: H. C. Southwick, 1813.

"Spafford's Name in Court Again," *Chicago Daily Tribune,* April 28, 1895.

"Still Long for the Holy Land. Overcomers Bent on Following the Teachings of 'Mother' Spafford, Despite the Opposition," *Chicago Daily News,* December 15, 1897.

Strachey, Ray. *Religious Fanaticism: Extracts from the Papers of Hannah Whitall Smith.* London: Faber & Gwyer, 1928.

"Sunday School Items," *The Quiver,* November 1888.

Surmont, Marius, "Letter to the Editor of the *Daily Telegraph*—The *Ville du Havre* Disaster." *The Glasgow Herald,* December 15, 1873.

"They Claim Title to Valuable Land," *Chicago Journal,* January 15, 1898.

"Total Loss of an Atlantic Steamer," *Daily Telegraph,* December 2, 1873.

Urquhart, W. W. *Reminiscences. The Merchant Marine. Ocean Travel in the Sixties and Now.* New York: Knickerbocker Press, 1910.

Vester, Bertha Spafford. *Our Jerusalem—an American Family in the Holy City, 1881-1949.* Garden City, NY: Doubleday & Company, Inc., 1950.

"The *Ville du Havre,*" *The Scotsman,* December 4, 1873.

"The *Ville du Havre*," *The Birmingham Daily Mail,* December 9, 1873.

"The *Ville du Havre*. Action of the Court of Appeals. Tribute to the Memory of Judge Peckham," *New-York Times,* December 5, 1873.

"The *Ville du Havre*. Interesting Facts Relative to the Lost," *New York Times,* December 4, 1873.

"The *Ville du Havre* Relief Fund." January 13, 1874. *Chicago Daily Tribune.*

Waite, C. Burritt to parents, November 29, 1873, in Culver (William B.) Memorial Scrapbook of the Shipwreck of the *Ville du Havre,* 1873–1874, Holt-Atherton Special Collections, University of the Pacific Libraries.

Weiss, Nathanael. *Personal Recollections of the Wreck of the* Ville-du-Havre *and the* Loch-Earn. New York: Anson D. F. Randolph & Company, 1875.

Whittier, John Greenleaf. "Chicago.*" The Complete Poetical Works of John Greenleaf Whittier.* Boston: Houghton, Osgood and Company, 1878.

Whittle, D. W., ed. *Memoirs of Philip P. Bliss.* New York: A. S. Barnes & Co., 1877.

Willard, Frances E. to Hannah Whitall Smith, December 22, 1897, Hannah Whitall Smith Collection, Asbury Theological Seminary Library, Special Collections.

Wolcott, Oliver, Jr. " 'A Sad Tale that Must be Told' Madeleine Curtis Mixter's Account of the Loss of the *Ville du Havre*." *The American Neptune* 57, no. 3 (1997):229–236.

ILLUSTRATION AND PHOTO CREDITS

Cover jacket and Frontispiece, *Portrait of Horatio Spafford,* ca. 1860–1880. American Colony in Jerusalem Collection, Manuscript Division, Library of Congress. http://memory.loc.gov/phpdata/pageturner.php?type=&agg =ppmsca&item=18412&seq=4

Page 1, *Portrait of Horatio Spafford,* Mayer & Pierson, photographers, Paris, France. ca. 1873. American Colony in Jerusalem Collection, Manuscript Division, Library of Congress. Part I, Box 1, Folder 9. http://hdl. loc.gov/loc.mss/mamcol.014

Cover jacket and Page 1, *Portrait of Anna Spafford,* Chicago, Illinois, ca. prior to 1873. American Colony in Jerusalem Collection, Manuscript Division, Library of Congress. Part I, Box 1, Folder 8. http://hdl.loc.gov/ loc.mss/mamcol.013

Page 1, *Home of Anna and Horatio Gates Spafford,* Lake View (Chicago), Illinois. Stone & Brooks, photographers, ca. 1875. American Colony in Jerusalem Collection, Manuscript Division, Library of Congress. Part I, Box 1, Folder 3. http://hdl.loc.gov/loc.mss/mamcol.006

Page 2, *Republic Life Building.* Reproduced by permission from Robert N. Dennis Collection of Stereoscopic Views, Miriam and Ira D. Wallach Division of Art, Prints and Photographs, The New York Public Library, Astor, Lenox and Tilden Foundations.

Page 2, *Business card of attorneys Horatio Gates Spafford, H. O. McDaid, and John P. Wilson,* Chicago, Illinois, ca. 1875. American Colony in Jerusalem Collection, Manuscript Division, Library of Congress. Part I, Box 1, Folder 4. http://hdl.loc.gov/loc.mss/mamcol.007

Page 2, *Upper and Lower Bay of New York*, Currier & Ives print. Reproduced by permission from Eno Collection, Miriam and Ira D. Wallach Division of Art, Prints and Photographs, The New York Public Library, Astor, Lenox and Tilden Foundations.

Page 3, T*he Sinking of the* Ville du Havre *and The* Loch Earn; page 5, *Captain W. W. Urquhart,* and *The American Ship* Trimountain; page 6, *The Rescue of Mrs. Bulkley.* Reprinted from Rogers (1957). All efforts were made to trace the copyright holder, believed to be the Estate of Stanley Rogers, have not been successful. Random House Group currently owns the copyright of books published by WH Allen, and they have given permission to reprint.

Cover jacket and Page 3, Photographic copy of lithograph *The Sinking of the Steamship* Ville du Havre. Currier & Ives, 1873. American Colony in Jerusalem Collection, Manuscript Division, Library of Congress. Part I, Box 1, Folder 5. http://hdl.loc.gov/loc.mss/mamcol.010

Page 4, *Portraits of Annie, Maggie, Bessie, and Tanetta Spafford,* ca. 1873. From Spafford family photograph album. American Colony in Jerusalem Collection, Manuscript Division, Library of Congress. Part I, Box 1, Folder 1. http://hdl.loc.gov/loc.mss/mamcol.001

Page 5, *Telegram, "Saved Alone" from Anna Spafford to Horatio Gates Spafford, December 2, 1873.* American Colony in Jerusalem Collection, Manuscript Division, Library of Congress. Part I, Box 1, Folder 6. http://hdl.loc.gov/loc.mss/mamcol.011

Cover jacket and Page 6, *Bulkley stained-glass window* photograph courtesy of Kathy Jarvis, Karen Klacsmann, and Mary Gail Nesbit, The Church of the Good Shepherd, 2230 Walton Way, Augusta, Georgia.

Cover jacket and Page 7, *Draft manuscript of hymn "It is Well With My Soul" by Horatio Gates Spafford,* ca. 1873. American Colony in Jerusalem Collection, Manuscript Division, Library of Congress. Part I, Box 1, Folder 11. http://hdl.loc.gov/loc.mss/mamcol.016

Page 8, *Portraits of Horatio, Bertha, and Grace Spafford.* From Spafford family photograph album. American Colony in Jerusalem Collection,

Manuscript Division, Library of Congress. Part I, Box 1, Folder 1. http://hdl.loc.gov/loc.mss/mamcol.001

Page 9, Photograph of *Dwight L. Moody*, ca. 1870s. From Spafford family photograph album. American Colony in Jerusalem Collection, Manuscript Division, Library of Congress. Part I, Box 1, Folder 1. http://memory.loc.gov/cgi-bin/ampage?collId=mamcol&fileName=mamcol001.db&recNum=8&itemLink=h%3Fammem%2Fmamcol%3A%40field%28NUMBER%2B%40band%28mamcol%2B001%29%29

Page 9, *Fullerton Avenue Presbyterian Church* and photograph of The *Reverend Dr. W. C. Young* reprinted with permission from Barry Smith, Church Historian, Lincoln Park Presbyterian Church, Chicago, Illinois.

Page 9, *Portrait of Dr. Samuel Hedges*. From Spafford family photograph album. American Colony in Jerusalem Collection, Manuscript Division, Library of Congress. Part I, Box 1, Folder 1. http://memory.loc.gov/cgi-bin/ampage?collId=mamcol&fileName=mamcol001.db&recNum=5&itemLink=h%3Fammem%2Fmamcol%3A%40field%28NUMBER%2B%40band%28mamcol%2B001%29%29

Page 10, *First American Colony building located within the Old City of Jerusalem*. American Colony in Jerusalem Collection, Manuscript Division, Library of Congress. http://www.loc.gov/exhibits/americancolony/images/ac0042s.jpg

Page 10, *Portrait of Rob Lawrence*. From Spafford family photograph album. American Colony in Jerusalem Collection, Manuscript Division, Library of Congress. Part I, Box 1, Folder 1. http://memory.loc.gov/cgi-bin/ampage?collId=mamcol&fileName=mamcol001.db&recNum=45&itemLink=S%3Fammem%2Fmamcol%3A%40FIELD%28SUBJ%2B%40od1%28%2Blaurence%2C%2Brobert%2Beugene%2C%2B1866%2B1885%2B%2Bportrait%2B%29%29

Page 11, *Portrait of Horatio Gates Spafford,* Jerusalem, ca. 1885. G. Krikorian Photo Studio, Jerusalem. American Colony in Jerusalem Collection, Manuscript Division, Library of Congress. Part I, Box 1, Folder 10. http://hdl.loc.gov/loc.mss/mamcol.015

Page 11, *American Colony Grave marker* ca. 2011, photograph courtesy of Marla H. Corts, Birmingham, Alabama, U.S.A., and Olga Smoldyreva, Jerusalem, Israel.

Page 12, *Upper Court, 1898.* [American Colony building (Pasha's palace)]. ca. 1898. American Colony Photo Department. American Colony in Jerusalem Collection, Manuscript Division, Library of Congress. LC-DIG-ppmsca-15830-00092 (digital file from original on page 27, no. 92 of photo album belonging to Grace Spafford). http://memory.loc.gov/phpdata/pageturner.php?type=&agg=ppmsca&item=15831&seq=27

Page 12, *Group portrait of Bertha, Grace, and Anna Spafford,* Jerusalem, ca. 1890s. From album of studio portraits of American colonists and friends. Visual Materials of John D. Whiting Papers, Prints and Photographs Division, Library of Congress. http://www.loc.gov/pictures/item/2008676305/

Page 13, *The American Colony kindergarten,* Jerusalem, ca. 1902. From album of members and activities of the American Colony (page 21, no. 72). Visual Materials of the John D. Whiting Papers, Prints and Photographs Division, Library of Congress. LC-DIG-ppmsca-15830-00072. (digital file from original on page 22, no. 92 of photo album belonging to Grace Spafford). http://memory.loc.gov/phpdata/pageturner.php?type=&agg=ppmsca&item=15831&seq=22

Page 13, *Corner of Grand Hotel showing American Colony stores and Dodge auto business (one of American Colony enterprises),* ca. between 1920 and 1935. G. Eric and Edith Matson Photograph Collection. American Colony in Jerusalem Collection, Manuscript Division, Library of Congress. LC-DIG-matpc-08827. http://www.loc.gov/pictures/item/mpc2005001003/PP/

Page 14, *Spafford-Vester-Whiting families, Jerusalem.* American Colony in Jerusalem Collection, Manuscript Division, Library of Congress. LC-DIG-ppmsca-18415-00001. http://lcweb2.loc.gov/phpdata/pageturner.php?agg=ppmsca&item=18415&type=contact

Page 14, *The Salon.* ["Pasha's room", American Colony, Mr. Sinson reading book (far left), Lewis Larsson and Anna Spafford, (center), possibly Amelia Gould (far right)]. From album of members and activities of the

American Colony (page 29, no. 105). Visual Materials of the John D. Whiting Papers, Prints and Photographs Division, Library of Congress. LC-DIG-ppmsca-15830-00105. http://memory.loc.gov/phpdata/pageturner.php?tImages=332&page=9&type=contact&agg=ppmsca&item=15830

Page 15, *Anna Spafford baby home in Jerusalem* [between 1924 and 1946], G. Eric and Edith Matson Photograph Collection. American Colony in Jerusalem Collection, Manuscript Division, Library of Congress. LC-DIG-matpc-13970. http://www.loc.gov/pictures/item/mpc2005008614/PP/

Page 15, *The raising of the siege of Jerusalem (bread distribution by nurses of the Anna Spafford Baby Home)*, October 22, 1938. G. Eric & Edith Matson Collection, Prints and Photographs Division, Library of Congress. LC-DIG-matpc-18871. http://www.loc.gov/pictures/item/mpc2010004360/PP/

Page 15, *Bertha Vester distributing food aid*, Jerusalem, 1916. From album of World War I in Palestine and the Sinai. American Colony in Jerusalem Collection, Manuscript Division, Library of Congress. Part I, OV 5. http://memory.loc.gov/cgi-bin/ampage?collId=mamcol&fileName=mamcol059.db&recNum=72

Page 16, *Buildings in Jerusalem.* The American Colony, air, ca. between 1950 and 1977, Matson Photo Service, Jerusalem. American Colony in Jerusalem Collection, Manuscript Division, Library of Congress. http://www.loc.gov/pictures/item/mpc2010000209/PP/. *American Colony Hotel* ca. 2011, photograph courtesy of Marla H. Corts, Birmingham, Alabama, U.S.A., and Olga Smoldyreva, Jerusalem, Israel.

INDEX

Made in the USA
Lexington, KY
28 February 2015